Florida's Golden Galleons

Formerly

Gold, Galleons & Archaeology

COVER: Designed by James N. Baker

Bernard Romans map of 1775 — one of the earliest references indicating the location of the wrecks. The authors have indicated the names and locations of each wreck site.

Florida's Golden Galleons

The Search for the 1715 Spanish Treasure Fleet

by
Robert F. Burgess and Carl J. Clausen

Florida Classics Library
Port Salerno, Florida

A Brief Resumé

N July 24, 1715, a Spanish treasure fleet sailed from Havana, carrying a cargo of 14 million pesos in gold, silver and jewels. In the Florida Straits, near present-day Cape Canaveral, the fleet ran into a hurricane, with the disastrous loss of ten ships and 700 lives. Little was salvaged at the time.

For more than two centuries, sand and sea held their secrets well. Occasionally, however, tides and storms tossed blackened silver coins up on the beaches, tempting would-be treasure hunters. Among the most successful was the Real Eight Company, contracted by the state of Florida to recover the valuable treasure and historical artifacts under the supervision of state underwater archaeologist Carl J. Clausen. Spurred by the unique finds on the ocean floor and curious about the full story behind the tragic event that had scattered this fabulous treasure along Florida's east coast, he and Robert F. Burgess determined to record the history of the ill-fated fleet.

In writing their book, the authors needed the answers to hundreds of questions. What was it like to cross the Atlantic in the eighteenth century? What precautions were taken against pirates? What caused the delays that led to sailing at a particularly treacherous time of the year? What really happened the night of the hurricane? How much treasure was lost? How many people survived?

The authors discovered that pieces of the historical jigsaw puzzle lay scattered all over the world. They examined hundreds of documents recovered from dusty archives: official statements, depositions, royal court orders, private and public letters, and ships' mainifests. After ten years of research, the authors finally had all the facts, which enabled them to reconstruct the story.

Florida's Golden Galleons is that stunning story, meticulously detailed and excitingly told, of the sinking of the great fleet and of the successful modern-day efforts to bring its treasure once more to the light of day.

Gold, Galleons, and Archaeology
Copyright © 1976 by Robert F. Burgess and Carl J. Clausen

Florida's Golden Galleons
Copyright © 1982 by Robert F. Burgess and Carl J. Clausen

Published by Florida Classics Library
by agreement with the authors

ISBN 0-912451-07-6

For Julie and Cynthia

About the Authors

Following his discharge from the U.S. Army Ski Troops at the end of World War II, ROBERT F. BURGESS returned to Europe to study foreign languages in Italy and Switzerland. Later he majored in Journalism at Michigan State University. Magazine editor, freelance writer/photographer, author of 14 books on ocean related subjects such as sharks, shipwrecks, treasure hunting and underwater archaeology, Mr. Burgess works closely with anthropologists, archaeologists, oceanographers and marine biologists. His magazine articles, books, photographs and audiovisual programs detail major research work in these fields. To gain material for his writing, he has dived on ancient treasure wrecks, photographed the unique beauty of Florida's underwater caverns and documented the scientific recovery of 12,000 year old Early Man remains from deep Florida springs. Since small boat sailing has long been his hobby, Mr. Burgess is presently writing a handbook on the subject. He and his wife live in northwest Florida.

Carl J. Clausen is a marine archaeologist whose principal interests lie in colonial-period shipwreck sites. He has served as Adjunct Professor of North American Archaeology at the American Institute of Nautical Archaeology, as well as a university lecturer and a consultant to private firms. Appointed Florida's first state underwater archaeologist, by governor Farris Bryant in 1964, his duties called for inspection of historical period shipwrecks and numerous dives involving observation and supervision of the activities of commercial salvagers working under leases and contracts with the State of Florida.

Mr. Clausen's present endeavors include: Visiting Assistant Curator (Social Sciences), Florida State Museum, University of Florida, Gainesville; Associate Professor (Geoarchaeology), Department of Geology, University of Miami, Coral Gables; Director and Principal Investigator, Little Salt Spring Research Facility, North Port, Florida and founder and president, CCC Enterprises, Inc. a cultural resource management firm primarily involved in terrestrial and marine cultural resource surveys and archaeological site evaluations (including historical period shipwreck sites). Mr. Clausen and his family reside in northwest Florida.

Contents

Other books by Robert F. Burgess

SINKINGS, SALVAGES AND SHIPWRECKS
— McGraw-Hill

SHIPS BENEATH THE SEA
— McGraw-Hill

THE SHARKS
— Doubleday & Co.

THE CAVE DIVERS
— Dodd, Mead & Co.

THEY FOUND TREASURE
— Dodd, Mead & Co.

EXPLORING A CORAL REEF
— MacMillan & Co.

THE MAN WHO RODE SHARKS
(With William R. Royal)
— Dodd, Mead & Co.

MAN: 12,000 YEARS UNDER THE SEA
— Dodd, Mead & Co.

SECRET LANGUAGES OF THE SEA
— Dodd, Mead & Co.

Preface

Our goal was to trace the voyage of a Spanish treasure fleet to its destruction by hurricane on the Florida east coast in 1715, then record the problems and events that occurred 250 years later when the shipwrecks and treasure were found by modern-day treasure hunters. To write the history of such a fleet, we had to know specific details about the circumstances involved. What was it like, for example, to make a transatlantic crossing in the early 18th century? What were the fleet's destinations? Who were the officers involved? What had caused the fateful delays that led to the disaster? How much treasure was lost? What really happened on the night of the hurricane? How did one ship traveling with the fleet escape doom? What was the survivors' fate on the hostile coast far from help?

Hundreds of such questions needed answering, but the pieces of this historical jigsaw puzzle were scattered through the archives of the world. In the search that followed, countless dusty documents, many of which had not been touched since the day they were stored in the archives 250 years before, had to be scrutinized for clues. Official statements, depositions, royal-court orders, private and public letters, ships' manifests, bills of lading-these were the pieces of the puzzle we needed. More than ten years of original research went into the quest for the necessary data. But once these were found, filmed, translated, taped, transcribed and finally filed in a more manageable form of organized chaos, we had the raw material to write the book.

In telling this story we have tried to strike a balance between the dry, unemotional historical facts and a dramatization of the material based on contemporary archaeological information relating to it. We hope the academicians among our readers will forgive us this effort to breathe life into what were assuredly very lively events. For those who might wish to peruse translations of original documents, we have included in the appendices a few of the most important ones consulted during the preparation of the book. Our principal sources of documentary information were: the Museo Naval and the Museo Nacional in Madrid; the Archivos General de Indias, Seville; the Archivo de Simancas, near Valladolid; the British Museum and the Public Record Office, London; the Netherlands Royal Archives in The Hague; the French National Archives, Paris; the Vatican Archives, Rome; the Archivos Generale de la Nacion, Mexico City; the Archives of Jamaica; the National Archives and the Library of Congress, Washington, D.C.; the North Carolina Collection of Spanish Documents in the North Carolina Department of Archives and History; the Stetson Collection of Spanish Documents in the P. K. Younge Library of Florida History, University of Florida, Gainesville, Florida; publications of the St. Augustine Historical Society, St. Augustine, Florida; and numerous books, pamphlets, articles and reference works of the last three centuries. Archaeological material relating to the Spanish fleets was assembled from records of the salvage contract program of the Division of Archives, History and Records Management of the Florida Department of State, from the site records of the Underwater Archaeological Research Section of the Bureau of Historic Sites and Documents, from excavations carried out by the Florida State Museum, and from the original research and publications of both authors .

This work could not have been accomplished without the cooperation and assistance of many colleagues. In appreciation we offer our gratitude to the scientists, scholars, writers, researchers, linguists, librarians, treasure hunters, divers, adventurers and friends who have in some way helped make our task easier. We would especially like to acknowledge the kind assistance of Louis Ullian, a friend and original member of the Real Eight Company; Marjorie Barnes, our always dependable research librarian; and Dr. Eugene Lyon, Professor of History, Indian River Junior College.

In addition, information for this book's revised edition could not have been possible without the kind assistance of many friends to whom I owe a special debt of gratitude, especially to members of Florida's Bureau of Archaeological Research, James Miller, Jamie Levy and Frank Gilson, who kindly provided me with help in all phases of my research with them; to John Durham, Alex Kuze, Randy Lathrop, Frank Giovenco, and Ron Hampton who generously shared with me their tales of treasure trove; to photographers Ernie "Seascribe" Richards, marine biologist/treasure salvor, John Halas, and Salvors Inc. conservator, Bill Moore, for permission to use some of their fine photographs; to my friends Russ and Christine Shoemaker who unknowingly furnished me information that filled an important niche in this story; and especially to my friends Bob and Margaret Weller whose vital information, warm hospitality and great shrimp salad were treasures enough for this author that July day when the "Royals" simply didn't show. To one and all, thank you for your help.

Florida's Golden Galleons

Prologue

On July 24, 1715, a Spanish treasure fleet comprised of five ships of the *Flota* under the command of General Juan Esteban de Ubilla, six vessels of the *Galeones* fleet commanded by General Don Antonio de Echeverz y Zubiza, and an accompanying French warship, the *Grifón*, had left Havana, homeward bound for Spain, when they were caught in a hurricane off the Florida east coast near present-day Cape Canaveral. All but the French ship *Grifón* were wrecked, seven hundred persons perished, and some 14,000,000 pesos' worth of treasure was lost.

To better understand the significance of this event to Spain, one must know something about the history of her treasure fleets, which were largely responsible for Spain's rise to a leading world power.

Their story begins in the late Middle Ages when European nations found they lacked the precious metals necessary to meet the demands of an expanding mercantile trade. It was this quest for new sources of wealth that sent Columbus sailing westward in search of a new route to the riches of the Indies. But instead he found the New World and returned to Spain, where he assured his sovereigns that he had discovered islands containing gold mines.

1

But in the next twenty years the only wealth that trickled back to Spain was a little gold panned by Indians from the streams of Hispaniola.

After Hernando Cortés conquered the Aztecs (1519–1521), the main flow of wealth was silver from the rich mines of New Spain (Mexico). Then Francisco Pizarro and his conquistadors conquered Peru (1527–1535), and the legendary cities of gold became glittering realities for Spain. In 1545, the Spanish discovered a veritable mountain of silver at Potosí in present-day Bolivia, which produced enormous amounts of the precious metal for Spain for the next fifty years. In addition, the discovery of other rich silver, gold and mercury mines in the New World began to pour an immense wealth into Spain up to the 19th century. Transportation of all these riches back to the Old World was entirely dependent on the success of Spanish treasure fleets.

Each year during the period of the *Flota* or fleet system in use from the late 16th century to the mid-18th century, two fleets were customarily dispatched from Spain to the New World. One was the *Tierra Firma Armada* or the *Galeones*, which collected the trade goods and treasure of South America; the other was the *Nuevo España Armada* or *Flota*, which collected merchandise and treasure accumulated in Mexico. Each fleet consisted of two heavily armed warships—the largest called a *Capitana* and the other an *Almiranta*—generally two *pataches* or patrol vessels, a supply or reinforcement ship, and the merchant vessels or *naos* sailing under their protection. In wartime, when the treasure fleets were threatened by enemy intervention, the number of protective warships might be increased to eight or twelve, and the merchant ships would travel more heavily armed than usual.

The *Flota* usually sailed in March and the *Galeones* in May or June, both fleets following the same general route to the New World. They sailed down the coast of Africa to the Canary Islands, where they left their escorting warships. These would, when practicable, rejoin them in the Azores for the return voyage. Then, with the help of the trade winds and the North Equatorial Current, the ships made their way westward across the Atlantic Ocean. About two months later the fleets sighted Trinidad or the Windward Islands in the West Indies and entered the Caribbean. The *Galeones* sailed to Cartagena in present-day Colombia to take on the South American treasure. Smaller vessels were dispatched to the island of Margarita to pick up the year's accumulation of pearls from the oyster beds there. Meanwhile, word of the fleet's impending arrival was sent ahead to the governor of Panama so that he could arrange for the Peruvian treasure to be brought north from Lima by other vessels, then transported across the Isthmus from Panama City to Porto Bello. It was then picked up by the *Galeones*, which usually returned to Cartagena to winter.

The *Flota*, which generally arrived in the Caribbean a month or two earlier than the *Galeones*, proceeded to Vera Cruz, where it took on the treasures and exports of New Spain, along with goods from the Orient that had been brought to Acapulco aboard the annual Manila galleon, then transported overland by mule train to Vera Cruz. Generally, after wintering in this port, the *Flota* left the following year, catching the prevailing westerly winds on a course that carried the fleet upward into the northern Gulf of Mexico, then southward down the west coast of Florida, passing east of the Dry Tortugas to Havana. There the *Flota* met the *Galeones*, which had crossed from Cartagena. Both fleets reprovisioned and then sailed up the Florida Straits, following the Gulf Stream until it veered eastward north of Bermuda, where they caught the prevailing winds that would carry them across the Atlantic to Spain.

Spain's economy was almost totally dependent on these treasure shipments from the New World. Since she manufactured nothing that was needed by other countries, the wealth she received from her New World colonies merely passed through her economy into the economies of other European nations that sold their goods to Spain to fulfill her needs. In a word, other countries benefited more than Spain from her New World wealth. Nearly 95 percent of the precious metals backing European monetary systems came from the Spanish treasure fleets. That is how important they were. When one of these fleets was lost, the whole European economic structure felt the effect. Wars or anything else that interrupted the flow of precious metals from the New World kept the Spanish in debt to international bankers, occasionally with the Crown's customary 20-percent share of the treasure pledged up to five years in advance. Once, when a fleet failed to reach Spain on schedule, Italian bankers threatened to stop all further loans to the Spanish Crown. King Phillip II was so disturbed by this news that he ordered most of the remaining treasure in the royal coffers distributed to various churches and monasteries in Spain for the saying of

3

masses to insure the safe arrival of the fleet. When the ships finally reached Seville, the event was said to have caused great rejoicing throughout the land.

But frequently the fleets failed to reach their destination. The ultimate success or failure of these long voyages depended on the weather. Hurricanes were the worst villains. Throughout the Indies they destroyed more ships, claimed more lives and were responsible for the loss of more treasure than all the pirates or privateers that sailed the seven seas. Between 1525 and 1825, dozens of Spanish treasure ships were lost in Florida waters alone. This is the story of one such fleet.

Chapter 1

Outbound to Oblivion

Standing at the taffrail of his flagship, twenty-seven feet above the water, General Don Antonio de Echeverz y Zubiza, commander of the *Galeones*, was watching his quartermaster supervise the loading of fruits and vegetables aboard the 700-ton frigate. The commander's fleet of six ships had waited eight months in Havana for the arrival of the *Flota*, General Don Juan Esteban de Ubilla's four vessels from Vera Cruz. The lengthy wait had been enough to vex a saint, but the fleet from New Spain had had difficulties. No matter how diligently commanders sought to avoid them, General Echeverz would have realized that certain delays were unavoidable. Above all, however, he must have regretted their happening to this particular fleet.

Although Spain customarily sent two annual fleets to collect the treasure of the New World colonies, the recent War of the Spanish Succession (1701–1714) had changed that. The usual sailings of the treasure fleets were curtailed by English and Dutch squadrons in the Atlantic. With the cessation of hostilities in 1712 and the signing of the Treaty of Utrecht, Spain was anxious to reestablish this rich trade with her colonies, particularly the viceroyalties of New Spain and Peru, which had long supplied the lifeblood of her economy—silver. The large amount of merchandise and treasure that had accumulated in the warehouses of the New World during the war was sorely needed in Spain to help defray the cost of that conflict.

The fulfillment of that need rested with the 1715 treasure fleet now assembled in Havana harbor with 14,000,000 pesos' worth of treasure and cargo aboard. The combined flotilla numbered twelve ships, including the French warship *Grifón*, commanded by Captain Antonio Darié. Most of the vessels were low-profile frigates, faster and better designed than the top-heavy galleons formerly used in the Indies trade. Though galleons as a ship type were no longer in use, the romantic term had survived as a name for treasure ships. The fleet's two flagships were large *Capitanas*, one commanded by General Ubilla, the other by General Echeverz. Next in size and importance were the two *Almirantas* commanded by admirals. During an attack or any other emergency in which the *Capitanas* were unable to fulfill their duties, the *Almirantas* took charge of the fleet. These four warships carried most of the treasure returning to Spain. By virtue of their size and total armament of some two hundred cannon, they would protect the convoy. The remaining vessels were smaller, lighter-armed *pataches* (tenders), *resfuerzos* (supply ships) and *naos* (cargo vessels).

During his long wait for the *Flota*, General Echeverz knew full well that the later the season, the greater the danger of hurricanes. Sailing late only increased the risk of being caught in the narrow passage between the Bahama Bank and the Florida reefs by one of those terrible tropical storms. Aware of this fact, the commander became increasingly distressed by the endless delays, particularly since it was now almost August.

This, however, was their final day of waiting, their last delay in loading. The ships would sail with the afternoon tide, and that was a blessing. The general's vessel already looked like a floating garden.

Stalks of bananas and plantains, hampers and sacks of oranges, limes, coconuts and a variety of other fruits and vegetables littered the frigate's main deck. Under the watchful eye of Echeverz's quartermaster, more came aboard on the backs of ragged Indian and Negro stevedores who swarmed alongside the ship in their boats and canoes. Enough water and victuals would be carried to sustain the vessel's five hundred passengers and crew for the almost two-month voyage to Spain. Most of the fresh food would be consumed quickly during the first weeks at sea, as would some of the main stores already laden below—large quantities of hard biscuits, salted meat and fish, dried beef, garbanzo beans, corn, flour, cheeses, oil, vinegar and wine. Pens on the main deck held pigs, chickens, goats, cattle and live sea turtles turned bottoms up. Water was carried in both large and small earthenware jars, wood casks, and six-foot-long sealed segments of bamboo as thick as a man's thigh. Some of these water containers were hung in the rigging; the rest of the supply was stored both above and below decks. For replenishing water stores during the voyage, the frigate carried plaited grass mats which, when leaned along the gunwales from one end of the ship to the other, would catch rainwater and pass it along split bamboo troughs into jars. This process and the dispensing of the vital water ration was in the charge of a seaman called the *alguacil de agua*, or "water constable." Once the fleet left Havana, it would not stop again to reprovision until it reached Spain.

By 2 P.M. the hot tropical sun beat down mercilessly on the stone and stucco red-tile–roofed buildings and wharves that lined the waterfront. Although it was already the siesta hour, Havana was in no mood to sleep. The departure of the treasure galleons was a day to be celebrated. Colorful flags flew from the somber battlements of El Morro Castle. Their vivid reds, yellows, whites and blacks were repeated in the long pennants and flags waving from the masts and sterns of the massed fleet below. People thronged the narrow cobblestone streets and stone quays at harbor edge. Their voices and guitar music drifted across the water of the bay. Dozens of boats moved back and forth between the quays and the great ships loading the last passengers. Gay crowds of elegantly attired people crossed to the vessels in slender, elaborately carved shallops with up to ten efficient oarsmen. The resplendent colors of the ladies' pastel parasols, broad-brimmed plumed hats and expensive silk dresses made a brave show in the bright sunlight. Not to be outdone, the bewigged gentlemen in their velvet or brocade waistcoats, ruffled shirts and silk pantaloons postured and preened with the nonchalance of peacocks. Less flamboyantly clad soldiers, sailors, servants and other people of lower social standing were transported in smaller, more modest cutters. Baggage for each passenger was supposed to be restricted to two or three trunks or leather-covered chests, a bottlecase or two for wine, and writing materials. Candy, biscuits or anything else could also be carried, so long as it could be kept under the bed. Passengers of some importance often exceeded these restrictions by simple agreement with the captain. The common people carried their belongings in wicker hampers or bags to be kept under their hammocks.

Aboard ship, persons of rank or nobility, frequently royal officials and their families returning to Spain after completing their terms of office in the colonies, were given the choicest accommodations, quite modest by modern standards—quarterdeck cabins the size of small prison cells. Lower-class passengers—men, women and children—shared the same quarters as the crew between decks, where each individual was allotted a tiny six-foot-long space to sling his hammock or lay a pallet, no one more than fourteen inches from his neighbor. The headroom in these quarters was usually five feet four inches or less. On General Echeverz's *Capitana*, the largest ship in the fleet, the gun deck was 160 feet long and less than 45 feet wide. More than 450 persons were relegated to this cramped, dark, damp space. At sea, when all hatches and ports would often be closed, sometimes for weeks, the air below decks would become foul enough to extinguish a candle.

Every cubic inch of space not occupied by a passenger was crammed with cargo or baggage. When the hold, cabins and companionways were filled, bales and chests were piled along the main decks, despite a law of 1608 that confined all cargo to the hold. Spanish treasure ships were frequently overloaded. Often cannon were detrunked and stored below along the keel in rows, muzzle to cascabel, to lower the ship's center of gravity and thus permit more cargo to be carried above. General Ubilla's flotilla was no exception.

Finally, the last passenger was aboard and the last official formality performed. The ships were ready, the men standing by. Spectators and passengers waited calmly, expectantly. Havana's cathedral bells signaled the last ritual. General Echeverz gazed across the harbor to the sea, but what he was really looking at was the sky. Nothing marred the flawless pale blue rim except a single wispy mare's-tail cloud on the northern horizon. Then he saw Ubilla's flagship hoist the signal to make sail. The commander of the *Galeones* murmured an invocation, turned brusquely away from the rail and gave the order.

A cannon aboard the flagship of the *Flota* boomed hollowly, relaying the signal to the more distant ships of the fleet. Officers bellowed orders, and bare feet pounded the decks as crews sprang into action. Men scurried up the ratlines and out the yards. Headsails blossomed from forestays and rose rippling and flapping, the breeze blowing down both sides. Clouds of canvas billowed aloft, while sweating men heaved the creaking capstan bars around to the rhythmic clanking of the capstan pawls. Slowly the thick hemp cables came home, water oozing out of the fiber strands and running down the decks. Seamen at the bows shouted when the massive oak anchor stocks hove into sight, streaming mud and silt from the harbor bottom.

On General Echeverz's *Capitana*, men at the sheets hauled the yards round until flapping canvas caught the breeze and boomed full foresails and mains. Slowly, ponderously, the great ship moved forward under reduced sail, gradually gaining speed, a "bone in her teeth" as she pushed a small hillock of water ahead of her stubby bows. On shore the crowds cheered and shouted farewells.

One by one the ships lumbered into line behind their respective flagships. The awakening of the massed armada was a spectacle long to be remembered as the *Flota* led the way: General Ubilla's 471-ton, 50-gun *Capitana*, *Nuestra Señora de la Regla*, followed by his three tenders and supply vessels; then the 315-ton, 40-gun French warship, the *Grifón*, and finally, the *Flota's* 450-ton, 54-gun *Almiranta*.

Then came the *Galeones* fleet: General Echeverz's 713-ton, 72-gun *Capitana*, *Nuestra Señora del Carmen*, leading his smaller *patache* and *resfuerzo*, then the two prize vessels captured earlier off South America—the small frigate *La Francesa* and the sloop *La Galera*. The last warship in line was the fleet's 312-ton, 40-gun *Almiranta*.

In majestic splendor the ships moved toward the sea, ghosting across the water like swans, the heavily armed men-of-war with their gunports raised to expose their tiers of menacing cannon.

High above the harbor a rumbling tattoo of drums rolled from the ramparts of El Morro Castle, where a black-robed archbishop blessed the fleet while impassive officials, bedecked in gold braid, hoped fervently that this flotilla of vessels, with its huge treasure so sorely needed by the Empire, would safely reach Spain.

Twelve times the fortress's cannon roared their measured salutes, and twelve times they were answered by the departing fleet.

The twelve vessels under sail were an impressive sight as they swung out of the harbor with their crested flags flying, their decks crowded with people waving a last farewell.

Once the ships were clear of the headland, crews scurried aloft to break out all sails. Topsails and gallants shook free and filled with a bang. The ships gained speed, heeling heavily into the coastal currents. From that moment on, the long-awaited Spanish treasure fleet of 1715 was set on a course destined for a rendezvous with modern history.

Chapter 2

The Gathering Storm

As treasure ships had done since the mid-16th century, the 1715 fleet would follow the New Bahama Channel, the straits between Florida and the Bahama Islands. But rather than go by the short, direct route north into the unknown reefs and labyrinthine Florida Keys, or even northeast up the safe deepwater axis of the Straits, it chose a longer, more devious route. The reason was simple. Navigation was still a hit-or-miss proposition. There were few straight lines in the sea lanes when ships were at the mercy of winds and currents, so there was much beating back and forth in the ocean to get anywhere. Since no one could be certain exactly where he was, once out of sight of land, Spanish pilots in charge of the fleet's navigation felt safer sailing for known landmarks or hazards so that they could see and avoid them, rather than confronting the unknown in the open ocean. Therefore, vessels taking the longer and supposedly safer way to reach the relatively narrow passage between Florida and the Bahamas steered a course that kept the fleet close to land. As soon as the ships left Havana harbor, then, they swung east along the coast of Cuba, traveling only as fast as their slowest vessel. With favorable winds and currents, the armada averaged almost six nautical miles an hour.

11

Twelve hours out of Havana, the lookouts sighted Punto Ycaco, a prominent point overgrown with coconut palms. For vessels following the eastern route to the Straits, this was their last view of Cuba as the ships altered course to the east-northeast for Cayo Sal, a small group of islands thirteen leagues* away where the Spaniards often made salt. Prior to leaving Havana, the fleet's officers had been soundly briefed on all the bearings, course changes and landfalls from Havana through the Straits to the point where the ships veered eastward across the Atlantic to Spain. For obvious reasons it was vital for the fleet to travel together and for everyone to understand the route that lay ahead. From Cayo Sal the course was northwest five leagues to Muertos Cayos (Deadman's Keys), more than a hundred great rocks the size of vessels that thrust up out of the ocean on the west end of the Double-Headed-Shot Keys; then north-northeast twenty-three leagues to Los Membros (Riding Rocks), barren rocks that look like wrecks. At this point the fleet would sail west-southwest across the Florida Straits for nineteen leagues until it approached the Cape Reef in latitude 25°2'N, directly east of Cayo Tabona (Tavernier Key) just south of Key Largo. Then it would begin a series of zigzag tacks northward as the ships beat their way up the narrow Straits against the prevailing northeast winds.

Knowing how important it was for the fleet to reach the mouth of the Straits and pass through them without delay, generals Ubilla and Echeverz saw to it that the armada made good time. Their ships sailed hard during the day but more cautiously at night, the lookouts always within sight of the next ship's stern lantern or topmast. Despite the fleet's haste, its officers were wary, for charts were often wrong and the penalty for carelessness could be a collision with an unmarked reef.

At night the ships reduced sail and slackened their speed. Double lookouts were posted aloft and in the bows. Every fifteen to thirty minutes by the glass, soundings were made with a 300-foot deep-sea lead line. The ship's speed was determined by a log line—a block of wood (cast from the bow) on a 150-fathom rope divided into knots representing part of a league. The number of knots that ran out during one turn of a quarter-minute sandglass

* A league is three nautical miles.

12

was multiplied to yield the distance the ship traveled in a given time.

By the early 18th century many ships carried a quadrant, but the earlier navigational instruments—the astrolabe and the cross-staff—were still in use for measuring the altitude of the sun or the polestar. The more accurate sextant and marine clock, so necessary for precisely determining longitude, had not yet been invented.*

Compasses told the ship's direction, and a trickle of sand through hourglasses, turned every half hour by ship's boys, told the time. These were tended diligently day and night. The ringing of a bell from one to eight times with each successive turn of the watches marked the passage of time. Half of the working crew—often 50 to 100 men on the large ships—was on deck at all times. There were sails to be tended, rigging to be adjusted, lookouts to be kept, soundings to be taken, log lines to be cast, supplies to be shifted, pumps to be manned, repairs to be made, and the ship to be sailed. No one was ever idle. When there was nothing else to do, sailors swabbed decks, mended sails or made rope. Crews stood their watches twenty-four hours a day, each man alternating four hours on deck with four hours below. A sailor coming off watch crawled to his hammock on his hands and knees so as not to disturb sleepers in the other hammocks. It mattered little that his hammock was wet or that his clothes were damp, because in the darkness between decks, everything dripped. It dripped from the humidity and from the exhalations of closely packed creatures. It dripped because all wooden ships, in fair weather or foul, leaked badly above and below the waterline. Sea water constantly seeped through seams and splashed through ports, scuppers, hatchways and gunports. Closing the openings did little to stem the flow. Water ran in through upper-deck planks, streamed down cross beams and dripped on passengers below. Neither the ship nor the passengers ever dried out completely. Water that was not caught or absorbed ended in the bilges and had to be pumped regularly. From flooded bilges the ship reeked of drowned rats, rotting wood, decaying garbage, scummy ballast rock and foul bilge water. Stale food, sour bedding, wet clothes and unwashed people added to the

---

* The sextant was invented in 1731; the forerunner of our modern chronometer, in 1765.

overwhelming stench below decks. A pigsty would have smelled sweet by comparison. By the end of a long voyage the holds had to be fumigated with iron pots containing a smoking mixture of gunpowder, vinegar and water, or pans of burning pitch or brimstone. The treatment temporarily disguised but never entirely eliminated the smell.

Quite possibly it was these conditions that brought passengers up on the open decks as often as the weather and deck space permitted. On General Echeverz's flagship some of the men passed the time by trailing baited hooks over the side and catching sharks. The small fish were saved for eating. The large ones were either quickly dispatched or tormented for the amusement of the upper-class passengers by being thrown back into the water with a board tied to their tails. Other men gathered in the lee of the mainsails to talk and play cards while the women gossiped and sewed. The children ranged noisily and happily around the deck. When they were not helping the men catch sharks or plying the sailors with questions about sailing the ship, they were playing tag around the masts or teasing the animals in the stock pens.

Throughout the ship there were rigid fire regulations. Men were allowed to smoke only above the "waist," or forecastle, on the lee side of the ship, either day or night. Even there, their pipes had to be well covered or their cigars in holders. When the wind was strong, smoking was permitted only under the forecastle, where jars of water were placed for any emergency. Any violation of these orders brought severe penalties. Anyone caught smoking in an unauthorized area was put in the bilboes* on bread and water for fifteen days. A seaman caught violating the smoking regulations was sentenced to a year's labor on the vessel without pay. As part of these same regulations, all fires aboard ship were to be extinguished before sunset, with the exception of well-covered lanterns. These alone were permitted above or below decks and were allowed to burn all night—one lantern before the door of each cabin, one at the entrance of the powder magazine but separated from it by a bulkhead, and another in the fore part of the ship between decks.

During the early part of the voyage, when provisions were abundant and fresh, everyone ate reasonably well. Breakfast might consist of boiled meal with molasses or flour dumplings fried in

*Iron bars with sliding fetters that shackled to the ankles.

pork fat. On meat days, fresh fruit and vegetables were often served with *Tassajos Fritos*—sun- or wind-dried jerked beef. Other meals included a thick bean soup cooked with salt pork, and various meat and turtle stews. The choicest food was served to the officers and upper-class passengers, who often feasted on roast fowl, wine and honey. The usual after-dinner treat for everyone above the rank of common seaman was a mug of chocolate, a favorite beverage among the Spaniards since the conquest of Mexico, when Cortés's men inherited the bitter cacao bean drink from the Aztecs and discovered how good it was when sweetened. On fish days, boiled fish supplemented the meat, along with a kind of kidney bean soup called *Mongos*. Saucer-sized biscuits made of wheat flour and dried-pea flour served as bread. In the course of the voyage these weevil-ridden disks would become hard as rock and could be skipped across the water like flat stones. When there was an ample supply of water, the total daily ration was three pints. A shortage reduced the allotment to a small coconut shell full. This was all that was allowed for drinking or bathing.

Toward the end of a long sea voyage, meals were not so eagerly anticipated as they were in the beginning. Passenger Gemelli Careri's daily account of shipboard life on the Manila galleon during a crossing just seventeen years before the 1715 fleet's voyage explains why:

"The Ship swarms with little Vermin," he wrote, "the Spaniards call *Corgojos*, bred in the Biskit; so swift that they in a short time not only run over Cabbins, beds and the very dishes the Men eat on, but insensibly fasten upon the Body. . . . Abundance of Flies fall into the Dishes of Broth, in which swim Worms of several sorts . . . in every Mouthful there went down abundance of Maggots, and *Corgojos* chew'd and bruis'd. On Fish Days the common Diet was old rank Fish boil'd in fair water and Salt; at noon we had *Mongos*, something like Kidney Beans in which there were so many Maggots, that they swam at the top of the Broth, and the quantity was so great that besides the Loathing they caus'd, I doubted whether the Dinner was Fish or Flesh."

When the treasure galleons cleared the Double-Headed-Shot Keys between Cuba and the Bahamas, they caught the prevailing easterly winds blowing across the vast expanse of shoal water off their starboard side, known as the Great Bahama Bank. While the vessels retained their ship-of-the-line formation that kept their cannon flanks clear, they tightened up, the lookouts warily watching the horizon for any sign of a strange sail. Privateers and Bahamian pirates openly roamed these waters, and the commanding generals were not taking any chances. News of the final peace in the recent war would be slow to reach all the participants, particularly some of the English privateers lurking in such far-flung colonial outposts as the Bahama Islands. Indeed, some would purposely ignore the end of hostilities for a while in the hope of taking a final war prize. One could not be certain what might appear from behind the large islands over the horizon to the east.

If there was any apprehension among the passengers, it was not apparent. Their days were long and languorous. Under the hot tropical sun and the refreshing easterly breezes, the incredibly clear, deep blue water rolled by endlessly. And in those fathomless depths there were always strange, wonderful creatures to behold: flying fish erupting from the water ahead of the bows like flushing coveys of quail, gliding and skimming with their wing-fins spread; schools of smiling porpoises leaping and tumbling in the waves like playful children; big hump-headed dolphin fish the color of rainbows darting and flashing from beneath the frigate's hull, almost too quick to see; lazy loggerhead sea turtles the size of tubs, floating on the surface and staring curiously at the passing ships; fleets of purple air-bladders called Portuguese men-of-war sailing the waves; hundreds of lavender jellyfish as big as dinner plates floating in layers; and always, somewhere nearby, either following in the shade of the ship or trailing in her wake, the malevolent shadow of the shark.

Only at night, when the wind fell and the waves calmed, was there any change in the things to be seen and the things to be done. The sea grew dark and somber everywhere but around the slowly moving ships, where pale light flared in the water streaming past the bows and glowed green with phosphorescence in the gurgling wakes of the sterns. Over this eerie phenomenon glittered the pale and wavering yellow lights of the ships' lanterns, somehow comforting, yet out of place on the lonely sea.

Entertainment in the evening was limited only by the passengers' talents and imaginations. In the pleasant downdraft of air from the big canvas sails, there was often singing and dancing aboard the treasure galleons. Impromptu plays, stunts, skits and buffoon shows were dramatically performed on the main deck for everyone's enjoyment. Or passengers might gather in the light of the lanterns to play "The Renegade Caxcara" and other innocent card games, all forms of gambling being prohibited. Toward the end of the voyage, after the ships had been at sea for nearly two months, there would come a day of joyous, unrestrained merrymaking. It was called the *fiesta de las señas,* a ceremonial occasion celebrating the first sighting of the "signs"—floating grass, sticks or other debris from land, or shore birds—that heralded their approach to land. The fiesta began sedately enough with the singing of a *Te Deum,* praising God for a safe crossing and an end to their wearisome journey. Then, to the accompaniment of drums and trumpets, everyone joined in an uproarious saturnalia (kept within the bounds of "decency and modesty") highlighted by a mock trial and punishment of ships' officers at the hands of the gleeful crews.

The flotilla finally reached *Los Membros* (Riding Rocks), on the northwest edge of the Great Bahama Bank, where the fleet was to change course and head westward across the Straits to Florida. Until then, the northward progress of the treasure galleons had been uneventfully routine. By a rather devious course they had now reached 25°15′ north latitude and had traveled some 150 nautical miles from Havana without mishap. Keeping well clear of the rocks, the ships swung one by one onto their new course and set out across the Straits.

At three o'clock that afternoon, the lookouts sighted white water over the Cape Reef, flanking the low-lying Florida Keys. Off *Cayo Tabona,* just south of Key Largo, the ships veered northward again. With the four-mile-an-hour Gulf Stream current pushing them, they beat their way up the coast, the overloaded frigates struggling to sail as closely as possible into the northeast winds, but managing not more than about a fifty-degree angle.

Finally the fleet reached the mouth of the Old Bahama Channel,* the beginning of the narrowest part of the Straits between the Florida shore and the Bahama Bank, where the ships would start tacking northward. But now the winds grew erratic. First they blew strong from one quarter, fell off, then gusted from another. Frequently they died altogether. Sails slatted, tackle rattled and the

---

* Believed to be just south of present-day Miami.

17

vessels wallowed in the choppy, uncertain seas. No satisfactory course could be held under such conditions. General Ubilla chose to wait for better sailing weather.

For the next twenty-two hours the ships tacked back and forth well out at sea. Then about 2 P.M. the following afternoon, the winds settled more steadily into the northeast and the fleet started its journey up the Straits. Ships' officers were kept busy watching for luffs in their sails and seeing that the crews leaped to their tasks with smartness and efficiency. Now, instead of going to whatever place work had to be done, each man of the watch had a special station. On the forecastle, an officer and two crewmen were in charge of handling the headsails and forward end of the ship. Another officer and two men in the waist of the vessel stood by to work the main tack and bowline, two others the foresheet and main. Other officers and men were responsible for seeing to the after yards and handling the lee fore and main braces, the main topsail, the topgallant and the weather cross-jack braces, while the rest of the watch stood ready at the main brace.

When the captain deemed the ship ready to tack, he gave the order, "Helm alee!"

The helmsman pulled the wheel around, and the ship slowly turned into the wind. As she did, the officer on the forecastle shouted an order, and the headsail sheets were let go; then, in rapid succession down the full length of the ship, fore tack and main sheets were let go, and the opposite braces hauled—the weather cross-jack braces were belayed on one side and hauled on the other. From the foremast to the mizzenmast and from the gallants down, the yardarms swung around one after the other, the sails first fluttering and slapping, then filling and pulling taut, and finally being trimmed, with the sheets all made fast and the ship beating to windward again on a new angle. As long as the wind came from the same general direction, the ships could remain on the same tack for hours. Back and forth they sailed, first from within sight of the Florida shore eastward until the lookouts reported the bright green shoal water and sawtooth reefs of the Bahama Bank; then, one after another, the vessels turned back on as much of a northwest course as they could muster against the northeast winds. As they sailed this zigzag course northward, each of the twelve vessels would tack once every three hours, night and day, for the next week.

On Sunday, July 28, the distance between ships gradually

widened as they moved up the passage. General Echeverz must have been annoyed to learn from his lookout that Captain Darié's frigate, the *Grifón*, had pulled out of line against orders and was now sailing well ahead and to the northeast of the fleet. Everyone knew that the brash young Frenchman had been forced to sail with General Ubilla's fleet from Vera Cruz to keep the *Flota's* sailing date a secret. And now the Frenchman was apparently showing his disdain for the slow-moving convoy by deliberately letting his ship take her head and pull away. It was an affront to Spain that Echeverz, an old knight, would not have taken lightly, but at the present there were more important things to worry about. On the south and southeastern horizon the rapidly growing banks of clouds had a strange, ominous quality about them. The evening sun sank into this somber setting, lining the western horizon hours before dark. Echeverz surely noted that the usually clear vial of shark oil, which he kept in his cabin to help him foretell the weather, was turning cloudy—a sure sign of approaching bad weather.

The next day—Monday, July 29—offered no improvement. In the distance, to the leeward of the armada, lay the Florida coast, but even in the midday sun a strange milky haze obscured the view. The sea looked leaden. The ships rolled on long, steady swells sweeping toward shore. With each ungainly rising and falling, rudder pintles creaked, blocks clattered, rigging strained or slackened, and passengers braced themselves against the wild, inverted pendulum swing of the masts. Sailors who claimed they could feel the coming of bad weather in their bones complained of aching joints. Aboard the fleet's flagship, General Ubilla spent more time than usual on deck, staring eastward.

By Monday night, the prevailing wind had slackened noticeably, and a few rain squalls dotted the horizon. Instead of reducing sail, as was customary at night, General Ubilla ordered the fleet to lay on all canvas available. Foul weather was coming, and this was no place to delay. Both commanders were well aware of their perilous position in the Straits and the danger of delay, but for the fleet's commanding general, Juan Ubilla, this realization undoubtedly was particularly poignant. From the inception of this combined fleet, there had been delays upon delays. Fateful delays. Each had seemed of little importance at the time. But now, on the night of July 29, 1715, if General Ubilla thought of anything other than how

19

to avoid their impending problems with the worsening weather, the commander probably remembered all too clearly the unfortunate circumstances of the last three years that had brought them to their present predicament.

Chapter 3
Prelude to Disaster

Events that were to shape the destiny of the fleet began in 1712 during a period of historical turmoil near the end of the War of the Spanish Succession. This conflict, which stemmed from the accession of Phillip IV of Anjou, a Bourbon and grandson of Louis XIV of France, to the Spanish throne as Phillip V, had been a long and costly one for Spain and her French allies. Although their armies had acquitted themselves well in the European campaigns, the French and Spanish navies were less than successful in opposing the powerful English and Dutch fleets at sea. By controlling the seaways, particularly during the latter years of the war, the Anglo-Dutch fleets had effectively prevented Spain from drawing on the rich resources of her New World empire when she needed them most. After the enemy had destroyed seventeen Spanish treasure galleons at Vigo Bay in 1702 and captured the entire South American treasure fleet off Cartagena in 1708, Spain was understandably reluctant to risk any more large fleets in the Atlantic or Caribbean. Although some sailings continued during the war, these were usually limited to dispatch boats or small groups of vessels—nothing comparable to the large fleets which had customarily carried on Spanish commerce in peacetime.

When it appeared that the war was coming to an end, however, Spain was anxious to pick up where she had left off. Even before the signing of the treaties at Utrecht in 1713, which officially ended the war, King Phillip V was moving to get the much-needed stored wealth from Spain's New World colonies. On March 3, 1712, he ordered the Council of the Indies to organize a flotilla of eight vessels to be ready to sail to New Spain. The king's directive was approved immediately in Madrid, and the powerful House of Trade at Seville, which controlled commerce and navigation in the Indies, began to enlist a *Flota* at the port of Cádiz.

It was not an easy job. When such fleets were organized in the latter part of the 16th century, there had been no difficulty in obtaining convoys of more than a hundred ships each to sail to the Spanish Indies; but now, in 1712, Seville was hard pressed to find even one ship to fill the order for a fleet to sail to Vera Cruz. Eventually, however, eight vessels were found for the voyage. An agreement was made on May 15, 1712, with Don Juan de Ubilla and Don Guyermo Con to prepare two of them as warships of 50 to 54 guns to serve in the New Spain fleet as *Capitana* and *Almiranta*. Ubilla, a veteran of many years' service in the Spanish fleets, became general. Since Guyermo Con declined to undertake the voyage, Don Francisco Salmón was named the admiral or *Almiranta* in his place.

The next few months were spent loading and provisioning the ships at Cádiz. In the cargo, the goods going to the New World were consignments of wine, brandy, olive oil, cloth, ironwork, books, two years' supply of officially letterheaded legal paper, and the royal monopoly of 3,999.5 hundredweight of mercury (just under 200 tons) to be used in the amalgam process for refining gold.

Although peace talks were under way by 1712, hostilities continued. General Ubilla was probably hesitant to risk the fleet while waters in Europe and the Western Hemisphere were still alive with enemy ships. Phillip V had ordered the *Flota* to sail by July 31, but it was delayed. On August 8 a report was brought to the general that five English warships of from 50 to 70 guns had been sighted near Cádiz. An armistice between England, France and Spain was signed on August 19, 1712, but official word of this settlement was not published until September 4. Now the Council of the Indies decided that, regardless of risks, the fleet should sail. General Ubilla held a meeting of his major officers with representatives of the merchants' association. They voted that the fleet should sail, with three smaller vessels scouting ahead for any ships that might not have heard of the armistice.

As the day of departure approached, passengers began coming aboard. They were merchants, government officials with their families, bishops, friars, missionaries, people seeking their fortunes abroad, and an incredible number of hopeful opportunists who had bribed minor ships' officers to hide them as stowaways. And, as was always so, there were late arrivals.

Finally, after many lengthy delays, General Ubilla's fleet of eight vessels was ready to sail. The House of Trade officials had given the ships their final inspection to make certain that none carried unregistered cargo for which export taxes had not been paid, and the church officials had given their blessing to the fleet before it weighed anchor. Even then, there was one more last-minute delay. A wealthy nobleman and his entourage from Barcelona almost missed the ship because they had been held up by floods near Valencia. In addition, the portly gentleman was afflicted by gout in his feet and had to be carried aboard the *Capitana* in a sedan chair, which he controlled by applying his cane to the ribs of his lead porter. One hundred fourteen barrels of water had to be disembarked to make room for the new passenger's baggage. The *Flota* delayed sailing until early the next morning.

At 5:30 A.M. on September 16, the ships hoisted anchor and cleared from Cádiz—the two guard vessels leading the way, while the others fell in line behind General Ubilla's *Capitana*, the *Nuestra Señora de la Regla*. Admiral Salmón's *Almiranta*, the *Santo Cristo de San Román*, brought up the rear.

The Marquis of Monroy was later to report in a letter to the Council of the Indies that by 10 A.M. the fleet had rounded the point of Rota. As the wind freshened, the ships soon passed out of sight of land. "May God grant a fortunate voyage for this fleet," said the Marquis.

At sea the routine of the voyage began. Each member of the crew had specific jobs to do. The pilots attended to navigational matters, the seamen controlled the sails, the helmsmen steered the ships, and the ships' boys scrubbed the upper decks, fed the stock and took care of the wants of the officers and wealthy passengers. The entire crew took turns standing watches. Only the idle passengers had time on their hands.

23

As soon as the *Flota* was out of sight of land, it was discovered that there were 134 *llovidos*, or stowaways, aboard the flagship. These people had come aboard secretly, with the understanding that if they did not show themselves until the ship was far offshore, they would not be thrown into the water or allowed to die of hunger or thirst. To the Spanish way of thinking, a trip to the colonies practically guaranteed one's fortune; therefore the fleets sailing to the New World always had a large number of stowaways aboard. Spanish historian Cesáreo Fernández Duro reported that on one early-18th-century ship clearing from Cádiz with the *Tierra Firma* fleet, some three hundred stowaways who had "embarked secretly to travel on the King's money" were discovered.

As overcrowded as ships normally were, this should have created enormous logistics problems for the commanders, but apparently it did not. Although Spanish officials frowned on the practice, stowaways were accepted as a minor nuisance of the Indies trade.

The presence of these additional people aboard General Ubilla's flagship increased the total number to over eight hundred. Since most of the extra water supply had been disembarked to accommodate the last passenger's baggage, there was now more than a distinct possibility that there would be some thirsty stowaways aboard the *Capitana* before the fleet reached Vera Cruz.

As the days passed with monotonous regularity, the passengers amused themselves as best they could. Some fished for gilthead and sharks, while others made a game of watching the sky for rain clouds. With every small shower they spread pieces of cloth to catch the vital drops. Cockfights and mock bullfights were popular events. The latter never failed to draw a crowd to cheer for the "bull."

If the weather was pleasant in the evenings, there were other kinds of entertainment on the maindeck beneath the great sails. On several occasions a troop of tumblers and jugglers, bound for the trade fairs, amazed and delighted everyone with their feats of agility and skill. There was also singing, recitations, and concerts with flute, violin and oboe. The Capuchin monks helped to lighten the spirits of those on board by holding a mission of nine days, a jubilee and general Communion. On General Ubilla's *Capitana*, moreover, there were two events uncommon to a warship: the wife of a prominent official en route to an important position in Vera Cruz presented her husband with their thirteenth offspring, and another woman gave birth to a healthy baby, but died in doing so.

For every death at sea, there was the ceremony of casting off the corpse, which ceremony the solemn and curious passengers always gathered to witness. While the priest performed his ritual, the crew stood at attention on deck; then with three shouts of "Bon voyage," the corpse was consigned to the deep. If scurvy or another deadly disease swept the ship, the ceremony was performed daily, and all the bodies were cast into the sea at once. At such times it is doubtful that the remaining passengers were much interested in watching these final rites being administered to their departed traveling companions.

Frequently the boredom of the voyage was broken by watching punishment meted out to someone for a crime or an infraction of the strict shipboard rules. Sometimes the offense was so minor that the punishment consisted only in making a man lie face down on the deck for a period of time. But for anything as severe as disobeying an order or stealing food or water from the supplies, the offender was beaten with a cat-o'-nine-tails. In all cases the captain-general of the ship decided the severity of the punishment—how many lashes should be applied, for example.

When the *Flota* reached the Canary Islands the two guard vessels left the fleet. General Ubilla sent two letters back to Spain on one of the ships, reporting that he had arrived there safely and was continuing.

Shortly after dawn on October 8, the *Flota* was about 250 leagues from Martinique in the West Indies when the lookout aboard the *Nuestra Señora de la Regla* sighted a sail on the western horizon. Now that the fleet no longer had its protective escort, the stranger's sudden appearance caused considerable apprehension until the vessel passed to leeward of the fleet and was identified as a French ship. In a letter to the Marquis de Monroy, the French sea captain mentioned sighting the fleet. The Marquis in turn reported the event to the Council of the Indies in his letter of December 13, 1712.

In the diary of a passenger making that transatlantic voyage, we read that after more than a month at sea the overcrowded conditions, the ennui, the stinking squalor below decks and the rapidly diminishing food supplies began to tell on the passengers. Tempers flared, and petty grievances became the main topic of conversations. The irascible old nobleman from Barcelona complained that all he ever got to eat at the general's table was a thick corn soup and a perpetual stew of garbanzo beans. The ship's boy learned early to stay clear of the gouty old man when he was carried on deck in his sedan chair, for he often took out his temper on whoever was within reach of his cane. On several occasions he was seen to apply it rudely to the ribs of some of the pages and irreverently to the backsides of some of the bishop's relatives. According to accounts, another individual on board who was the recipient of wrath was the officer controlling the water ration. As the daily allotment grew smaller, the general resentment grew greater. No longer did the passengers call him by name; they simply referred to him as "the executioner of the thirsty." They said he was cruel, inexorable, incorruptible and given to argue even over the general's special orders dealing with the gouty old nobleman's chocolate mug. Before the voyage ended, the water officer would be thoroughly hated by all.

One day the first *patache,* the *Nuestra Señora de las Nieves,* began taking on more sea than usual through her teredo-riddled timbers, and the fleet stopped in midocean to make repairs. While divers went down to mend the hull, General Ubilla ordered a meeting aboard the flagship of all the ships' captains and pilots. The commander pointed out that since there was a shortage of drinking water, he wanted them to determine whether it would be feasible to sail for one of the Lesser Antilles and replenish their supply. The pilots got together and checked their navigation. Those from the *Santissima Trinidad* said they were 140 leagues from the islands. The chief pilot on General Ubilla's flagship set the distance at 135 leagues, and the second pilot at 100 leagues. With repairs completed, the fleet sailed on, but the discussions and debates about the pilots' accuracies continued until the islands had been passed.

The *Flota* stopped for water at San Juan, Puerto Rico, but passengers were not allowed ashore. The fleet then continued along the northern coast of the island, swung southwest through the Mona Passage and followed the southern coast of Hispaniola. In the latitude of Cabo Tiburon, General Ubilla opened his sealed orders and called another meeting of his fleet officers, in which everyone agreed that conditions seemed safe enough in the Indies for the convoy to go on to Mexico. The ships sailed along the southern coast of Cuba, crossing the Yucatán Channel to pick up Cabo Catoche, then stayed within sight of the Mexican mainland until they reached Vera Cruz on December 3.

The *Flota* anchored at the island of San Juan de Ulúa, directly opposite the town where a fort had been built to protect the fleets. Despite the importance of Vera Cruz as a New World trade terminus for Spain, the seaport was little more than a shantytown. Originally it had been located fifteen miles up the coast where Hernando Cortés and 508 conquistadors had first landed in 1519, but this was a poor choice. The open harbor was exposed in the winter to northern gales. Moreover, its entrance was blocked by a treacherous sandbar, which allowed the passage of small vessels but forced large ones to anchor at San Juan de Ulúa down the coast. Cargo was then transferred to smaller boats and brought to Vera Cruz. Finally, in 1599, the town was moved to its present location opposite the island. For almost two hundred years, Vera Cruz had dealt in the wealth that had enriched an empire, yet in 1712 it still looked like a transient town which wealth and progress had simply passed by. Since the trade fair would not be held until the following spring, Ubilla found the place virtually deserted. The general intended to winter his fleet there and get on with the business of discharging his cargo, selling it at the trade fair and loading for his outbound trip in the spring. But neither the commander nor the impatient king of Spain could have envisioned how long a delay fate was about to impose on the expedition.

A series of unfortunate incidents at Vera Cruz prevented the fleet's leaving for the next two years and five months. Although some of these events have been pieced together from official letters and documents of the period, they still present a fragmentary picture of the factors leading to the *Flota*'s ultimate end.

Primarily, it appears that the *Flota* had trouble disposing of its cargo at the Vera Cruz trade fair in the spring. This was probably due to the presence of several French vessels that had special trade agreements with the Spanish king. The French frigate *Grifón* arrived at Vera Cruz in May 1713 with three hundred tons of goods, which Captain Darié may have been able to sell at lower rates than Ubilla's, thereby making it more difficult for the commander to dispose of his merchandise. It is also possible that the Viceroy of New Spain was unprepared for the *Flota*'s arrival and had not yet readied all the goods and treasure that would be going back to

Spain. In any event, complications delayed the fleet through the summer and into the fall hurricane months of 1713, when it would have been unwise for the *Flota* to try to reach Havana.

On May 18, 1714, officials of the House of Trade complained to the Crown that Seville was badly in need of funds. They said they had twice received word that the fleet would sail by February after needed repairs, but that it had not. Consequently, the House of Trade tribunal went unpaid, and there were back charges on the fleet's revenues owing since 1711.

In September the fleet was damaged by a storm at Vera Cruz and so required further delay for repairs. On December 8 the Council of the Indies reported to the king that Ubilla's fleet had twice been ready for loading, but the outbound cargo was still in the warehouses. Once again the star-crossed fleet was forced to winter in Vera Cruz.

By spring of 1715, however, the *Flota* was finally being loaded. Most of the Mexican treasure consisted of 1714 silver coinage. The viceroy had ordered the mints into overtime operation that year so that the fleet could carry back to Spain as much silver as the Mexican mines had produced up to then. The entire process, from mining to minting, had been slow and laborious. In previous centuries the rich veins had been closer to the surface, where the high-grade ore was easier for the Indian slaves to obtain. But by the 18th century, some of these mines had become as deep as nine hundred feet; the risks were greater, the accident rate was higher, and the grade of ore was poorer. Working in these narrow, dangerous mine shafts under the worst conditions, the Indians hammered the ore loose from the surrounding rock, hauled it to the surface in baskets and crushed it into fine powder for refining. Prior to the 1555 discovery of the amalgamation process in which mercury was used to simplify the refining of precious metals, powdered ore was mixed with lead and carbon, placed in crucibles and melted over wood fires fanned by large bellows. The lead and impurities were skimmed off with ladles, and the liquid silver was poured into molds to solidify. But with the amalgamation process, the powdered ore was mixed with mercury to separate the precious metal from the impurities. The silver and mercury amalgam was then cooked until the mercury evaporated and only the silver remained. This was either left as wedges or remelted and poured into round disks or bars. These were inspected by an assayer who either passed them as an acceptable grade of silver, cutting a mint or mine-owner's mark into the surface, or returned them for additional refining. Up to 20 percent of the precious metal mined, often called the "Royal Fifth," was subtracted as the Crown's share. Since mercury was indispensable to the refining process, the Crown monopolized the Empire's entire production of this metal and furnished it to the New World mines from the Empire's two major mercury mines, one in Almadén, Spain, and the other in Huancavélica, Peru.

Actually very little silver was sent to Spain as bullion. That an accurate inventory of the precious metal being purified and sent home might be kept, most of it went to one of the mints to be converted into coinage. In this process, pieces of silver the approximate size and weight of the intended coins were clipped or chiseled from the ends of flat strips of silver. These were then hand struck between two dies, which embossed them with the cross of Spain on one face and the royal coat of arms on the other. Although the handmade dies carried the date, the coins were minted so carelessly that the date seldom showed on the finished coin. The most important thing was that the coin be of the right weight and purity; consequently it was desirable to show the mint mark and assayer's initial. All silver coins were called reals* and during this period were struck in denominations of ½, 1, 2, 4, and 8 reals—the largest denomination being known as a piece of eight. The irregularities of the strip gave each cob coin an angular, irregular shape, and no two were exactly alike. The crude coins were probably reminted in Spain. In the early 18th century, a piece of eight (or 8 reals) was often a peso,** a monetary unit which at that time had a purchasing power equal to about $12 in our present currency.

Essentially similar refining and minting processes were used for gold, except that the weight was watched far more closely. If the gold was minted into coins, they were called escudos through the 18th century and doubloons from that period on. Doubloons were minted in the same denominations as silver coins, but they were struck more precisely. Since gold was worth approximately sixteen times the same weight of silver, the purchasing power of a gold

* In the early 18th century, one silver real, the equivalent of 12½ cents, could buy so many groceries in the Mexico market that the purchaser needed a cart to carry them home.
**9,000 pesos could buy a ship complete with crew and supplies.

8-escudo doubloon in the early 18th century was equal to approximately $200 in today's currency.

The *Audencia*, New Spain's colonial council, had tentatively set the date for the *Flota's* departure for Havana in late March. Following this decision the officials, as required by law, halted the issuance of licenses permitting other vessels to leave Vera Cruz before the *Flota* sailed. This was done to prevent knowledge of the exact sailing date of the treasure fleets from falling into the hands of pirates or belligerents who might capture small or lightly armed merchant vessels and force this information out of those aboard.

One of the vessels detained by the closing of the port was the French warship *Grifón*, commanded by Captain Darié. Early in 1712, when it became obvious that peace was imminent, Darié had applied for and received—as indicated above—a special license to trade with New Spain. These special trade permits granted to the French by the Crown were apparently a natural outgrowth of the two countries' wartime alliance and the fact that Spain was gradually losing the trade monopoly she had always enjoyed with her New World possessions. Captain Darié had paid the considerable sum of 50,000 pesos (equal to about $600,000 today) for the license, and he was understandably annoyed at not being allowed to get his merchandise back to France—especially since he could reasonably expect a profit return of from four to eight times his original investment in fees and cargo.

With his ship nearly loaded and ready to go, Darié appealed to the *Audencia* to make an exception in his case. He argued that an unnecessary layover would cause additional expenses to himself and other investors; that since his vessel was a warship it was unlikely to be a target for pirates; and finally, that he was a French national, and the ruling applied only to Spanish subjects.

The council turned a deaf ear to his appeal. He was told that the *Grifón* could either sail with the fleet or sometime after. Darié reluctantly agreed to accompany the fleet.

Early in March, when it became apparent that the fleet would not be ready to leave on time, a new date, April 11, was set for sailing. Then on March 28, when the ships were about half loaded, a particularly violent storm struck Vera Cruz. Hurricane-force winds swept across the exposed harbor and hurled twelve ships against the coast, smashing them to pieces or holing their hulls. Two ships of the *Flota*, one of the *pataches* and another small vessel, were lost.

The second *patache* pitched and rolled and came out badly damaged. The *Urca de Lima*, which had become the fleet's *resfuerzo*, snapped one of her cables and ended up six leagues away from her mooring with several broken timbers. It took eleven days to return the vessel to her position. The *Capitana* was blown from her mooring and ran into a reef, and General Ubilla ordered the masts chopped down to save the lives of those aboard. The ship managed to drop anchor and remain afloat. Both the *Grifón* and another French warship, the *Française*, snapped their cables and drifted. Darié's men got the *Grifón* anchored again, but the ship was badly shaken. The *Française* drifted off so far that she left the other vessels behind. Only the *Almiranta*, sheltered by the fortress of San Juan de Ulúa, escaped undamaged.

The *Flota* was now forced to lay over another five weeks for repairs and final loading. If this unfortunate turn of events rankled, General Ubilla kept the fact to himself. What the commander could not foresee, however, was that four months and three days later, this and previous delays would be largely responsible for troubles that would confront his fleet in the Florida Straits.

Finally, on May 4, 1715, the *Flota* sailed from Vera Cruz for Havana, accompanied by the French ship, *Grifón*. After the storm losses, the fleet was down to four vessels, the *Capitana*, the *Almiranta*, the *resfuerzo* and the *patache* of Soto Sanchez. These ships were heavy-laden with treasure, most of it aboard the two well-armed warships, the *Capitana* and the *Almiranta*. They alone carried the king's treasure, 1,222,824 pesos 3 tomines 5 grains in silver coins and bullion. In addition, General Ubilla's flagship, the *Nuestra Señora de la Regla*, carried 8,076 small chests and sacks of silver coins comprising privately registered treasure, plus sixty-two chests of gifts and one small chest of gold bars, doubloons and pearls. There were also considerable amounts of worked silver, cochineal, indigo, vanilla, chocolate, copper, Chinese porcelain, brazilwood, balsam and other miscellaneous cargo.

Besides the royal treasure, Admiral Salmón's *Almiranta*, the *Santo Cristo de San Román*, carried 2,076,004 pesos in silver for private interests, plus 684 small chests and sacks of gifts, Chinese porcelain, worked silver and other less valuable riches. The *resfuerzo*, the *Urca de Lima*, carried 252,171 pesos of privately registered silver, and the *patache*, the *Nuestra Señora de las Nieves*, carried 44,000 pesos in coined silver and bullion.

31

The *Flota* sailed northward with the winds and the current into the Gulf of Mexico, following the coast on a course that more than a month later would bring the vessels to Havana and the long-awaited rendezvous with the *Galeones* fleet of General Echeverz.

Meanwhile, the *Galeones de Tierra Firma*, waiting for the *Flota* in Cuba, had had far less difficulty keeping to its schedule. In 1712, while the *Flota* was being enlisted at Cádiz, the king granted registries for a fleet of privately owned vessels to sail to Cartagena and pick up the treasure of South America. These contracts to civilians were issued in the name of Don Antonio de Echeverz, Don Manuel Lopez Pintado and a few other influential speculators. The fleet consisted of four vessels, the *Nuestra Señora del Carmen*, Echeverz's flagship; the *Nuestra Señora del Rosario*, his *Almiranta*; and two *pataches*, the *Nuestra Señora de la Concepción* and the *El Señor San Miguel*. In the contract signed June 23, 1713, Echeverz agreed to take 1,000 quintales of mercury, 150 troops and 471 packets of sealed paper to the New World, returning in one year with all the silver, gold and royalties from the South American mainland for the Crown loaded aboard his flagship.

Ubilla's *Flota* had left Cádiz in September 1712. Echeverz was ordered to leave the following spring—in May 1713—but as usual there were delays in preparing the ships for departure. When the vessels were not ready by mid-May, the sailing date was moved to June 3. The spring floods that ravaged Spain that year, making it difficult to obtain food supplies, caused further delay. Finally, the ships were loaded and sailed from Cádiz on July 9, 1713. Most of the cargo they carried was general trade supplies, including hundreds of tons of English manufactured goods, books, cloth, wax, iron-work and nails. There was the usual livestock brought along for food during the voyage, but General Echeverz had got out of carrying several camels aboard the *Capitana*. Although the animals were to have been sent to the Marquis de Villarocha, president of the High Court of Panama, with the intention of acclimating them to serve as replacements for mules used to transport silver and other cargo across the Isthmus, they would now have to go by another fleet.

With the signing of the last treaties at Utrecht that year, war tensions eased and the galleons sailed westward across the Atlantic without an additional escort and without mishap. Once they entered the Caribbean and were following the warm westerly currents off the Lesser Antilles, General Echeverz sent one of his *pataches*, the *El Señor San Miguel*, on to Havana to purchase in advance the large amount of tobacco he intended to pick up there the following year. The remaining three ships maintained their course along the north coast of South America, sighting their landmark at Cabo de la Vela and sailing southwestward past Cabo de la Aguija and Santa Marta, where the voyagers offered their prayers of thanks for a safe crossing to the sanctuary of the Virgin Mary built high in the hills. On August 29, after fifty days at sea, the galleons sailed through the narrow Boca Chica pass into the fine ten-mile-long harbor at Cartagena, New Granada.

Ever since its founding in 1533, this important port on the northern coast of present-day Colombia had been the first stop for most of the ships in the *Tierra Firma Armadas* coming to the New World. Officially it was called Cartagena de las Indies to differentiate it from the port of Cartagena on the Mediterranean in southeastern Spain. Within two years after the Caribbean town was founded, it was actively engaged in the shipping business. Although other ports along the Spanish Main were closer to the routes used to transport gold and emeralds from the interior, none offered such an excellent harbor as Cartagena. The harbor is formed by an indention of the coastline enclosed by two long islands lying parallel to the mainland. Originally there were two entrances—the Boca Grande (large mouth) and the Boca Chica (small mouth). The more than ten-mile-long harbor with its two entrances could easily shelter hundreds of ships. The only disadvantage was that entry was so easy that Cartagena was attacked and sacked three times by sea-rovers before the Spanish got around to building adequate defenses.

Considering the seaport's past, it is understandable that the port resembled a veritable armed fortress when General Echeverz and the galleons arrived there in 1713. The town, about three-quarters of a mile long and half a mile wide, was surrounded by a heavy wall, in places forty feet thick. Several formidable-looking forts, including the turreted battlements of Fort San Felipe, stood ready to defend it.

The arrival of the *Tierra Firma* fleet at Cartagena was the big event of the year. It heralded the forthcoming trade fair, the long-awaited *feria*, with its special emphasis on business and pleasure.

As soon as the ships were moored and the official preliminaries over, General Echeverz dispatched a boat northwestward across the Gulf of Darien to the small town of Porto Bello, to carry the news that the fleet was in. The intelligence was sent by courier across the Isthmus to the president of Panama, who relayed it by boat to Peru so that the gold and silver shipment could be started north. To make certain that Peru got the word, native runners were also sent overland with the message to the viceroy at Lima.

For the next two months the galleons remained in Cartagena. Cargo was disembarked for the port, fresh water and victuals were taken aboard, and a small boat was sent to collect the annual pearl harvest at the island of Margarita off the coast of present-day Venezuela. When Echeverz learned that the treasure shipment from Peru had reached Panama City and was being transported across the Isthmus for the annual trade fair at that port, the fleet weighed anchor on November 4 and sailed to Porto Bello.

In the early 18th century this small Caribbean seaport on the Isthmus of Panama was both uncomfortable and unhealthful. The intense heat, the encroaching jungle and the prevalence of tropical fevers made it a difficult place to live, especially for unacclimatized foreigners. Originally the main trade terminus on the Isthmus had been Nombre de Dios, a small town several miles up the coast. But this unwalled settlement had a shallow, hazardous harbor and such a high mortality rate from tropical fever that it was called the "Graveyard of the Spaniards." Although Nombre de Dios was close to Panama City and the treasure traffic from the south, conditions were so bad there that Phillip II ordered the town moved to its present site at Porto Bello, which after 1596 became the main port of call on the Isthmus for the *Tierra Firma* fleets. Though Porto Bello did have a better harbor, the move did not change the sultry climate or cut down the fever fatalities.

To visitors and citizens alike, however, these matters were of little concern once the Porto Bello trade fair began. Rum flowed freely, merriment was the order of the day, and business was brisk in the shade of the great sailcloth tents erected in the city square. The fleet remained in Porto Bello through the winter, and on April 24, 1714, with the ships heavy-laden with goods and treasure, it returned to Cartagena, arriving there on May 15. During its stay some of the ships had sailed in patrol of the local coast and had had the good fortune to overtake and capture two foreign vessels engaged in smuggling. One was the French frigate *El Ciervo*, which

34

General Echeverz renamed *La Galeria;* the other was a Dutch sloop, *La Holendesa,* which he renamed the *San Miguel.* The crews were taken prisoner and the vessels added to the fleet.

Through the summer months the remaining treasure and goods for Spain were loaded aboard the ships. Finally, on September 7, when the fleet cleared for Havana, General Echeverz's *Capitana* was carrying 7,766 pounds of cacao;* 33,600 pounds of brazilwood; 79,967 pesos 22 reals in gold bars and doubloons; 309 castellanos;** 7 tomines;*** 6 grains of gold dust; 18 marks† 5½ ounces of silver; 1,175 pesos 8 reals of plata doble†† and three gold chains worth 380 pesos 14 reals. The *Almiranta* carried 15,514 pesos 13½ reals in gold bars and doubloons, 175 pesos in plata doble, chests of gifts and general cargo which included brazilwoods, cacao, chocolate, dry goods and hides. Along with similar goods the merchant *nao,* the *Nuestra Señora de la Concepción,* carried 8,503 pesos 3 reals in gold bars and doubloons. The remaining ships were to be loaded in Havana.

The *Galeones* reached this Cuban port on October 2, 1714. It was too late in the year to expect General Ubilla and the *Flota* from Vera Cruz. However, Havana was a far better place than Cartagena to winter the fleet. It had a well-defended deep-water harbor capable of sheltering hundreds of ships, the balmy climate was agreeable to Europeans, and in the early 18th century this fast-growing city of almost 50,000 was a far cry from the primitive settlements at the other ports of call along the Caribbean.

As the early months of 1715 passed, General Echeverz loaded 1,500,000 pounds of tobacco aboard his ships while he impatiently awaited the *Flota.* Then, a month after it arrived, the combined flotilla sailed.

If either commander had any foreboding of doom in those final days of July as the fleet pushed on through the treacherous Florida Straits under threatening skies, he undoubtedly kept his fears to himself. But the prelude was over. It was the beginning of the end.

---

* Seeds of the cacao tree used to make chocolate, cocoa and cocoa butter.
** One-fiftieth of a mark of gold.
*** A unit representing 12 grains.
† A measure of weight, approximately ½ pound or 230 grams.
†† Mixed denominations of silver 4- and 8-real coins.

Chapter 4

The Sea Came
Like Arrows

On Tuesday, July 30, dawn broke on an oppressively hot, humid day. People's hands felt clammy; their clothes stuck to their bodies. The fleet had made little progress during the night. Winds were erratic, often changing directions, sometimes ceasing to blow at all. During these lulls the creaking rigging of distant vessels could be heard over the water. The sun seemed enveloped in thin yellowish gauze. The unceasing swells grew larger and the ships rolled with more abandon. By noon there was not a man, woman or child in the fleet who did not sense that there was grave trouble ahead.

Gradually the wind picked up out of the northeast. The ships leaned into the steepening waves, but their northward movement was slow and awkward. Much time was lost on long southeastward runs necessary to gain sea room to tack northward along the coast. Shreds of grayish clouds scudded across the sky, gathering in an ominous black mantle that blotted out the sun. The wind blew increasingly stronger; the waves grew foaming crests. Pilots conferred with their captains to decide the best tactics to follow. If they reduced sail too much, they might lose valuable sea room and end up on the Florida shore. Yet if they did not reduce sail and were suddenly hit by high winds, they might lose both sails and upper masts. Ubilla's decision aboard the *Capitana* of the *Flota* was to reduce sail. Aboard Echeverz's flagship the proper signals were made and both watches were called out. Hatches and ports were closed and battened down. The crow-jack yard was lowered and reefs taken in the topgallants.

By midafternoon it had grown so dark that stern lanterns were lighted. Sporadic rain squalls lashed the fleet, the heavy downpours completely obscuring the ships. Suddenly the wind veered to the east and shrieked across the Straits at forty knots, wind across current—an awful combination to sail in. The rolling, rushing water thrust up jagged peaks that the gale instantly whipped into white spindrift and foam, driving it across wave troughs to mottle and streak the angry gray-black sea like veined marble.

With the storm's first powerful blast, the ships staggered and heeled over sharply. Sheets of spray blanketed the bows, spurted from around closed gunports, hawseholes and scuppers to race wildly across the decks. The ships no longer obeyed their helms but were forced around into the wind, righting as they swung bows on into the weather. Headsails flogged violently; standing and running rigging thrummed like strings on a giant harp. With a hissing rush, a solid wall of rain advanced on the fleet, the wind-driven drops hammering the foaming seas so hard that they seemed to smoke. Crews were ordered aloft to furl the topgallant sails. Shielding their faces against the stinging fury of the squall, the men clawed their way to the ratlines and climbed upward into the howling black nightmare where ropes, yards, tackle and sails thrashed, slapped, banged and clattered in wild confusion. The rain and the wind tore at their flimsy jackets and duck trousers. Attempts at speech were impossible, for words were whipped from lips and drowned in the shattering discord. Hand over hand the men went out on the swaying yards 130 feet above the dizzying deck, going by feel alone, their feet sliding along a single slippery wet rope arcing through space while they gripped the thick yard with fishhook fingers and knew that a single missed grip or misstep would send them plummeting into eternity. The driving rain seemed determined to pin them to their swaying perches in the sky, while the sharp wind tried to scrape them off. There was no such thing as turning their faces to windward, for the weather pounded them mercilessly from all sides. With outstretched arms they tried to smother the violently flapping sails, clutching and pulling canvas to them, getting it halfway in, only to have it ripped from their grasp, but grabbing again with fingers numb from fatigue, and fighting it in. Finally the sails were bunched on the yards and gaskets passed over them as snugly as possible before the men slid down the shrouds to the deck. For some there was a few minutes' rest; for others it was forty minutes on the pumps, trying to keep the already excessive volume of water in the bilges under control.

Half the watch went below, where there was little more comfort than in the hell they had just left. Down the full length of the gun deck, upper beams rained steady streams of water on the miserable folk huddled row after row in their soggy hammocks. Children cried, the devout or terrified prayed, the sick moaned. And now the stifling air had another overpowering odor added to it: the stench of vomit.

At least the wet hammocks offered some small relief, for their swaying was far less violent than that of the rest of the ship, whose decks, bulkheads, timbers, knees and beams were in constant motion, tilting forward and back and rolling from side to side, sometimes the parts working against one another in agonizingly shrill discord. Below decks the whole ship creaked, groaned or screamed in torment. To this was added the muffled sliding, scraping and bumping of shifting cargo, the jolting thunder of bows crashing into waves, the hiss and gurgle of water rushing past the hull, the thud and rattle of tackle dropping on the deck overhead, and the screeching of the rows of cannon straining at their lashings along both sides of the gun deck.

The weary sailors had hardly slumped into their hammocks when there was a sudden sharp, booming explosion topside, as if a 24-pounder had fired, then a banging on the scuttle and a cry for all hands on deck. The men scrambled for the ladder and stumbled back out into the storm. The fore-topsail had split from clew to earing and was blowing to pieces. The first watch was already aloft, fighting to control the topgallants that had blown free from the gaskets and were streaming loose from the yards.

Once again the men climbed up into the reeling darkness of thrumming rigging and careening yardarms. It took more than a half hour to drag in the tattered sail and furl it around the yard, lashing it with double gaskets and tightening the rolling tackle until it looked like a crudely bandaged broken limb.

Two hours later the rain passed as quickly as it had come, but the wind moved into the northeast and blew harder, gusting to fifty knots. Mountainous white waves crashed over the bows. The men were aloft constantly in their endless battle against the wind and the sails. Officers strained to see the arcing amber glow of lanterns on the vessels ahead and behind as the specks of light rose, lurched and disappeared behind the heavy seas. The commanders knew that the worst was yet to come. If they had not been caught in the channel between the Bahama Bank to the east and the inhospitable Florida coast to the west, they could have run south or southwest, away from the storm. But they were trapped unless the wind shifted. Although they could not maintain sail in the rising winds, their only hope was to go on, to try to pass what is now Cape Canaveral rather than collide with it at the mercy of a full-blown hurricane.

By midnight the fleet had been pounded by five vicious gales, each worse than the one before. Safety lines stretched fore and aft kept the watches from washing overboard as they went to and from the rigging, but the strain of fighting the storm had already left its mark on the ships and the men. All the vessels had badly opened seams; water rose in the holds. Pumps had to be manned constantly. Two seamen had fallen from swaying yards on Ubilla's *Capitana* and been lost at sea. The general's *Almiranta* had to jury-rig a mainsail, the first two having been blasted to shreds during the squalls. Echeverz's *Capitana* had lost its jib-boom and part of its bowsprit from plowing into the unyielding seas. With them the topgallant mast and sails had crashed down and enveloped the forecastle, part of the debris dragging in the water until it was slashed free and allowed to go by the board. There was no hope of repair. Each time the flagship's bows went under, tons of water were scooped up and flung across the forecastle onto the maindeck. Trunks, bales, barrels, livestock—everything washed about in confusion. Yet, somehow, each time the vessel managed to pull her head free, to rise up out of the foaming abyss with water gushing from her scuppers, the deck cargo settled momentarily into a new pattern of disorder, until the ship plunged down again into the next onrushing wall of water.

Having failed to finish the fleet with its first vicious onslaughts, the storm grew worse. The wind blew harder, the waves piled higher, the rain came in torrents. The ships were now completely out of control. General Echeverz's *Capitana* shipped a sea at her stern that almost finished her. It blasted in the cabin windows and bulkheads of the poop, sending tons of water rushing through the officers' quarters and down companionways, the blow knocking pilots and officers off their feet on the deck just above. The last sails tore loose from their gaskets and split open. Sailors aloft did what they could to jury-rig the remains, but it was already too late.

At 2:00 A.M., Wednesday, July 31, the hurricane struck with all its fury, roaring out of the east with winds in excess of seventy-five miles an hour. Nothing withstood its wrath. One moment jury sails were bowed rock hard from their improvised yards; the next instant they were gone, atomized, the sounds of their passing no more heard above the howling holocaust than the crash of splintered masts or the screams of maimed men. The air was filled with foam, the wind-driven spray flying like arrows. Once recognizable waves were now towering white moving Matterhorns of destruction that overwhelmed and crushed whatever ships they encountered, while pushing others inexorably closer to the seething maelstrom of water thundering over the Florida shoals.

The fleet was helpless; each ship was on its own. Some wallowed broadside to the waves and the wind. The land was near. Dismasted ships broached to, touched bottom and were torn apart, every living thing swept away. On other vessels the end took longer, and there was time for prolonged pandemonium. Crazed livestock reared and plunged on decks littered with men trying to free themselves from fallen rigging. People driven by fear swarmed out from below decks into the black tumult of destruction and added to the confusion. Ships that survived the moment were given but a temporary reprieve. But in those moments, crews drew on the last reserves of mind and limb in an effort to try to save their vessels by jettisoning cargo, cannon and anchors and frantically slashing away rigging that had already gone by the board, its weight threatening to drag the ships over on their beam ends.

On General Ubilla's flagship, the *Nuestra Señora de la Regla*, the crew tried to chop down the masts, hoping to lighten ship enough to let it float closer to dry land, for if the vessels could not save themselves by avoiding the shoals, their only hope was to reach shore to save lives. But for the big *Capitana* it was too late. The 471-ton vessel struck bottom with such force that her entire lower hull was sheared away. Ballast, cargo, cannon, passengers and 120 tons of registered silver coins in boxes plummeted to the bottom of the rampaging sea, while the superstructure continued shoreward, breaking up as it went. General Ubilla, commander of the armada, and some 220 others drowned.

Santo Cristo de San Román, the 450-ton *Almiranta* of the *Flota,* also lost the lower part of her hull after striking bottom; the upper works broke to pieces near shore. One hundred twenty persons drowned. Two of the *Flota's* tenders, Ubilla's recently purchased small frigate and the *Nuestra Señora de las Nieves* were literally torn apart in the surf. On the former, twelve persons perished; on the latter, two dozen drowned as the deck lifted off the hull, but some one hundred survivors rode the wreckage ashore like a raft. The *Flota's* supply ship, the *Santissima Trinidad,* called the "*Urca de Lima,*" was the only vessel to remain virtually intact. Although she lost her foremast, her crew managed to anchor her between two rock ledges lying parallel to the shore near the mouth of a river. In trying to reach shore, thirty-five drowned. The *Urca* remained afloat until eight o'clock that evening, when a second violent storm caused the seas repeatedly to lift and drop the vessel on her own foremast tangled underneath until she holed her hull and sank on the spot. General Echeverz's flagship, the *Nuestra Señora del Carmen,* was more fortunate than the other large warships. The crew lightened her sufficiently for the vessel to reach the shallows near shore, where she sank, listing, but with little loss of life. General Echeverz was among the survivors. His *Almiranta,* the *Nuestra Señora del Rosario,* was totally destroyed near shore a little farther south; 124 perished, including her captain, General Echeverz's son.

In a few short hours the hurricane took its terrible toll on the Spanish treasure fleet of 1715. Eleven vessels, more than 14 million pesos of registered treasure, and seven hundred lives were lost in one of the worst sea disasters in history. Of the twelve ships that sailed from Havana, only one escaped—the French frigate *Grifón,* whose captain, Don Antonio Darié, had slowly pulled away from the fleet and was sailing so far to the northeastward at the time of the disaster that he was out of the hurricane's path. In fact, when he reached Europe, he was unable to report that there had even been a storm! When the fleet failed to appear off the Carolina capes where it would sail east for Spain, Darié, who had waited several days at that latitude, thought the ships had simply been delayed by a "prolonged calm."

41

Chapter 5

Castaways in the Land of the Ays

The hurricane was so severe and turbulent that, according to what he heard from old sailors, they had never seen one like it. Such was the violence of the sea waves that they seemed like arrows even to those on land, so that many who managed to reach the shore also were killed. It is calculated that more than 600 other persons drowned or were missing from all the ships in these coasts and beaches, with the added misfortune that, after some of the ships and part of the cargo of others had been washed ashore, the furious swaying to and fro of the sea waves would drag everything back into the ocean, where it disappeared, so that the coast was bare again.

From the deposition of Father Francisco de León y Cabrera, August 12, 1715

For the next eight hours the wind and the rain tore at the coast, the waves thundered into the beaches, and, to the south, one ship after another smashed upon the shoals. The living, the dying and the dead were cast up indiscriminately on the beach, along with broken planks, shattered timbers, tangled rigging, boxes, barrels, chests, and anything else that the capricious waves spared. Wreckage and people were scattered for almost thirty miles along the bleak, uninhabited coast. Wherever a ship was crushed between surf and shoals, the tragic flotsam washed ashore. Most of the women and children never made it. Neither did some of the seamen, who, though good swimmers, sank like bar-shot, their pockets bulging with the heavy silver coins rifled from passengers' baggage or from the boxes of treasure carried aboard ship. Dazed and disoriented survivors whose lives had been spared by the sea crawled up the narrow strip of sand to face the nightmare of the storm on land. Many stumbled over each other in their scramble up the dunes to the scrub palmettos and palms. Others, lost and confused in the dark, too exhausted or injured to drag themselves away from the water's edge, stayed where the waves had washed them. The sea was impartial. Whoever was unable to move out of its reach was swept back into oblivion.

At daybreak the beach was strewn with wreckage and bodies. Other bodies tumbled grotesquely in the waves with waterlogged barrels, bales and debris. There was no sail on the horizon. All one saw was grim skies, heaving seas and the terrible evidence of what had happened. Survivors later reported seeing seamen on the beach bent over bodies as if searching them for signs of life. But that was not what they were looking for. They were robbing the dead of rings and valuables. Others were observed eagerly pulling clothing out of a large trunk, until some officers and marines came down from the dunes and made them stop. After a while the seamen began dragging some of the boxes and barrels into a pile well above the tide line. The bodies were laid in rows below the dunes and covered with torn sails. Several seamen collected wood and started a fire on the beach. As the wind slackened, more people left the palmettos, and a large group soon gathered around the fire.

This scene was repeated in nine other places along the narrow barrier island that parallels the southeast Florida mainland from what is now Cape Canaveral to a point south of present-day Fort Pierce. This region was known to the Spanish as *Palmar de Ays*, or palm grove of the Ays, named for some two thousand troublesome Ays Indians who lived along the mainland in this area. Since the survivors were uncertain just how hostile the Ays might be, they were wary of venturing any farther into the island than the sand dunes. In the first few hours after the worst of the storm had passed, they were unable to do much more than care for their injured and bury their dead, scratching shallow graves in the white sand to be blessed as a matter of course by surviving priests. Then they took what comfort they could from the driftwood fires they built on the beach.

That evening at eight o'clock, a second violent storm sank the *Urca de Lima*, aground near the mouth of the old Indian River inlet, the only vessel that had remained afloat.

Now only her maindeck showed above water. Although the longboats and some provisions had been taken off before she filled with water, most of the supplies were still in her flooded hold. A similar situation existed several miles to the north, where General Echeverz's *Capitana* had come to rest near a sand point. The few perishable provisions that had not been swept overboard during the storm only tantalized the hungry survivors camped on the beach opposite the wreck. However, these people and those near the *Urca* fared far better than survivors at the other camps, who found that most of the provisions had either gone down with their ships or had been swept away from the beach by the strong coastal currents. They were lucky to get some water from the few casks and bamboo containers that drifted ashore to slake their thirst temporarily.

But at least one good thing came of the night: the realization that they were not alone, that there were other fires and probably other survivors scattered along the distant beach.

At the southernmost wreck of the fleet, where the *Flota's patache*, the *Nuestra Señora de las Nieves*, had gone down, Captain Soto Sanchez took a careful fix on the wreck's latitude with a quadrant he had salvaged, and determined that he and his companions were 137 miles south of the only civilization in these parts—the Spanish settlement at St. Augustine. After sending a sergeant and two seamen down the coast a way to see if there were any other wrecks, and learning that there were no survivors in that direction, Sanchez immediately started leading his party north along the beach to find the commanding officers of the devastated fleet.

Four miles up the coast, on the south side of the inlet, the Sanchez group met Captain Miguel de Lima and his men, who were preparing to burn off the upper deck of the *Urca* so that they could haul up valuable provisions stored inside the supply ship's flooded hold. Two of the vessel's longboats had been salvaged, and although they were in need of repair, Don Miguel assured Sanchez that they would soon be made serviceable enough to help transport injured passengers and provisions.

At Sand Point, near present-day Rio Mar, survivors from General Echeverz's *Capitana*, the *Nuestra Señora del Carmen*, were busy salvaging what they could from the badly damaged ship that had sunk near shore. The vessel was listing, but her upper works were still out of water and relatively intact. Carpenters hoped to repair one of her large launches, which had not been claimed by the waves. As yet no attempt had been made to salvage any of the waterlogged provisions from inside the wreck.

That afternoon a runner arrived from the north with the news that General Ubilla was dead and that his admiral, Francisco Salmón, second in command of the *Flota*, was now in charge. Admiral Salmón sent word that the remaining officers were to organize their people and move them up the beach to his camp at the *Bara de Ays*.

Throughout this period everything was totally disorganized. Some looting was occurring at all the camps opposite each wreck along the coast. Those mainly involved were seamen and lower-class passengers. Risking no more than a reprimand from ships' officers who were largely unarmed and vastly outnumbered, the looters wandered the beaches, taking pretty much whatever they wanted from unclaimed baggage or corpses.

On August 2, Captain Soto Sanchez and his advance party from the south reached the northernmost camp opposite the wreck of Ubilla's *Capitana*, the *Nuestra Señora de la Regla*, at the *Bara de Ays* (sandbank), two and a half miles south of the present-day Sebastian Inlet. Sanchez immediately reported to Admiral Salmón the loss of his vessel and the general extent of the destruction. Salmón had already moved his people up the beach from the wreck of the *Almiranta* to take charge of his camp. Despite the commander's suspicions that the fleet's losses had been severe, he was visibly moved by Sanchez's description of the scope of the disaster. But this was no time for emotion; there was considerable work to be done. He knew that to bring all the survivors together in one group was going to aggravate the shortage of rations, but it would also strengthen the defense capabilities of the castaways.

In anticipation of the growing number of people who would soon arrive at the sandbank, the officers tried to make the men enlarge the camp. The whole width of the island from ocean to river would be needed to accommodate everyone. The work went slowly, however, for many were still too weak to accomplish much. A few

45

shelters were built with wreckage hauled up the dunes from the beach; some of the thickets were partially cleared with salvaged boarding cutlasses and lean-tos were constructed and roughly covered with palm fronds or pieces of sail. Clouds of mosquitoes and sand flies plagued the party day and night. The insects were so bad that some of the men buried their wives and children up to their necks in loose sand in an effort to protect them from the perpetual tormentors. Others, notably those who obviously had been accustomed to a more sheltered existence, were almost driven mad by the stinging and biting insects. Smudge fires helped only those few brave enough to crowd closest to the clouds of acrid smoke. There was little choice. One either smothered in smoke or suffered the bites of the pests. Driven by hunger, everyone welcomed the opportunity to forage for food and water.

Although provisions were scarce, there were rabbits, raccoons, opossums, deer, bears and turkeys on the island, which had long been a popular hunting ground for Indians, who frequently came over from the mainland to hunt bear. The fat was rendered from their kills and carried back to their main settlements on the mainland. Since virtually all firearms and shot had been lost at sea, the survivors were limited to the few small animals they could snare, catch by hand or run down. But there was an abundance of fish and shellfish in the waters. Indian River contained many catfish, drum, rays, flounder, mullet, clams, oysters and conches. Piles of refuse shells littered the sandbank, left by generations of Indians who had enjoyed the river's rich bounty. At various times the recalcitrant Ays customarily came there to live and to fish. It was on one of these occasions that the survivors had their first encounter with the Indians.

Admiral Salmón had sent out twenty groups of men to fish for the camp. Having fashioned crude spears from gum saplings, they pursued their quarry into the shallows of the river. And there, quite by accident, the foragers stumbled upon a small fishing party of Ays. The sudden confrontation must have been unsettling to both sides. Early etchings show these Indians with part of their long black hair drawn up into characteristic topknots held in place with slender bone pins while the rest curled around the sides of their heads, so that they seemed to be wearing helmets. Clad in plaited loin belts tied in back with short, arched grass tails, and carrying longbows, with sheaths of bone-tipped arrows slung across their backs, the Indians surely presented a formidable appearance to the Europeans. Despite the Ays' reputation for dispatching an occasional shipwreck victim for whatever goods he might have been fortunate enough to salvage, however, the large number of survivors apparently discouraged, at least for the moment, any similar mischief. Both parties simply withdrew. As uneventful as the encounter was, Admiral Salmón was certainly well aware of his people's precarious position and what the consequences might be if the savages returned in force. Now, more than ever, he must have felt the need to be wary of the unpredictable Ays.

Chapter 6
The Secret Letter

Any hope of help for the castaways would have to come either from St. Augustine about 120 miles to the north, or from Havana, some 360 miles by water to the south. Admiral Salmón knew that he must count on St. Augustine for immediate, temporary assistance; but the main effort would have to come from Havana. It was most important that word be gotten out to these places as quickly as possible.

As soon as the salvaged boats from the *Urca* and the *Nuestra Señora de la Regla* reached the main camp, they were immediately made ready to go for help. These were fairly large boats. The launch was about twenty-four feet in length, with a seven-foot beam and a three-foot depth. Each of the boats could be rowed or rigged with lateen sails and could carry up to fifty people. The survivors selected to go on the first boat to St. Augustine were mainly women, children and the most seriously injured, who needed immediate medical attention. There were few of the latter, however, for those who survived the initial ordeal, despite their injuries, died from water inhalation shortly after reaching the beach. The unpleasant task of deciding who would go and who would stay fell to the officers, who now were confronted with another serious problem. Admiral Salmón announced that looters were to return any treasure they had taken to the ships' officers, who would place it under safekeeping, with no questions asked. The offer of amnesty in exchange for their ill-gotten plunder did not impress the looters. Some had collected enough silver and gold from wealthy passengers' luggage to make them rich. And since there were more looters than officers, the former simply disobeyed the commander's order and demanded to be allowed to leave on the boat to St. Augustine. Admiral Salmón refused. The men openly tried bribing some of the subordinate officers for a place on the vessel. When this failed, they attempted to seize one of the launches by force. This might have succeeded but for the quick thinking of an alert lieutenant and a handful of the *Capitana*'s marines armed with several salvaged matchlock muskets.

Finally, as a last resort, the worst of the looters left camp and headed north with their ill-gotten gains. All they had to do, they reasoned, was last until they reached St. Augustine and they would be rich men. Possibly it was the intoxication of new-found wealth in their pockets that numbed them to the fact that they had a 120-mile trek and the wrath of Spanish officialdom ahead of them.

On the morning of August 4, Admiral Salmón took out a leather-bound writing case Captain Lima had rescued from the *Urca* and carefully composed an open letter to Governor Francisco Corioles at St. Augustine:

Dear Sir:

I have not communicated our mishap to you before because I did not have a vessel at my disposal. I do it now with deep sorrow in my heart since this disaster has been the worst that has occurred in many a year. Not a single ship, whether from the naval escort or from the galleons, has been spared, and because my general Ubilla perished in the Capitana (Flagship), I have taken his place to recover this treasure, which is something of great importance to the service of the King and to the common good. Inasmuch as I am on an island, where we became lost, and we are all so desperately in need of supplies, I am begging you to help me by sending to us as much as you can, or else everyone here will perish. In addition to food supplies, I would like to receive twenty rifles with their bullets, as much powder as possible, half a dozen axes, another half a dozen shovels and some hoes to remove the sand in order to see whether I can manage to dig out some of the silver and break open part of the hull. His Majesty's treasure and that of private persons, both of

49

which were carried in the hold, sank with the ship in five fathoms of water, in a spot we have duly marked. I am sending my pilot along with this message. I hope and trust that you will help me as soon as possible with some vessels from your garrison. May God grant Your Lordship a long life. August 4, 1715.

Your most humble servant,
Don Francisco Salmón

When he had finished, the admiral wrote a second, secret letter to the governor which apprised him of the seriousness of their condition.

Dear Sir:
I wish to communicate to you, in confidence, after having sent to you another letter with the pilot, that my men have revolted and are leaving this camp for your garrison heavily loaded with the silver they have stolen. Please, have them arrested and deprived of what they have unlawfully taken. I advise your Lordship that this letter is being carried by the pilot and that on his prompt [return] may depend our ability to remain here watching over His Majesty's treasure and that of private persons, because up to now, nothing has been recovered. I hope our efforts will not be in vain. May God grant Your Lordship a long life. At the Sandbar of Ays, August 4, 1715.

Your most humble servant,
Francisco Salmón

These dispatches were given to Ipilito Sebastián Méndez, pilot of the *Nuestra Señora del Carmen*, who had been given command of the longboat going to St. Augustine. A few minutes later the select few who were going for help hoisted sail and set out to sea, while those who remained behind called farewells and wished them Godspeed.

Between the 4th and the 10th of August, the two remaining boats were made ready to leave, one of them for St. Augustine. The largest of the three, a launch, was provisioned and loaded with salvaged cargo to sail directly to Havana, Cuba—Spain's most important link with the New World. Admiral Salmón was both anxious to let the outside world know about the fleet's predicament and eager to evacuate from the camp as many nonproductive survivors as possible. Thirty joined Father Francisco de León y Cabrera, chaplain of the *Nuestra Señora de la Regla*, in the second longboat that sailed for St. Augustine on August 7 under the command of Captain Fernando Ignazio Barriga. And the following day, the large launch, commanded by one Captain Perdomo, left for Havana with most of the nobility, the royal officials and other important personages of rank or wealth. One may well imagine that, when this last vessel set sail, the leavetaking was a bit strained. Because of its social standing, one group was exuberantly escaping the deprivations of the castaways' lot while the other was gloomily preparing to embrace it.

As soon as the vessel was dispatched, Admiral Salmón returned to the problem of expanding the main camp at the Barra de Ays for the remaining large population, which now had to establish a more permanent, defensible community there.

Although few cutting tools had been salvaged from the wrecks, work parties began slashing and burning out large clearings in the almost impenetrable thickets of scrub oaks, sea grapes and cabbage palms behind the island's steep sand dunes. Palm- and palmetto-thatched lean-tos were built around the perimeters of these areas, and despite the humid tropical heat, fires were kept burning or smoldering in the middle of the clearings in an attempt to ward off the swarms of mosquitoes and other insects that plagued the castaways. In time, the camp would expand to cover an area over 3,000 feet long, divided into two major camps on the riverside, a network of forty to fifty clearings. Each clearing would hold from ten to fifty and each would be linked to adjoining clearings by tunnel-like trails hacked through the dense undergrowth.

Admiral Salmón had made a wise choice in selecting this site for his main camp. It was a strategic position in case of attack, and it enabled him to keep an eye on the area where the king's treasure had gone down aboard General Ubilla's flagship. The camp could be protected by pickets to the north and south, and since it was on a narrow part of the island, it could not be attacked by surprise from either the river to the west or the ocean to the east. It was the best and most logical choice in the entire area.

While the camp was being enlarged and made more livable, the first longboat of survivors heading for St. Augustine was making good time. The hurricane had cleared the air and the weather was fine, with brisk favorable winds. They covered the 120 miles in three days, arriving at the inlet to St. Augustine on August 7. As the boat rounded the headland and crossed the treacherous sandbars at the mouth of the inlet, the survivors saw in the distance the sloping coquina walls of El Castillo de San Marcos. It was a welcome sight indeed.

When they sailed into the inlet and landed at the quay, a crowd of curious soldiers, settlers and minor officials, informed of their coming by Indian signal fires down the coast, was already there to meet them. Eager hands helped the bedraggled survivors ashore, with particular care for the few women and children, who had especially suffered from the ordeal. Everyone seemed to be speaking at once, questioning, answering, gesturing, gradually learning the terrible news that the combined fleet had been wiped out by the same hurricane that had swept St. Augustine a week before, taking the roofs off many houses and destroying crops, but sparing the settlers the terrible toll of death and destruction it had brought the ships. News of the disaster spread quickly through the town. Crowds grew larger. Boys ran through the streets calling out exaggerated rumors. "All the ships lost! A thousand perish! Few survive!"

Already hard pressed from the deprivations of the recent war* and the destruction wrought by the same hurricane that had sunk the fleet, St. Augustine citizens shared what few comforts they had with the survivors. The injured were immediately taken to homes and cared for, clothing was found for those who needed it, and everyone was fed—with the first decent food they had eaten in over a week.

Accompanied by crowds of curious people, Ipílito Sebastián and the other representatives of the fleet were escorted down the narrow, crooked streets, past rows of whitewashed coquina-rock houses, directly to the governor's residence. The house was a large, sturdy two-story structure well designed for the Florida climate. A wide, covered second-story balcony occupied a large part of the front. There was no chimney, nor were there glass windows. Instead, a projecting frame of wood rails covered the windows. On the northwest side of the house, there was a lookout tower surmounted by a flagstaff bearing the royal flag.

* In America, called Queen Anne's War.

Authors Robert F. Burgess (left) and Carl J. Clausen (right).

Ship models showing the kind of vessels used in the Spanish
plate fleets during the 17th and 18th centuries. Ship number
4 has the low-profile lines of the frigates used as men-of-war
with the 1715 fleet.

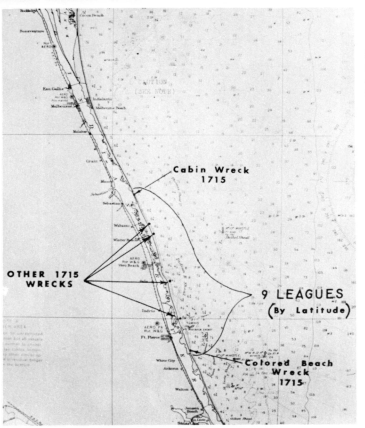

Section of United States Co[ast] and Geodetic Survey map of [the] middle Florida east coast show[ing] the locations of the 1715 wreck[s].

Cabin Wreck
1715

OTHER 1715
WRECKS

9 LEAGUES
(By Latitude)

Colored Beach
Wreck
1715

Aboard the Real Eight salv[age] boat, Clausen and treasure di[vers] pause while fresh air tanks [are] readied for another dive on on[e of] the 1715 wreck sites.

Dubbed "royals" by treasure hunters, gold coins such as this perfectly struck, round 8-escudo piece were extremely rare on the Spanish fleets. Because they are both rare and well made, such coins sell for more than $3,000 apiece. This one came from the Colored Beach Wreck, site 8–UW–1. (Scale in inches.)

Working in a blizzard of sand and limestone particles kicked up by the idling blowers, a diver searches the bottom for treasure.

Reverse of an 8-escudo gold "royal" minted in Mexico City in 1714 and recovered from the Colored Beach Wreck, 8–UW–1.

Six silver wedges arranged as they may have been packed for shipment on the 1715 fleet. Such wedges weigh from one to five pounds each. These came from the Cabin Wreck (8–UW–2) south of Sebastian Inlet.

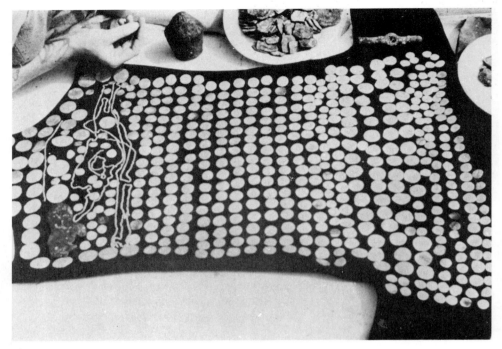

The morning's find of gold coins from the Colored Beach Wreck lie atop a wetsuit jacket. The coins were recovered by Treasure Salvors from their boat *Dee-Gee*.

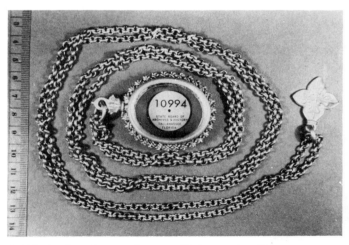

Gold locket for religious relics on gold chain with gold cross motif on counter-pendant, recovered from site 8–UW–4, the Rio Mar Wreck located just south of Vero Beach, the probable site of the *Capitana* of the *Galeones* fleet.

Small gold bee with emerald. This artifact was recovered near the Colored Beach Wreck site (8–UW–1) by a beachcomber. The emerald is believed to be Colombian, because of the characteristic fault discernible in the gem. (Millimeter scale.)

Happy treasure hunter Rupert Gates of Treasure Salvors, Inc., sorts silver coins in a vault of a Vero Beach bank for division among the owners.

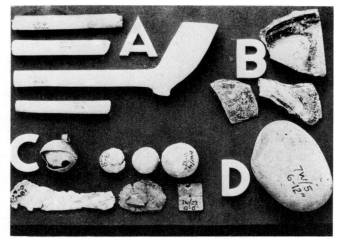

Stem fragments and bowl of English pipe (A); broken glass from Spanish bottles (B); hawk's bell, lead bullets (C); and stone (D) from camp of the survivors and salvagers of the 1715 fleet excavated by archaeologist Clausen in 1966 and early 1967.

Gold pendant once contained a painted miniature under glass surrounded by precious stones. Gold earring bearing likeness of head of Christ has cups for missing pearls. Both were recovered from the Cabin Wreck.

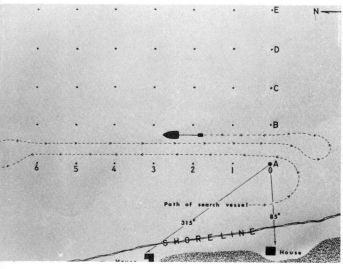

Plan showing the method of searching an underwater site for a shipwreck by towing a magnetometer head along a plotted grid course. This procedure is called "magging."

When Governor Corioles read the dispatches from Admiral Salmón, he immediately started the official machinery that would hasten relief to the people at the Barra de Ays. His first act was to write a formal statement to the king summarizing the recent events. In this document, dated August 7 and signed before Juan Solana, the court clerk, the governor reported that a longboat had arrived carrying two letters from Admiral Salmón dated August 4. From these he learned that the commander of the *Flota* portion of the fleet, General Ubilla, had gone down with his flagship, and that in order to recover the king's treasure, which was in the hull of this vessel at a depth of five fathoms in the spot knows as "El Palmar de Ays," located forty leagues to the south of the garrison, Admiral Salmón had requested immediate help in the form of food and other supplies. "Steps are being taken," said the governor, "to send this help by repairing the longboat and dispatching other vessels." He added that very little could be sent, however, since there had been a long drought and, consequently, a crop failure, besides the damage done by the storm. He said that he had issued the necessary orders to secure depositions from the pilot and other survivors and learn exactly what had taken place.

Next, to prevent St. Augustinians from going after the treasure, the governor issued a decree forbidding all persons to leave St. Augustine to travel either north or south, unless they had special permits. He ordered everyone who owned a vessel—a pirogue,* a canoe or a flat-bottomed boat—to bring it to the main Guard House within six hours. Failure to comply could mean a fine and imprisonment. This decree, also signed on August 7, was designed to keep looters away from the site until official salvage operations could be put into effect.

Following this, Governor Corioles issued a proclamation, announced by the beating of war drums through the town, asking the royal treasurer to "open the warehouse containing maize and corn meal in order to help the survivors of the wreck." The royal treasurer reluctantly complied, but emphasized that the amount of stores in the warehouse was "hardly enough to attend to the needs of the garrison."

A sworn statement was then taken from Captain Sebastián Méndez, pilot of General Ubilla's flagship, the *Nuestra Señora del*

---

* A boat made from a hollowed tree trunk.

Carmen, which outlined the events from the time the fleet left Cuba until it was lost in the hurricane on the Florida coast.

Finally, Governor Corioles met with Francisco Melendez Marques, the royal auditor, and Salvador Garcia de Villegas, the royal treasurer and acting chief of supplies. It was agreed that food and supplies would be sent to the survivors despite the shortage in the garrison; a large sloop and several pirogues would be dispatched as soon as possible. After arriving at the camp, the sloop would be used to search for the remains of the wreck containing the king's treasure. Further, in support of the admiral's request, it was decided that the royal auditor should go to the watch post on the Sand Bar of Matanzas to instruct the officer in charge to intercept looters coming up the beach and to confiscate stolen goods. The auditor was to see that those items for which the beach-walkers lacked proof of ownership were collected and sent back to the royal treasury in St. Augustine.

The following day, August 8, the governor wrote Admiral Salmón the letter that was to accompany the relief party to the Barra de Ays:

Dear Sir:
I received your two letters of the fourth with a feeling of sorrow and regret, which I now share with Your Lordship, for the deplorable misfortune represented by the loss of the two fleets, the navy ships and the galleons, a very severe blow to the Monarchy, since His Majesty, to whom may God, Our Lord, grant a long life, must be awaiting the arrival of these treasures to help ease some of the heavy burdens of the Crown. Since these are things that occur because of decisions from Above, we as Catholics have nothing left to do but to accept the Divine Will, which is what we ask Him for every day in our prayers.

For the past three years, this garrison has suffered under grave hardships, both because of the belated arrival of the provisions from New Spain and because of the general drought that, having lasted for that period of time, did not allow us even to collect seeds. In addition to this, the latest hurricane, which caused such havoc in the fleets, destroyed and ruined all the plantations, as the men you have sent here will testify when they return.

The longboat, which arrived yesterday, will leave today carrying the provisions and supplies that Your Lordship requested; I hope you will understand that this is all we can send at the present time. Since we do not have any firelocks, none are included in the shipment; neither are there muskets or arquebuses,* because your emissary refused them on the grounds that they were of no use to him. In regard to vessels, the Royal Officials and myself have agreed to send the large bilander,** inasmuch as the other is rotten and, therefore, entirely useless. We have begun to caulk the large one, and the shipwrights have taken out six boards. Others are being looked for to replace them, but even if they should be found, God only knows whether or not there will be an artisan to put them in place, because I do not have masters or workmen in any field, my repeated requests to have some sent from Havana or New Spain having come to naught.

His Majesty's treasure may be brought up a river and eight leagues over land—thus without having to go out into the ocean—to this garrison. This task can be accomplished little by little, it being my duty as governor to apprise you of all this, with the warning that in the months from August to October the side winds and hurricanes are frequent in these shores. I do not doubt, therefore, that, as in the past, Your Lordship will now show the same understanding and experience, together with the evident zeal to do what is best for the royal service, and will, therefore, adopt the safest course, because the risks involved in taking the treasure to Havana at this time and hence to Spain are too great. I cannot avoid to remind Your Lordship of all these things because, having thus done my duty, nobody will be able in the future to level any charges or claims against me. On the other hand, I hereby offer all the help that I or this garrison can give in the way of pirogues, people acquainted with the rivers and swamps, and anything else needed for the recovery and safety of the royal treasure, as it is my duty to do. I am well aware of the meagerness of the provisions I am sending and of those I will be able to send—they amount to almost nothing considering the large number of victims. But I must limit myself because of the shortage we now face and the pressing needs of the garrison. Since everything comes from abroad, there being no resources here, I must be careful now and until such a time as the *situado*** arrives, specially in the months ahead, which are dangerous to navigation in this coast, as I have already stated. So that if the *situado* is lost—God forbid!—or is late, it will be necessary (to avoid dismantling the garrison) to resort to the strictest ration-

* A heavy portable matchlock gun invented during the 15th century.
** A small two-masted sailing vessel.
*** A support dole.

ing, as I had to do in the past, when in desperation the infantry and inhabitants of this garrison had to eat horses, dogs and cats in March and April of the year 1712.

The bilander will leave as soon as it is ready, and I am doing all I can to have it repaired in the shortest possible time. In it, I will send you all the provisions that our circumstances permit. I regret not to have the means at the moment to extend any other help to Your Lordship; but, as you know, I had to hastily send the longboat to you today and, as I have already stated, we are lacking in almost everything here. I am very sorry about the death of General Ubilla and the other victims. May God, Our Lord, grant them peace and rest, and to you a long life.

Florida, August 8, 1715.

Your most humble servant,
Don Francisco de Corioles y Martínez
To: The Admiral Francisco Salmón

The same day the governor wrote to Admiral Salmón, Melendez, the royal auditor, left by boat for the watchtower at Matanzas Inlet, sixteen miles south of the settlement. This outpost guarded the city's southern water access to the sea. The inlet was a natural barrier to anyone moving north up the coast.

When Melendez reached the outpost at sunrise, Friday, August 10, he found that a number of the survivors from the wrecks were on the south side of the inlet, where a petty officer, Luis Rodrigo, and his guard at the watchtower had kept them until he arrived. Melendez and the soldiers took boats across the river and immediately searched the party. In a letter written to Governor Corioles the same day, the auditor reported that he had collected four hundred pesos from the looters. In addition, he requested the return of a canoe "in view of the fact that the survivors can hardly walk because of sore feet, so that some of them are unable to walk overland to the garrison"; and additional food supplies, "hardtack and fifty pounds of corn, because I had to distribute the quantity I brought with me among the survivors."

In his letter of reply, which returned with the requested canoe and supplies, the governor ordered Melendez to proceed as soon as he could to Admiral Salmón's camp and inspect the hulls that contained the registered treasure. Once he had appraised the situation, he was to return immediately to St. Augustine and report to the governor. Before Melendez could leave the watchtower for the survivors' camp, however, he was approached by Father Manuel de Quiñones, Notary Public of the Ecclesiastical Court, who asked by what authority he was there. Melendez replied that certainly the Father knew that he was there by virtue of the governor's decree in response to Admiral Salmón's request that the looters be intercepted and relieved of stolen goods.

Father Quiñones admitted that he was aware of the decree and that he understood the survivors had opened all the cases and taken out all the silver and gold they contained. Therefore, he said, it was the duty of representatives of the Church to see that all recovered goods be turned over to the Commissary of the Holy Crusade at St. Augustine. Furthermore, anyone who dared interfere with the Church's wishes, including the governor, was subject to excommunication.

Melendez quite obviously had no wish to oppose the strong authority of the Spanish Church in this serious matter. Avoiding the issue by following the governor's order, he left at once for the camp at the Barra de Ays.

Meanwhile, the first help from St. Augustine arrived at the survivors' camp in the form of small boats and canoes with food, tools and, most important, a number of Indian militia composed of Yamassee, Guali and refugee Apalachees, dispatched by the governor to help the castaways by foraging for food. Needless to say, their arrival created considerable excitement among the stranded people. It represented their first glimmer of hope since the disaster. The relief party also reported the good news that it had passed Father de León and the second boatload of survivors that was making its way to St. Augustine.

Conditions on the Barra de Ays had gradually improved, largely through the efforts to make more substantial shelters in the clearings. What had been insufferable hardship soon became routine. Still, everyone was forced to remain on extremely short rations.

Not long after the boats had departed for St. Augustine and Havana, Ays Indians visited the island. They apparently came in peace in spite of their fierce reputation, and Admiral Salmón encouraged them to supply the camp with fresh fish and game in exchange for trinkets and other trade items. Although the fifteen hundred or so survivors surely could have held out against all the Ays in existence, living along the coast between Cape Canaveral and Jupiter Inlet, the commander undoubtedly knew that these Indians could be trusted only as long as they believed that any trouble they caused would bring certain retribution from the Spanish garrison. Without this veiled threat, however, and perhaps even with it, Admiral Salmón had no way of knowing how long the Indians would remain peaceful.

As the camp grew larger and better organized, one of the first necessities was to find a better source of drinking water. The river was brackish, and there were no springs or creeks on the island. It had not taken much investigation by the more knowledgeable officers to discover that the sloping west bank of the sandbar was satisfactory for building Spanish surface wells. Although the departure of the boats had reduced the camp's population by about a hundred, the number of wells would have to be increased to fill the needs of the remaining fourteen hundred. This job was undertaken by several groups of men who would concentrate the building of wells on the points extending into the river, as close as possible to various main camp clearings. The size of the wells depended upon how many people they needed to accommodate and the amount of building material available. Smaller wells were no larger than barrels, and their construction was simple. A hole was dug down through the soft sand to the water table, which on the west side of the island was never more than four feet below the surface. Loose sand and dirt were scooped out until the hole was large enough to allow a good seepage of water. A barrel with its top and bottom knocked out was then set halfway down into the water-filled hole to prevent the sides from caving in. Sand was filled around the outside of the barrel up to its rim, creating in effect a small reservoir into which water trickled and could be dipped out.

Larger wells required more work, but the method was just as simple. Once a hole was dug and cleared, salvaged ship timbers and parts of cargo cases were dragged up from the beach and placed one atop another around the sides of the hole to form a box. Both inside and out, the timbers were shored with short segments of hickory or sea-grape poles. Sand was then packed around the exterior to make a box-shaped well so substantial that modern archaeologists found several of them intact at the campsite almost 250 years later. The survivors probably needed about twelve such wells.

With the axes, tools, muskets and food from the first relief party from St. Augustine, rapid improvements were made in the camp.

The Indians quickly eased the crowded conditions in many of the clearings by constructing numerous thatched huts. They also hunted and fished for the survivors, teaching them how to sun-dry and smoke meat for preservation and how to prepare and eat sea grapes, palmetto berries, and the hearts of cabbage palms for nourishment.

Although Melendez, the royal auditor, was the first outside official to visit the site and dispassionately appraise what was happening, the fleets' officers were not overly enthusiastic in welcoming him. Admiral Salmón was more concerned when he read Governor Corioles's dispatch suggesting that he deliver the king's treasure to St. Augustine. His concern grew when Melendez told him of the Church's demand that it all be turned over to the Royal Commissary of the Crusade unless one wished to risk the punishment of excommunication. The commander told Melendez that he and the trade agents represented by General Echeverz had already decided that it would be inadvisable to send the treasure to St. Augustine and that when it was recovered, it should be sent directly to Havana. To absolve the royal auditor of any blame, Admiral Salmón and the trade agents spelled out their intentions in an affidavit which they signed.

Melendez stayed at camp only long enough to note that nothing had yet been done about salvaging any of the treasure; then he left for St. Augustine to turn over the confiscated valuables to the Commissary of the Crusade. Throughout that day the church bells of St. Augustine tolled and edicts were published threatening to excommunicate anyone who interfered with the Commissary's efforts to collect the stolen goods. By then the Commissary had instructed Governor Corioles to order the officer at the watchtower of Matanzas to cooperate fully with their representative, Captain Sebastián Lopez de Toledo, who had taken over the royal auditor's job of collecting plunder from the stragglers stopped at the inlet.

While these things were taking place in Florida, other events were occurring in Cuba that would soon sharply alter the fate of the castaways at the Barra de Ays. At 2 A.M. on August 15, the first survivors of the disaster reached Havana in the large launch. Despite the hour, Governor Casatores was awakened immediately and told the news. In disbelief he read Admiral Salmón's letter explaining what had happened. Then, dressing hurriedly, the governor asked that Captain Perdomo and other officials in the party meet with him at once so that he could learn the details and determine what must be done.

The weary survivors told him that there were about 1,400 men, women and children stranded on the Barra de Ays with little food and water, but that some help had probably already arrived from St. Augustine. When the governor asked if any of the king's treasure had been saved, all they could tell him was that two of the ships had been lost close to shore but nothing had yet been recovered.

Not long after daybreak, news of the disaster spread through Havana. The citizens were appalled by the great loss. Cathedral bells tolled the message long and mournfully throughout the day. Meanwhile, Governor Casatores did what he could to cope with the situation. After meeting with his government officials, he ordered the Sergeant Major of Havana, Don Juan de Hoyo Solórzano, to find and provision vessels at once to sail for the Barra de Ays to assist in the rescue, equipping some of the ships for lengthy salvage operations. He wrote the king two letters notifying him of the loss. These were dispatched the same day, along with some of the more prominent survivors aboard the frigate *Francisco*, which was about to sail for Rochelle, France. Although Phillip V would not learn of the disaster until September 7 when the letters would reach him, Governor Casatores knew the king would expect him to act with the utmost speed. And this he did, as far as the conditions of the time permitted. Seven ships were found, provisioned and made ready for sea in a remarkably short time—no simple task, considering that some of the vessels were to remain on the Florida coast for an indefinite time. Thirty experienced divers were enlisted. Most were Indians from the coast of South America; the best of these were ex-pearl divers from the Island of Margarita. These men were eager to go, knowing that for each chest of silver they recovered they would be well paid. All they would be expected to give in return was a full day's work under water from sunup until sundown seven days a week for the next few months. And to facilitate that task, special salvage equipment had been loaded aboard the ships: quantities of hemp and chain, grappling hooks, baskets, dredges, long-handled rakes, diving bells, empty chests and all the other necessities required for a prolonged salvage effort. Finally, the ships cleared from Havana and followed the fleet's route northward. Guided by several officers and returning crew members, the vessels reached the Barra de Ays on September 10, 1715, anchoring a safe distance offshore from Admiral Salmón's camp.

It was a happy day for the remaining survivors. Boatloads of food, water and supplies were landed immediately to ease their need. In the following days a steady stream of cutters and long-boats began transferring survivors to the rescue vessels. As each was loaded, it departed, either going to St. Augustine or returning to Havana, where passage could be arranged for the people going on to Spain. Then the fleet's officers and crews were removed to Havana and their depositions taken in an effort to determine the details of the disaster.

At long last the ordeal of the castaways was over.

Chapter 7

Of Pirates and Salvagers

The Spanish quickly prepared to recover the treasure lost with the 1715 fleet. Although Hoyo Solórzano was in charge of the salvage operation, the man in charge of diving was a veteran named Clemente, whose first responsibility was to the king's treasure. The salvagers knew the location of General Ubilla's *Capitana*, and they soon searched for and found the remains of his *Almiranta*. These two ships had carried the bulk of the royal and private treasure and were therefore the salvagers' primary targets. But locating the wrecks and finding the treasure were two different things. Clemente knew that when some of the ships struck, their hulls were ripped open and cargo strewn over a wide area, while the wreckage came to rest elsewhere. In some instances, hulls and decks had completely separated, the bottoms winding up in one place and the upper works, if they had not disintegrated, in another. To complicate matters further, it was the time of year when salvage conditions on this particular coast were at their absolute worst. Strong northeast winds kept echelons of cold, slate-gray Atlantic waves rolling over the wrecks and thundering ashore relentlessly. With the very best conditions, underwater visibility was little more than an arm's length, but now Clemente's divers would be lucky to see their hands twelve inches in front of their faces. Nor could the large salvage ships be brought in over the wrecks. The salvagers would have to work from the longboats and cutters. These vessels, capable of carrying thirty to forty men each, were more maneuverable and less likely to get into serious trouble in the tumbling surf.

Pry bars, rakes, ropes, baskets and grappling hooks were loaded aboard the boats, and the men started searching for the *Capitana's* treasure. While some of the boats concentrated their efforts on the main part of the wreck, others dragged light grappling irons back and forth along the course Clemente estimated the ship had taken coming in.

Sharp-eyed helmsmen stood at the tillers ready to angle the boats into particularly large waves. The Indians bent to their oars, and the hooks bit easily through the soft white bottom sand. If the hooks snagged rocks, the boats were backed down until the obstacles were disengaged. Then the procedure was repeated as the vessels gradually moved into deeper water. Clemente's boat was two hundred yards from shore, working between two broad ridges of shell-rock outcroppings, when the hooks grabbed solidly, then came up with fragments of oak on their tines. The cutter dropped anchor immediately, and divers were sent down to investigate. Minutes later Clemente had the news. The hooks had struck the shattered under-hull of the flagship. Collision with the bottom had sheared it off at the turn of the bilge. The weight of the ballast rock and tons of silver loaded on the orlop deck had sent it straight to the bottom the moment it separated from the upper works. With any kind of luck, the divers should find most of the treasure intact, stacked on the very timbers that had supported it aboard ship.

Clemente signaled nearby boats to assist him, then dove down himself to evaluate the situation. As best he could tell, the hulk lay in a sand valley between outcroppings of limestone, but the diving engineer could hardly stay with the wreck. Visibility was close to zero. The surge threw him in one direction and the strong offshore current whipped him in another. Three times he was forced to surface for air before he had any idea of how the cargo lay in the cold, swirling blue-gray world below. But finally he felt the chests; some were still stacked in precise rows, whereas others lay buried or broken amid the complex jumble of broken timbers, tangled cordage and scattered ballast rock.

When Clemente finally came out of the water, he was not pleased with the prospects. It was the time of year when there would be no calming of seas, no hope of the water's clearing. The coast would be punished by unrelenting winds and waves throughout the fall and winter, with no real letup until the following summer. If the boats were to be effective, they would have to remain over the wrecks, rolling and pitching in the surf while the heavy chests were being fished up from the bottom. And no man knew better than he what his divers could expect, working blind and fighting the currents, the numbing cold, the quick fatigue, the fatal exhaustion.

Despite Clemente's apprehensions, his divers must have been eager to go. Now that only four fathoms separated them from their goal, the attraction had to have been overpowering. Perhaps Clemente saw it on their faces, the mixture of eagerness and fear flashing momentarily across their dark features each time the wave-tossed cutter tilted dangerously close to capsizing. But as quickly as danger passed, they would have thought only of the rich reward that lay almost within their grasp. Each man would receive a percentage of what he found and Clemente knew that before this was over they would have earned it. Naked, they stood waiting at the gunwale. Clemente nodded and they plunged over.

On the bottom the Indians fought their way through the blue murk, towing the long hemp ropes behind them. Each time the surge swept shoreward, they clung like leeches to the nearest rock ledge or broken timber. When the rushing wall of water passed they thrashed forward, scrambling through the wreck's debris, grabbing onto chests of silver, then fumbling to untie the ropes around their waists while the new surge swept in, lifting and twisting their bodies in its cold embrace. Two minutes passed into three as numbed fingers knotted the ropes securely to chest handles. Then with the air hunger finally growing to a sharp, insistent pain, they started up the ropes hand over hand, exhaling a steady stream of bubbles from their bursting lungs.

In the cutter, as in the other longboats that had converged over the wreckage, men strained at the lines in their effort to haul the chests up, almost capsizing the craft. At length the first chests emerged and were with difficulty hoisted aboard. Many more followed. The divers were flushed with their first success, but it was to be short lived.

Three hours later the wind freshened and began shifting directions erratically. It gusted from all points of the compass until the boats were pitching and rolling wildly in the welter of colliding waves. Finally, Clemente saw that it was useless to remain where they were. Several boats had already dragged anchors and were in danger of being swept into the same oblivion that had claimed the fleet. Reluctantly he ordered his divers up and back to the ships.

For the next five days the steepening gray seas were whipped into a fury by a succession of northers. A safe distance at sea, the salvage fleet rode them out on double bow and stern anchors. Even when the winds finally abated, there was no noticeable change in the rampaging foam-crested hillocks of water that thundered through the surf to crash onto the narrow, weed-strewn beach at the foot of the dunes.

Only after the winds shifted to the south did the waves slowly subside, and on the eighth day Clemente's crews returned to the wrecks.

Now their difficulties were compounded. The water was as opaque as pea soup. The wreckage and the silver were still there, but the storm seas had done their dirty work. Many of the chests were buried under six inches of sand. What could not be seen had to be felt for and then dug out with bare hands and crowbars. The divers went to work with less enthusiasm than before. Although the Indians were accustomed to hardships, the rigors of diving under these conditions soon sapped their strength. Few could stay underwater more than three minutes before having to surface for air. In those brief moments on the bottom, they wasted precious time and energy simply struggling to keep from being washed away while they blindly dug and tugged to free half-buried chests from the sand so that they could be recovered. Sometimes while the chests were being hauled to the surface, ropes slipped and the prize plummeted back to the bottom again. Clemente faithfully noted in his records that in the first week of salvage he lost three men. Two were crushed by falling chests and a third expired in what the salvage master termed an "unfortunate incident." He was devoured by a shark. Still, Clemente drove the men hard, scrupulously recording that despite losses he was getting results, recovering many chests of the king's treasure. In the following weeks, both the returns and the divers' mortality rate climbed. Clemente was getting results, at a price.

The divers working on the *Almiranta* were confronted with similar hardships. The vessel was relatively intact, but the treasure was not easily accessible. The men worked in such shallow water that each time a wave lifted a longboat on its crest, then dropped it into its trough, the salvage vessel was precariously close to crushing its bottom on the upthrust wreckage of the sunken ship. The first things the divers recovered were the valuable brass swivel guns mounted on the warship's gunwales. Then they began dismantling the wreckage so that they could gain easy entry to the hold, using iron bars to pry loose deck planking. If a diver surfaced and said he believed there were chests buried under a segment of hull, the big grappling hook went into service. It was a five-foot-long heavy iron implement with four to six tines angling up from one end like boughs on an inverted Christmas tree. The hook was dropped overboard, and divers positioned it in the wreckage. A line was run from the grappling hook to the capstan of the nearest ship, which hauled it in until the hull section was moved. These hooks were also used to tear up decks or to pull hulls apart when it was necessary for the divers to get inside without too great a risk to life or limb. At least one of the hooks was lost by the salvagers and lay undiscovered on the shifting sand bottom for the next 250 years.

The necessity of having the larger ships in close to shore, where the capstans could be utilized for pulling apart the wrecks, petrified the Spanish. A shift of wind or current could swing the big salvage vessels onto one of the wrecks and cause damage they could ill afford.

After several weeks of intensive work, the salvagers had accumulated a large amount of silver. The coins were originally packed in cloth sacks inside wooden chests. As soon as possible the chests had to be opened, the sacks removed and the silver washed carefully in fresh water to prevent corrosion. This was done at Admiral Salmón's camp on shore. After the silver had been washed, it was repacked in clean bags and put into dry chests which had been brought for that purpose. Clemente ordered a small storehouse built on the west side of the island, where the salvaged treasure was kept under armed guard. Despite every precaution to prevent divers from pilfering coins, such pilfering undoubtedly occurred, not only among the Indians but among some of the Spaniards as well. The opportunity was there, and the best Clemente could do was make it as unattractive as possible. Anyone caught with treasure not belonging to him was promptly executed. Pilfering, however, was the least of his worries.

News of the disaster had traveled quickly through the Caribbean. In such places as the Bahamas, Barbados and Jamaica, people listened with more than casual interest when they learned that an entire treasure fleet had foundered on the Florida east coast and that a small band of Spanish salvagers was even then fishing up enormous sums of silver and gold. To many seafaring scallywags the particularly appealing part was all that wealth lying there virtually unprotected, a prize for anyone willing to go after it. Clemente anticipated trouble. The question in his mind was, "When?"

The king of England was kept well apprised of the loss of the Spanish vessels by intelligence reports from the New World. Governor Spotswood of Virginia wrote to the Crown: "There is advice of considerable events in these parts that the Spanish Plate Fleet, richly laden, consisting of eleven sail, are, except one, lately cast away in the Gulf of Florida to the southward of St. Augustine and that a barkalonga* sent from the Havana to fetch off from the continent some passengers of distinction who were in that fleet, having recovered from the wrecks a considerable quality of plate, is likewise cast away about forty miles to the northward of St. Augustine. I think it my duty to inform his Majesty of this accident which may be improved to the advantage of his Majesty's subjects by encouraging them to attempt the recovery of some of that immense wealth."

Few Englishmen in the colonies needed any official encouragement to tweak the beard of the Spanish king whenever such an opportunity arose. On November 21, 1715, Governor Archibald Hamilton of Jamaica commissioned two ships, the *Eagle*, commanded by Captain Edward James, and the *Bathsheba*, commanded by Captain Henry Jennings, to go to sea for six months to hunt pirates. But Jennings, a successful privateer from the recent war, had other plans. Instead of suppressing piracy, he intended doing a little pirating of his own. Furthermore, Lord Hamilton was undoubtedly aware of Jennings's scheme, and it was later widely believed that he had been its architect.

In any event, history relates that Jennings's fleet of two ships and three sloops, outfitted in Jamaica and Barbados, sailed directly to the site of the Spanish salvage camp on the Florida east coast and

---

* A single-masted open boat forty to fifty feet long.

landed three hundred men. The raiders drove off two commissaries and the sixty soldiers guarding the storehouse, seized the accumulated treasure and headed back toward Jamaica. On the way they met a Spanish ship bound from Porto Bello to Havana with a rich cargo, including bales of cochineal, casks of indigo and 60,000 pieces of eight. After plundering the vessel, Jennings let her go. The rovers repaired to Jamaica with their plunder and divided some 120,000 pieces of eight among all concerned.

Clemente returned to his salvage duties, driving his divers all the harder and gradually accumulating more treasure in the storehouse on the beach. Periodically, salvage vessels carried the wealth to Havana. Some of the ships made the crossing without mishap; others, however, fell into the hands of raiders. Jennings meanwhile waited for the Spanish at the Barra de Ays to stockpile a goodly amount of treasure before he deemed it profitable enough to make a second attempt. Finally, on January 26, 1716, two months after his first successful raid on the Spanish camp, he struck again. This time he sailed to the Florida coast in the *Bathsheba*, dropped anchor offshore and waited until night to land his men. The next morning the force moved on the camp with drawn arms. Clemente looked at their weapons and asked if England and Spain had resumed the war. Jennings said no, that he and his men had come to fish on the wrecks. Clemente replied that the wrecks belonged to the king of Spain and that he and his people were trying to find the lost treasure. But Jennings was obviously in no mood to quibble over who owned the valuable property, especially since he had the salvagers at a disadvantage. Hoping perhaps that he could buy them off, Clemente offered the raiders 25,000 pieces of eight to leave the wrecks and the salvagers alone. Jennings responded by taking the 25,000 and all the rest of the silver in the storehouse. He also stripped the salvagers of their valuables, helped himself to four small cannon, two of which were brass, and plugged the muzzles of two others left behind. Again the pirates made a clean getaway with their plunder, which according to the Spanish amounted to some 120,000 pieces of eight and wrought silver, though others said it amounted to far more.

Havana responded to this final indignity by sending Don Juan Francisco de Vale to complain to the governor of Jamaica. Lord Hamilton's probable response was to commission another ship or two to go forth and "suppress" the freebooters. But Havana's emissary was no fool. He recalled that when the Spanish captured an English vessel on the coast near Porto Bello because it was trading where foreigners were not allowed to trade, the English captain had told him that the governor owned a fourth part of the English raider. Vale said he had also heard it mentioned openly by gentlemen in Jamaica that the governor was part owner of all vessels sent to prey on the Spanish camp. Later he reported that he had traced some of the stolen wealth to the governor's house.

Despite this seemingly continual involvement in such matters, however, Jamaica's Lord Hamilton was by no means the only instigator of the frequent depredations on the Spanish salvage fleet on the Florida coast. Jennings's successes simply opened the door wider to greater excesses. As an example of the busy intrigues in the English colonial island communities, witness the deposition of one John Vickers of the island of Providence:

In November last, Benjamin Hornigold [an infamous pirate who once served under Blackbeard] arrived in Providence in the sloop *Mary* of Jamaica belonging to Augustine Golding which Hornigold took upon the Spanish coast. Soon after taking it he took a Spanish sloop loaded with dry goods and sugar, which cargo he disposed of at Providence. But the Spanish sloop was taken from him by Captain Jennings of the sloop *Bathsheba* of Jamaica. In January, Hornigold left Providence in said sloop *Mary*, having on board 140 men, six guns and eight *pattereros* [small breechloading cannons] and soon after returning with another Spanish sloop from the Florida coast. After he fitted out said sloop at Providence he sent Golding's sloop back to Jamaica to be returned to the owners and in March last sailed to Providence in the Spanish sloop, having on board 200 men but bound on a secret mission.

Somehow, despite the depredations of the English pirates, Clemente's men managed to salvage about 80 percent of the lost treasure during their first major salvage effort from September 1715 to the middle of April 1716, when the operation temporarily ended. Governor Corioles, who had been supplying the Spanish salvagers from St. Augustine, was notified by officers at the Barra de Ays that further assistance was no longer necessary, that he need not send the Indians that he had intended since there would be sufficient personnel arriving with the Spanish fleet from Havana to load the treasure. Further, they did not think that the returns of salvaging on the wrecks would pay for the cost of maintaining themselves any longer on the Florida coast, and they were therefore withdrawing to Havana.

On June 11, 1716, the governor of Havana, the salvage officers and the royal officials of Cuba held a meeting to determine how best to transport the salvaged treasure back to Spain. They decided to divide the risks between two ships, the 60-gun *Nuestra Senora del Carmen* and the 44-gun *Principe de Asturias*. Since the *Carmen* was the more heavily armed of the two, she would carry two-thirds of the treasure; the remaining one-third would go on the *Principe*. At another meeting, officials and shipmasters ratified the decision. Loaded aboard the *Carmen* for the royal account were: 680,697 pesos in silver coins packed in 227 cedarwood chests; 152,428 pesos 7 reales in 181 silver bars in 37 chests; 16,000 pesos in 1,000 doubloons of 8 escudos, Mexican serrated. Total: 849,125 pesos 7 reales. The grand total for the king on the two vessels amounted to: 1,273,688 pesos 7 reales. The fact that this much treasure was being returned to Spain indicated not only how effective the first Spanish salvage effort had been, but also that despite a shortage from pirating, Havana had made up the difference from its own coffers so that the king's share would be complete. The two ships carrying the treasure to Spain crossed the Atlantic without mishap and arrived at Cádiz on August 25, 1716, four years after the *Flota* and the *Galeones* had set out to get it from the New World. Most of the private and unregistered treasure was still missing.

As soon as the Spanish left the salvage site, the English swarmed in to "fish" on the wrecks. Most of the vessels were probably from New Providence in the Bahamas; others were from Jamaica and the Carolinas. Some idea of how the English responded to news of the Spanish pull-out is indicated in a letter about the situation in Jamaica written to a Mr. Burchett on May 13, 1716, by a Captain Belchin of H.M.S. *Diamond*: "There have been at least twenty sloops fitted for the wrecks and if I had stayed [in Jamaica] a week longer I do not believe I should have kept enough men to bring the ship home. I lost ten in two days before I sailed, being all mad to go a-wrecking as they put it."

Not one to miss such an opportunity, Captain Henry Jennings returned again to the scene of his former triumphs, this time acting as guard and overseer of the operations as stated in a document of April 22, 1716: "Captain Jennings arrived at Providence and brought in a prize of a French ship mounting 32 guns which he had taken in the Bay of Hounds, carrying a very rich cargo of European goods for the Spanish trade. He then went in said ship to the wrecks where he served as commodore and guard ship."

On June 3, 1716, Governor Spotswood of Virginia complained to the Council of Trade that pirates were taking over complete control of the Bahamas. He committed to prison one Captain Forbes for beating the Spanish from their batteries on the Florida coast while they were guarding the wrecks, and because he was also an accessory to the taking of a French ship. But the temptation to join in the illicit salvaging was apparently too great even for Governor Spotswood, who on June 15, 1716, ordered Captain Harry Beverly, commander of the sloop *Virgin of Virginia*, to go to the wrecks to fish up what he could. And in another document from Jamaica we read: "It is evident that under the pretext of a report that there were pirates on the coast of America, there fitted out in Jamaica fourteen sloops manned by 3,000 men to clear those seas. But the remedy was worse than the disease." The entry describes how one sloop commanded by "a tawny Moor named Fernando Fernandez" openly practiced piracy, the commander giving as his excuse that he was under orders from the governor of Jamaica. "The English plunder under the pretext of clearing the coasts of pirates," continues the entry, "[but] against all equity [they] have been diving for the silver which was lost on the *Flota* at Palmar." Thus the English helped themselves to the Spanish wrecks from early 1716 until early 1718, when the Spanish decided to launch another salvage attempt on the wrecks they had not officially abandoned.

On arriving at the Palmar de Ays, the Spanish found the English firmly ensconced there. The trespassers had already erected some dwellings and were proceeding to create a fortified town surround-ed by earthwork and fascines, with four cannon. The Spanish opened fire immediately, killing one and wounding several others, but they were no match for the superior number of English. Eventually they yielded and returned to Cuba. On learning what had happened, the governor of Havana urged citizens to finance a new and more powerful expeditionary force to drive out the English. This they did, mustering a sufficient number of men and ships to return to Florida and make short work of the intruders at the Palmar de Ays. According to a Spanish account, "On September 18, 1718, the new expeditionary force returned to Havana with the following prizes: five excellent bilanders [sloop-rigged sailing vessels], 98 Negro slaves, 86 British prisoners, 80 pesos in coins and wrought silver and other things of less importance. Before they could be arrested, more than 60 of the British managed to get away in canoes. Twenty escaped later to the island of Providence after they overpowered a Spanish crew of six on the vessel in which they were being taken to Havana. But our expedition left a garrison of 140 men to the defense of the post, provisioning them with supplies that had been wrested from the English; and four of our vessels with which to continue the diving operations."

This was the Spaniards' last big salvage effort on the wrecks. It is doubtful that they recovered very much, because the first attempt had claimed most of the treasure. Two years after the loss, the wrecks were broken up and scattered; most of the material sank into the sandy bottom and was lost. What little had not been salvaged by the Spanish the first time had certainly been picked over extensively by the English. The second attempt continued through the summer and fall and terminated sometime in 1719, followed by gradually diminished fishing for treasure from passers-by until the locations of the wrecks began to fade from man's memory.

Interestingly, the notorious Captain Henry Jennings never paid for his crimes of piracy. When Captain Woodes Rogers, renowned among other things for having captured one of the Manila galleons, became governor of the Bahama Islands, he posted a royal proclamation dated September 5, 1717, pardoning all pirates who would surrender before September 5, 1718. Jennings wisely turned himself in and never again returned to his nefarious career as a freebooter. Instead, the ex-pirate retired to Bermuda and lived out his life as a respected gentleman of means—a life made all the more bearable, perhaps, by an ample supply of Spanish silver.

Chapter 8
Romans's Clue

After the last Spanish salvage effort, all evidence of what had happened to the Spanish Plate Fleet of 1715 gradually disappeared into the musty pigeon-holes of time. Survivors of the drama lived out their lives and died. Carefully kept Spanish records were filed away and forgotten. Legions of hungry teredo worms consumed every exposed piece of wooden wreckage, and the shifting sands of the Atlantic buried the rest. On the Barra de Ays, nature's reclamation of the old Spanish salvage camp and the camp of the English was equally swift. Wood structures and palm-thatched roofs crumbled to dust. The man-made scars were healed with new vegetation, and the earth claimed all that remained.

Half a century after the disaster almost everything was gone, but the incident was not quite forgotten. In the late 1760s, English cartographer Bernard Romans passed through the area and was obviously well aware of what had occurred there, despite inaccuracies in some of his facts. Later, he described the event in his book, *A Concise Natural History of East and West Florida*, published in 1775. On page 273, Romans details the topographical aspects of the Indian River near Cape Canaveral; midway down the page he notes:

No rivers of any note fall into its northern branches, except St. Sebastians, directly opposite to whose mouth happened the shipwreck of the Spanish Admiral [*sic*], who was the northernmost wreck of fourteen galleons [*sic*], and a hired Dutch ship, all laden with specie and plate; which by stress of northeast winds were drove ashore and lost on this coast, between this place and the bleach-yard, in 1715. A hired Frenchman fortunately escaped by having steered half a point more east than the others. The people employed in the course of our survey, while walking the strand, after strong eastern gales, have repeatedly found pistareens and double pistareens, which kinds of money probably yet remaining in the wrecks, are sometimes washed up by the surf in hard winds. This *Lagoon* stretches parallel to the sea, until the latitude 27:20, where it has an out-watering, or mouth: directly before this mouth, in three fathom water, lie the remains of the Dutch wreck. The banks of this lagoon are not fruitful.

Romans spelled it out, but it would be a long time before anyone paid attention to this particular piece of information. Centuries passed; storms, wars and generations came and went, but the sand and the sea kept their secret well. Occasionally, however, the elements revealed more clues—a few encrusted silver coins dredged up from the bottom and tossed on the beach or eroded from the dunes by a storm tide, a scattering of pottery fragments washed from the soil by a heavy rain, a shell-encrusted iron cannon uncovered by a rampaging surf. The clues were there for anyone capable of interpreting them. And eventually someone proved capable.

The forebears of our modern treasure hunters were simply people with a penchant for picking up the odd items the sea sometimes casts ashore. These weekend beachcombers were not treasure hunters in the usual sense: they were curio hunters. But the germ was there. All it needed was a little encouragement. Once someone had identified a blackened, misshapen wafer of metal as a Spanish piece of eight, the die was cast. Once local inhabitants had noted the frequency with which strange coins appeared along a lonely stretch of beach, it was not difficult to let one's imagination run to Spanish galleons and shipwrecked treasure fleets lost somewhere "out there." The legends and rumors persisted, and so did the growing number of weekend beachcombers. They came, they searched and they left again, rarely any richer for the experience and seldom any wiser. Yet among them were a few notable exceptions, men who followed the clues several steps further and found answers to the centuries-old mystery.

One of the first was amateur historian Charles D. Higgs, a retired astronomer who had spent many years surveying the Florida area for early historical materials. In 1941, his researches led him to the Cape Canaveral region and eventually to a specific area on the offshore bar or island lying between the Indian River and the Atlantic Ocean from two to three miles south of Sebastian Inlet on Florida's east coast. There, curio hunters had been finding various articles belonging to the Spanish colonial period, and Higgs had come to investigate. He listened to the local legends, he studied the clues, he sifted the sands; when he had finished, he wrote of his findings in a report* he read to the archaeology session of the annual meeting of the Florida Historical Society on March 6, 1942.

"Down in the Indian River country, several miles below Cape Canaveral," reported Higgs, "there lies, half buried in the shifting sands, a sizable portion of a wrecked ship. This for some years has been ballyhooed as that of a Spanish galleon although its construction would render such belief very dubious. [Higgs based his belief on his observation that the seasonal growth rings evident in both the ribs and the planking of the wreck suggest our own northern woods rather than those of continuous growth that would have been used in the Spanish and Spanish-Indies ship construction. An eminent tropical forestry expert in Miami who examined specimens from the wreck expressed a similar opinion. Yet, noted Higgs, local legend had even associated this wreck with a fleet of the *Adelantado*** himself, with all the usual connotations of treasure.] It is my firm conviction that this particular hulk has no connection whatsoever with the findings in this report. It may, however, be quite pertinent to these findings that in placid weather other wrecks may be discerned along the adjacent reefs and shallows. Several cannon have been retrieved along the beach, and under favorable conditions of weather and tides, beachcombers and treasure hunters have picked up various articles of naval equipment and other relics undoubtedly of the Spanish colonial period."

* Charles D. Higgs, "Spanish Contacts with the Ais (Indian River) Country," *Florida Historical Quarterly*, 21 (1942), 25–39.
** The founder of St. Augustine and first Spanish governor of Florida, Pedro Menéndez de Avilés.

During his investigation Higgs had been told that brass culverins (a kind of heavy cannon used in the 16th and 17th centuries), which from the description might be Spanish, had been removed. All the cannon he had personally seen were of a later period, though he noted certain characteristics that indicated they were made before 1800.

His curiosity aroused by this knowledge, Higgs took a closer look at the bluff behind the beach, searching for some clue. As he moved along the sandy escarpment paralleling the coast, he suddenly found what he was searching for. Four-tenths of a mile south of the wreck, a portion of the bluff had been eroded away by the wind and rain. Protruding from the sand were pieces of human and animal bones. The bluff at this point was from twelve to fourteen feet high. A little poking around revealed iron spikes, clay pipes and a peculiar assortment of pottery sherds. A scrutiny of this escarpment showed an abundance of this material, stretching back toward Indian River and along the bluff for some 500 feet. Later Higgs found that the fragments were scattered through the sand all the way to the river, a distance of some 800 feet from the Atlantic side of the bluff. Their relation to the rate of erosion and sea encroachment clearly indicated to Higgs that the site was formerly centered more conspicuously on the river than on the ocean front.

Searching for more clues, Higgs dug a few test holes a short distance back from the bluff and found the ground increasingly fertile in European artifacts. The material lay in a stratum of charcoal-impregnated beach sand two and a half to three feet thick. He established a point of reference at the approximate center of the site, then worked outward from it. Attempting to plot his finds on a grid, he found the procedure "rather purposeless, as there is every evidence that the site had been destroyed and scattered by storms prior to its burial in the drifting sands."

Hoping that a competent archaeological survey might later be made of the area, Higgs disturbed the site as little as possible, limiting his work to sifting the piles of loose debris left by treasure and souvenir hunters. Yet he obviously wondered just how worthwhile further study would be when he wrote: "Since the finding of relics here has become common knowledge, perhaps much of the station's archaeological value has been and is being destroyed, and inevitably, key findings dispersed."

Higgs had unknowingly found what was left of the southern portion of the old Spanish salvage and survivors' camp. It had been damaged by storms, partially eroded, and mauled by curio hunters; yet in the rubble that remained there were still tantalizing clues.

As the evidence mounted, Higgs discarded the idea that his finds were debris from a shipwreck, because the site was on a bluff ten to twelve feet above sea level. He thought instead that he had found some evidence of a European structure having been built there. "At the center of the station," he said, "there is a considerable area of tabby floor* at a depth of three and one half feet. Beneath this floor is found an occasional sherd of incised or stamped Indian pottery. The choicest of the Spanish remains lie above and scattered around at a higher level; while still higher, about a foot below the surface, there is an abundance of the cruder, undecorated, recent Indian pottery. Scattered over a distance of 320 feet along the bluff there are four other deposits rich in brick and mortar fragments. It is only in the vicinity of the floor in the center of the station that the largest assortment of European articles is found, particularly the finer Spanish pottery and Chinese porcelain fragments."

The appearance of several varieties of Chinese porcelain at the site puzzled Higgs. In attempting to explain its presence, he made a surprisingly accurate observation: "We might suggest that the period involved was concurrent with the china mania in Europe . . . china was of great value, and doubtless many treasure ships from the Philippines carried it in cargo. This was packed overland from Acapulco and transshipped at Vera Cruz into homebound fleets, vessels from which might later be wrecked in the Bahama Channel."

Higgs also found quantities of various old glass fragments, mostly bottlenecks with lead screw-tops and the bottoms of "spirit" bottles; Indian pottery; Spanish crockery from grain, oil and water jars; Spanish pottery—mostly glazed in blues, greens and browns; Spanish-Mexican pottery glazed inside and out; clay pipes bearing the trademark "R. Tippet" in cartouche, or the lettering "R.T." or "R.R."—the former was later found to be an 18th-century English pipe maker. Heavily corroded iron objects were the most common

---

* What Higgs thought were the remains of a crushed shell floor were large lenses of compacted oyster shells from intensive Ays Indian occupation years before the loss of the 1715 fleet.

items he uncovered, but with the exception of ships' spikes, they were rusted beyond recognition. The cannon he identified at the site was later turned over to officials at St. Augustine.

Higgs's work was intentionally preliminary. He drew no conclusions from his finds. He knew, however, that the area had once been the territory of the Ays Indians, and his earlier research indicated that the tribe often enriched itself on gold and silver taken from Spanish treasure ships lost along their coast. The shipwreck evidence Higgs examined in the dunes was apparently too recent to be scientifically significant, nor did he venture a guess at why there might have been an early European structure built in this hostile land.

The amateur historian knew more than he was telling, however, or at least more than appeared in his published report. A study of Higgs's work papers for the 1940–1942 period indicates that he had seen a copy of Bernard Romans's 1775 chart of east Florida on which the English cartographer had printed this notation near the St. Sebastian River: "Opposite this River, perished the Admiral, commanding the Plate Fleet of 1715, the rest of the fleet, 14 in number, between this & Yᵉ Bleech Yard."* Nearby were the words "el Palmar," followed by tiny drawings of five palm trees. On a portion of a U.S. Coast and Geodetic Survey chart for this area, Higgs marked the exact location of the wreck near Sebastian Inlet, which years later would be known as the "Cabin Wreck." He also pinpointed the locations of several other wrecks of the 1715 fleet farther south. The historian's work papers indicate that he had found examples of "clipped Mexican silver real coins" on the land site he was investigating, but again this fact did not appear in the historical-quarterly report. The oversight may have been intentional in that Higgs was not interested in encouraging treasure hunters to despoil the site further. Whatever answers there were to the riddle, however, he knew would have to come from a more detailed archaeological search of the area.

Four years elapsed before this occurred. Then, in 1946, Dr. Hale G. Smith, acting as Assistant Archaeologist for the Florida Park Service, took an archaeological team to the Higgs site. Accompanied by Higgs, Smith surveyed the area. The island was so densely

---

* Higgs believed this to be patches of open sand on the high dunes just north of St. Lucie Inlet, about thirty miles south of Sebastian Inlet.

covered with palmetto, sea grape, yucca and cabbage-palm growth that the team was forced to confine its efforts mainly to the beach escarpment, where it was clear enough to work. Their test trenches revealed that the site ran not less than 343 feet along the escarpment and 800 feet across the width of the island on the east-west excavation axis established by Higgs in 1942. Carefully digging and sifting five-foot squares along these base lines, the workers found their greatest concentration of artifacts nine to twenty-one inches below the surface. Most of the Indian pottery sherds were a type called San Marcos, which has been assigned by archaeologists to the St. Augustine Period (1565–1750). A partially formed stone pipe made from limestone, similar to fragments found around the site, was uncovered 213 feet south of the east-west axis. Eventually, the archaeologists' painstaking efforts turned up animal bones shaped into crude tools; a variety of Mexican ceramics; clay figurines; Chinese porcelain; Spanish and what were then referred to as "Moorish" ceramics, but which are now called *Majolica* or tin-glazed wares; glass from old wine and case-gin bottles; a handmade stemmed goblet; clay pipes; three bone or ivory dice; nails; spikes; knife blades; iron bands from chests; "line snubbers" for mooring boats; buckles; parts of flintlock pistols and lead musket balls. In addition there were limestone building materials, an alabaster bottle stopper and two coins bearing the Spanish coat of arms with the quartered lions and castles of Leon and Castile.

Smith now had a few more clues. The big question in his mind was how these objects came to be there. Remember, neither Higgs nor Smith knew the history of what had taken place on the Barra de Ays. They had only a few pieces of a complicated puzzle from which they dared to reconstruct the past. It would be many years before the full story of those historic events would be revealed from long forgotten documents buried in Spanish archives. Yet the archaeologist's deductions were remarkably accurate.

To explain his mixed collection of European and Indian artifacts, Smith saw three possibilities: 1) The Higgs site was once an aboriginal Indian village which continued to exist after the arrival of the Europeans; 2) it was a European settlement which drew the Indians to it; or, 3) the Europeans and a group of Indians, not necessarily native to the region, settled there simultaneously. Since the Indian, Spanish, Mexican and Chinese artifacts were all found in the same occupational stratum, he reasoned that the Europeans and Indians had lived there at the same time—and wondered when and why.

Smith's training as an anthropologist specializing in archaeology uniquely qualified him to date the artifacts. Still, he needed assistance with the rare porcelains. Corresponding with Kamer Agla Oglu, an expert on Chinese porcelain, he learned that the majority of these fragments from the site were of the K'ang Hsi period and made between 1662 and 1722. This indicated that the site could not have been established earlier than 1662. The Spanish-Mexican ware dated from the period 1543–1723, indicating that the site had probably not been occupied much later than 1723. An English clay pipe marked "R. Tippet" was made in the early 18th century. Considering only these three items, Smith narrowed the date of the site to a fifty-year period between 1675 and 1725. When he learned from his research that the English Quaker Jonathan Dickinson had not reported any European settlement in that area when he passed through in 1696, he reduced the probable range even more, to 1697–1725. Still, the presence of the English pipes bothered him. What were they doing in a predominantly Spanish site? The Spanish had never been a pipe-smoking group, and few of their red clay pipes had been found in Florida. Also, considering the friction between the two countries, he thought it doubtful that the Spanish were getting pipes from the English.*

These facts suggested to Smith the possibility that the site may have been an intermittent hangout for pirates—probably English or Dutch. It was known that the English and Dutch privateers traded with the Ays and used their inlets as bases for their raids against Spanish shipping. Besides affording good harbors, these places offered a source of fresh water that was out of reach of the nearest Spanish garrison.

The next very significant piece of evidence was Bernard Romans's reference to the loss of the 1715 Spanish Plate Fleet on his 1775 Florida chart, accompanied by the words "el Palmar." From an old Spanish source given him by Higgs, Smith learned that in 1716, a year after the Plate Fleet wreck, there was supposedly a pirates'

---

* Smith was working in the formative period of Florida archaeology. It would be many years before our knowledge of Spanish shipwrecks and salvage camps would enable archaeologists to expect that up to 20 percent or more of the artifacts from such "Spanish sites" would, during this period, tend to be of English origin.

hangout at "Palmar de Ays." Surely this was the same "el Palmar" shown on Romans's chart.

Summing up the results of his research in 1949, Smith wrote:

Earlier, using the Dickinson data and the dating from the artifacts, we came to the conclusion that the site must fall between 1696 and 1725. Here we have two documentary references [Romans's chart and the Spanish mention of pirates at the Palmar de Ays] which would readily explain the amount of European material present in the area, and dating from about the middle of the postulated time range. Considering all the data it seems very likely that the Higgs site represents materials from the Plate Fleet of 1715 and/or the pirates' hangout of the following year. It must also be borne in mind that Indians, possibly Ays [and in a footnote he included Yamasee] were associated with the site, probably drawn there by the wrecks.*

Smith could not have been closer to the truth.

* Hale G. Smith, "Two Archaeological Sites in Brevard County, Florida," *Florida Anthropological Society Publications*, No. 1 (Gainesville: University of Florida, 1949).

Chapter 9

The Trail to Treasure-Trove

The next character to figure in this drama was a building contractor from Miamisburg, Ohio, named Kip Wagner.

At the end of World War II, Wagner came to the small east-coast Florida town of Wabasso to build a motel. Wabasso is six miles from Sebastian, and both communities are situated in the general area shown on the Romans chart as the Palmar de Ays. Wagner said that when he arrived in the area, he had no clearer idea about treasure hunting than anyone else whose only association with the subject was a vaguely remembered youthful enthusiasm for Robert Louis Stevenson's *Treasure Island*. But if anything could rekindle that enthusiasm, it was the stories of treasure lost and treasure found that Wagner heard from old-timers in the Wabasso-Sebastian area. What particularly interested him was the rumors that blackened Spanish coins sometimes turned up on the beach after a howling northeast gale.

Captain Steadman A. Parker was apparently the first to tell Wagner about the coins. Parker, a retired steamship captain, was renowned in the area for his thrilling tales about transatlantic crossings and European adventures. He told Wagner that a Spanish treasure fleet had foundered on the coast nearby, and over the years the long-lost treasure kept washing ashore just east of Wabasso. Parker said he had found some of the coins on the beach. Furthermore, the ex-sea captain insisted that there was a big treasure somewhere offshore just waiting to be found and that one day he intended to find it.

Wagner said he did not know whether to believe the story or not, but one weekend he surreptitiously spent an afternoon at the beach looking for coins and finding nothing but sea shells. The experience did not allay his curiosity, however, especially after his hearing other yarns from scattered sources. Whether fact or fiction, they fired Wagner's imagination and whetted his curiosity even more. There was, for example, the postmaster of Sebastian who in the early 1900s was said to have found a fortune in silver and gold coins which he kept hidden in a cigar box until the night he was murdered. The box and hoarded coins were never found. Another tale concerned a Mr. Kragle who ferried mail from the mainland to an island in the Indian River near Sebastian Inlet and once saw cannon on the bottom during one of his trips. It was also reported that he once found a heavy "brick" in shallow water and used it in building a fireplace. The first time he started a fire, the brick melted. And then there was the old man who Wagner said told him he had found plenty of the blackened odd-shaped pieces of metal on the beach. He didn't know what they were, but he said their shape made them fine "skipping stones" when he sailed them out to sea—as he judged he had done with some two thousand of them.

In 1949 the ex-steamer captain, Steadman Parker, told Wagner that he had located the remains of a shipwreck near shore. Wagner and three others quit their jobs and agreed to help him recover it. First they used a dragline on shore and tried to scoop up the wreck from the shallow water. When this failed, they bulldozed piles of sand into the Atlantic, and at low tide moved the dragline out on to this makeshift pier in an effort to extend its reach. Each full tide washed away their sandy platform, and each day they rebuilt it. It was during one of these times that the bulldozer unearthed a coin, but according to Wagner it was a Spanish copper maravedi dated 1649, which he said he later gave away to one of the workers more impressed with it than he.

By summer's end, the group's salvage attempt had proved to be an expensive fiasco. After dredging up tons of ocean bottom, the men had found only a few wood fragments, ships' fastenings and metal spikes. They gave up and returned to their jobs.

But the following spring Wagner again felt the urge to search. Borrowing an old Army-surplus metal detector from Parker, he prowled the ocean front between Wabasso and Sebastian Inlet. As the summer passed, the detector zeroed him in on the usual junk—rusty tin cans, bottle caps and other useless items. Then, one day, the instrument enabled him to discover his first silver coin. It was an 8 real the size of a half dollar. At that moment, Kip Wagner became addicted to treasure hunting.

In the following months he found other coins, but his method was slow and plodding. His hunting ground was the six-mile strip of sand between Wabasso and Sebastian Inlet. It was a desolate coast where the full tide always lapped the dunes, while the ebb tide left a smoothly washed strand just a hundred feet wide. On weekends Wagner avoided the beach, then dotted with vacationers. But during the week, when the visitors were gone, he usually had the place to himself. Then he worked at his leisure, trudging the long, empty miles under a hot, glaring sun while he studied the beach. Nothing escaped his eyes. He learned to skim debris, broken shells and rusty bottle caps at a glance, hardly seeing them. But if among those items he glimpsed even the partially exposed edge of an irregular black shape, he subconsciously glanced back at it, singling it out for closer investigation. At least forty times in the next few months, these objects were old Spanish coins. Before long he had a small collection of the heavy, sulphided pieces of eight and a few small irregular gold coins. These he hoarded like a miser, lest word get out and Federal agents make him turn in the precious metal to the government. Years later Wagner learned that hidden or unclaimed objects found on the beach are considered treasure-trove and not liable to seizure. Meanwhile, however, he jealously guarded his growing collection and continued to beachcomb the productive strip of sand between Wabasso and Sebastian Inlet, which he fondly called his "money beach."

As his finds increased, so did Wagner's curiosity about where they had come from. Had the coins always lain on the beach, or were the waves of a storm-driven Atlantic casting them up from somewhere offshore? Wagner waded around in the surf, dragging

This dragon pendant was the single most valuable item to come from the wrecks. It is a combination whistle, toothpick and ear spoon which hung on a complicated floral-pattern gold chain. The artifact was recovered from site 8–UW–2, the Cabin Wreck south of Sebastian Inlet. It was sold for $50,000.

Enlargement showing the exquisite detail of the 11½-foot-long gold chain that accompanied the dragon pendant. The detailed floral pattern has been identified as olive blossoms.

(A) Pistol, (B) deck cleat, (C) chisel, (D) deck spikes, (E) shears handle. These artifacts from the 1715 fleet have been cleaned and preserved at Florida's archaeological laboratory and are ready for museum display.

Mel Fisher and Rupert Gates of Treasure Salvors, Inc., assist Clausen in weighing and measuring copper ingots recovered from the Cabin Wreck. These ingots were probably being shipped to Spain to become Spanish copper coins.

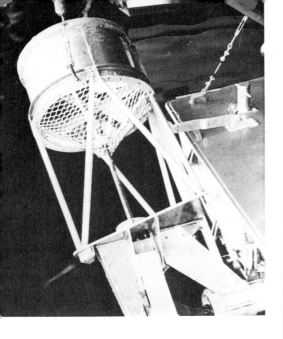

One of the early prototypes of the underwater excavating devices was this model, which had its own propeller. Power came from a motor mounted on the boat.

The original "mailbox," the revolutionary excavating unit used by Treasure Salvors in their startling 1964 recovery of treasure from the Colored Beach Wreck (8–UW–1) near Fort Pierce.

Fisher's original "mailbox" excavating device evolved into these effective units, called blasters, blowers or dusters. In use, they swing down so that the screened ends of the elbow pipes fit over the vessel's propellers. The prop wash is then directed toward the bottom in a swirling tornado of water that rapidly excavates holes in the ocean floor.

Silver bar found at the Colored Beach Wreck bears the markings "UUCCLV" and the name "Cevallus" followed by the Roman numeral XC.

At Florida's Underwater Archaeological Research Section, Burgess and Clausen examine a series of cleaned and catalogued silver coins recovered from the 1715 wrecks and retained by the state after division with Real Eight.

Tools recovered from the 1715 shipwreck sites as they appear when cleaned before preservation.

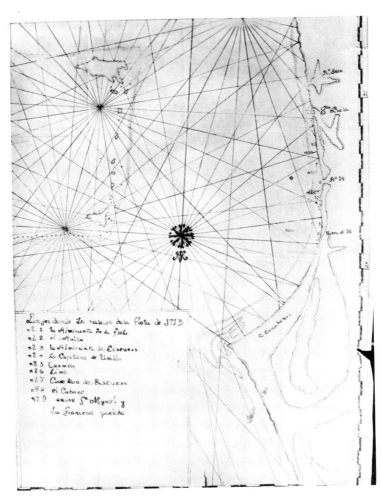

Despite its authentic appearance, this map purporting to locate the ships of the 1715 fleet is a fake drawn by Clausen. Treasure hunters must be on the lookout for such phony documents.

Clausen and artifact preservationist Curtiss Peterson examine an encrusted sword recovered from a Spanish shipwreck. Artifacts are kept in water until processed by the preservationist at the state laboratory.

Two sacks of silver coins from the Cabin Wreck which broke out of one of their shipping chests, fell on one another and were "frozen" in this shape by saltwater corrosion.

Brass navigational dividers recovered from the Colored Beach site in 1964. The globe-headed pair at the top, formerly with steel tips, is a rare type for this period.

Kip Wagner examines two silver wedges. Near his knee is a "pie" of similar wedges that weigh from one to five pounds apiece, possibly shaped this way to fit more easily into their wood packing keg.

Samples of the K'ang Hsi porcelain recovered intact from the wrecks of the 1715 fleet. These pieces originated in the Orient, crossed from the Philippines to Acapulco, Mexico, and were loaded aboard the fleet at Vera Cruz.

Composite photograph shows a variety of K'ang Hsi blue and white porcelain recovered intact from the Cabin Wreck site south of Sebastian Inlet.

his feet and trying to find other coins, but with no success. Still, he felt that they were washing in.

One of his close associates in those days, Dr. Kip Kelso, disagreed, believing the old coins had lain for centuries under the sand of the beach until the pounding surf unearthed them. Wagner apparently resolved the question by hiring a ditch-digging machine and digging three separate trenches seventy-five feet long and several feet deep across a usually productive stretch of beach. When no coins appeared, he and Kelso were convinced that the pieces of eight were washing ashore. After that, the two men got down to some serious treasure hunting.

First they had to establish what exactly they were looking for—a broken chest of coins, a single wreck or an entire fleet? When and where was the treasure-trove lost?

The best clues they had were the coins themselves. None that Wagner had found or had seen in other people's collections was dated later than 1715. As the two men cast about for information, someone told Wagner that a Spanish fleet carrying $14,000,000 in treasure had gone down in a hurricane off Cape Canaveral in 1715. But when he sent a 1714 coin to the Smithsonian Institution and asked if it was possible that the silver piece could have come from that fleet, the response was confusing. Mendel Peterson replied that the coin could not have come from that fleet, since it had been sunk 150 miles farther south in the Florida Keys, a sinking about which he was then writing a book. Treasure maps circulating during this time commonly carried a notation indicating that the fleet lost in 1715 had sunk on Carysfort Reef off Key Largo.

After receiving that news, Wagner and Kelso decided they had better start doing some research of their own. Instead of searching the beach, they started searching their local libraries, reading everything they could find that had anything to do with treasure or shipwrecks off the Florida east coast. Not surprisingly, they found themselves mired in records covering many such wrecks, but not one fitted the picture of a fleet sinking in a hurricane near Sebastian Inlet in 1715.

Finally, after a fruitless search of several Florida libraries, Kelso went to Washington to see what he could find in the Library of Congress. One of the works he encountered there was *A Survey of Indian River Archaeology* by Professor Irving Rouse of Yale. In it,

Rouse not only gives a detailed account of the 1715 fleet disaster on the Barra de Ays but also discusses the work of Higgs and Smith. The author mentions as one of his sources Bernard Romans's *A Concise Natural History of East and West Florida*, published in 1775. Kelso quickly located the volume in the library's rare-book collection and so was in possession of the information that many people, it appears, had had but no one had yet put to use.

Romans's book and chart established the general area of the shipwrecks. Now Wagner and Kelso needed more specific information. What were the circumstances surrounding the disaster? What and how much treasure had the various ships carried? Had any of it already been salvaged?

From reading various treasure-hunting books, Wagner learned that the richest storehouse of Spanish-American historical documents is the General Archives of the Indies in Seville, Spain. He wrote its curator, Dr. José de la Peña, requesting specific information about the 1715 fleet. When the reply arrived, the treasure hunters were disappointed to find that it told them nothing about the fleet that they did not already know. They tried again, this time through a friend who was visiting Spain and who agreed to talk to Dr. Peña and show him some of the silver coins they had found.

Months passed before they learned that this direct approach had been successful. The welcome result, according to Wagner, was 3,000 feet of microfilmed documents written in archaic Spanish that detailed the background of the late-17th- and early-18th-century Spanish treasure fleets. With the occasional help of National Park Service historian Luis R. Arana, an authority on archaic Spanish, Wagner and Kelso took about a year to decipher most of the script and translate it into English. But the effort bore fruit. The documents provided the names and numbers of the ships, their sailing dates and routes, and the events surrounding the loss of the fleet in 1715. What particularly pleased the treasure hunters was the remarkably detailed manifest lists recording the silver, gold and jewelry the fleet had carried: 14 million pesos' worth of treasure.

Fragmentary though it was, the story was there, including references to the early salvage camp and the amount of treasure the Spanish had successfully salvaged.

With these clues and a war-surplus metal detector, Wagner intensified his search of the beaches, hoping to pinpoint the old Spanish salvage camp. If he could find that, he supposed he would be within reach of the wrecks. His excursions into the thick palmetto and cabbage-palm undergrowth on the bluffs behind the beach brought him eventually to a sandy depression that looked more man-made than natural. He started working over the area with his metal detector and within an hour had turned up a ship's spike and a cannonball. Then he began marking the places that gave his detector the highest readings. The metal concentrations were spotted over half an acre.

What Wagner had stumbled onto was the Higgs site, which the amateur historian had investigated in 1940–1942 and Hale Smith had worked archaeologically in 1946, concentrating his efforts mainly along the beach escarpment because of the area's dense undergrowth.

Apparently unaware of the University of Florida's historical and anthropological publications concerning the site, Wagner wrote the South Florida Historical Society, explaining what he had found and asking for an opinion. The Society sent two of its representatives, who looked over the area, examined his finds and agreed that the place could be the old Spanish campsite.

With that green light, Wagner went to work. He posted off a half acre of the land, hired a bulldozer to clear away the palmettos, then settled down to shoveling and sifting his way through the sand. By the end of several months' hard work he had uncovered hundreds of fragments of Mexican ceramics, Chinese porcelain, Spanish olive jars, bricks and some cannonballs. His finds were almost identical with those of Higgs and Smith, with these notable exceptions: Wagner also unearthed parts of a small early-19th-century coffee mill, a bullet mold, musket balls, a pair of rusty cutlasses lying inches apart as if they had been in a leather case, three rectangular fragments of blackened silver, thirteen silver pieces of eight and a crudely made gold ring with a 2½-carat diamond mounted in it and six tiny diamonds set around the band. This last was his most valuable find.

Occasionally, Wagner broke the routine of his work ashore to swim out through the surf and look at the bottom through a window he had installed in a homemade surfboard. He always went hoping to find a shipwreck, but he did not really have any idea what one would look like. One day, however, as he was paddling along looking at the bottom, he saw something he had not seen before. Just below him, in eight feet of water, was a cannon. Beside it were four more. Wagner quickly dove down to inspect them. Each cannon was about nine feet long. Though they were covered with a brown patina of marine growth, there was no mistaking what they were. Nearby lay a huge ship's anchor. Wagner stayed with his find until his breath gave out; then he surfaced, panting more from excitement than exertion. To be certain not to lose the spot, he lined it up with marks on shore. Then he swam ashore and bulldozed through the palmettos a swath that pointed straight at the spot.

Now that he had found what he suspected might be a wreck site, he wondered if there might be others nearby. Thinking that perhaps he could spot them more quickly from the air, he leased a single-engine Taylor-Craft and had the pilot fly him along the beach while he squinted at the shallows below. Whenever he sighted unidentifiable objects or peculiar dark areas on the bottom, he dropped weighted coconuts to mark them. Then he had the plane land on the beach so that he could swim out and examine the areas more closely. Both Higgs and Smith had written that wrecks could be seen in the calm waters adjacent to the campsite, and Wagner found this to be true. The trouble was, the coast was so littered with shipwreck debris that he could not tell the difference between the old and the new.

Wagner acquired swim fins, mask and scuba gear and made several dives on the wreck site south of Sebastian Inlet. As he looked over the bottom he realized that if there was any real treasure to be found there, salvaging it was going to be a bigger job than he could handle alone. The wreckage was badly scattered, most of it buried under the sand. It would take men, money and machinery for a proper salvage job, and these things were then beyond his reach. The best he could do for the time being was make a mental note of the wreck's size and distribution. The rest would have to wait until another day.

Wagner himself, however, did not wait. He went to Fort Pierce to investigate another site. This was a shipwreck so well known that almost every skin diver in the area had dived to it. Wagner swam out to it several times to see what he could find. The site contained tons of ballast rocks, a formidable barrier to anyone curious about what might lie beneath them. Wagner reported that his repeated trips netted him a handful of 1715 silver coins, but again he knew that any serious salvage effort would require assistance. He said he then made up his mind that he either had to find what he needed or get out of the treasure-hunting "business" entirely. And at that point Wagner was not about to quit. He believed he was sitting on the biggest jackpot of his life; all he lacked was the means to secure it.

But there were other considerations. So far his treasure-hunting activities had been on a relatively small scale. He knew that when he went into it in a big way, he would have to observe certain legalities; for example, securing the right to salvage on state-owned submerged land. In preparation for that day, he decided to make application to the state for a search-salvage lease.

Wagner met Van H. Ferguson, director of Florida's Internal Improvement Fund,* in Tallahassee and discussed his plans with him. He said he was interested in working several sites on the Florida east coast and would like to make application for the necessary lease. Ferguson outlined the prerequisites for such an agreement and discussed its various parts with Wagner to be sure he understood what was involved. Simply stated, the standard policy then in effect was that the governor of the state of Florida, and his cabinet, as owners of all submerged lands under the state's navigable waters, could lease the same for search or salvage operations. A single lease could not include more than fifty square miles of submerged land, but other leases of land within the area could be secured until a specific find was made; then the lessee might define a one-acre area and request that his lease of this area be exclusive so that no other individual could work it. The cost of the annual lease was $100, payable in advance. In addition, the agreement called for a $500 bond and quarterly reports to the Florida Internal Improvement Fund detailing operations and listing all finds. For granting this search and salvage privilege, the state would retain 25 percent of whatever was recovered from the submerged land (subject to state selection). If the lessee broke any of the terms of the agreement by either failing to report finds truthfully or selling or otherwise disposing of finds before making a division with the state, then the lease would be subject to forfeiture and cancellation by the state.

The arrangement satisfying Wagner, Ferguson started the paper-work in 1959. Wagner's application to the Florida Internal Improve-

* The state body then issuing salvage leases.

ment Fund was for an exploration lease covering a fifty-mile area from Sebastian Inlet to a point near Stuart, Florida, with exclusive pinpoint salvage-right leases on the specific wreck sites he had investigated. As Wagner recalled later, applying for the lease was one of the smartest moves he ever made.

Chapter 10

Cannon's Silver Pie

In 1959 a series of events occurred that would have a long-lasting effect on the future of Florida treasure hunting. The catalyst responsible for this chain reaction was Boston-born Louis J. Ullian, who grew up in Fort Lauderdale, Florida. Like most boys, Ullian was steeped in stories of pirates and treasure-trove, but unlike most he lived within sight of the old Spanish Plate Fleets' homebound treasure route and was accustomed to beachcombing for pieces of eight along the ocean front by the time he was twelve years old.

With a degree in mechanical engineering from Purdue University, he joined the Navy in 1955. Knowledge he gained in handling explosives during some of his diving experiences brought him an assignment to ordnance engineering, and he was trained in the disposal of explosive ordnance. When he completed his service in 1959, this training qualified him for the job of Ordnance Engineer at the Air Force Missile Test Range at Cape Canaveral. Each time the Air Force fired a rocket there, Ullian was responsible for seeing that its destruct system was operative in the event that range officers deemed it necessary to destroy the rocket before it threatened land areas.

Whenever time and finances permitted, however, Ullian continued his hobby of treasure hunting. He had explored what he believed to be the wreck of a 1733 Spanish treasure ship and over the years had found just enough artifacts and adventure to whet his appetite for more.

One day in 1959, Ullian stepped into the diving shop at the base and met the owner, Delphine Long, a diving enthusiast with a talent for repairing anything mechanical. Long was the ground power equipment supervisor at Patrick Air Force Base, but his real love was the sea. He had organized a skin-diving club at the base and in 1958 had actually poked around in the ballast rock and scattered debris of the 1715 wreck near Sebastian Inlet without knowing what he had found.

Since the two shared an interest in diving and bottom-scratching for artifacts, Long persuaded Ullian to join his diving club. Several days later at a meeting, Ullian met Ervin Taylor, another diver, who lived at Micco, near Sebastian. When Ullian described some of his treasure-hunting experiences in southern Florida, Taylor mentioned that he lived near someone whom he thought Ullian should meet. He said the man's name was Kip Wagner and that he had been hunting treasure for years.

The four men eventually got together at Wagner's home and talked treasure. For many nights through the winter of 1959–1960, they met and compared notes, examined one another's finds and discussed the methods that might be used to salvage the sites Wagner was eager to explore. They planned to try a group effort the coming spring, pooling their manpower and equipment to see what they could do. But when they took stock of what each of them had to offer the enterprise, it became obvious that they lacked the essentials for even a modest operation. They needed help in both manpower and equipment.

Finding divers willing to go treasure hunting was no problem, but finding reliable persons who had something more than diving experience to offer the venture was another thing. But Lou Ullian had someone in mind—Colonel Dan F. Thompson, one of his bosses at the base. Thompson was not only an expert diver but a graduate electrical engineer finishing up a distinguished twenty-four-year career in the Air Force as director of operations at the missile test center. When Ullian told him of their plans, Thompson was eager to join the group.

The next recruit was Lieutenant Colonel Harry Cannon, who

worked for Thompson as chief of the Range Safety Office. Cannon's Air Force experiences included flying B-24s and C-47s over the Himalayas from India to China during World War II. After the war he was trained extensively in electronics and communications. In 1959, one of his jobs at the Cape was to push the destruct button on any wayward rocket and blow up the multimillion-dollar missile before it got into trouble. Cannon was also in charge of a special task force for recovering astronauts downed at sea, but he was not a diver. He owned a twenty-one-foot boat that the treasure hunters felt would be useful for ferrying them to the wreck sites. And shortly after joining the group he was initiated into the mysteries of diving. One cold night in January his companions strapped him into scuba gear, briefed him on what he was supposed to do, then tossed him into the icy waters of the Officers Club swimming pool. Cannon quickly became an accomplished diver.

There were now eight of them. They all came from different backgrounds and they were all skilled in an interesting assortment of specialties—Louis Ullian, diver, treasure hunter, explosives expert and ex-Navy ordnance engineer; Delphine Long, diver, treasure hunter, mechanical and electrical specialist; Ervin Taylor, diver and top mechanic; Colonel Dan Thompson, diver, electrical engineer, legal and organizational expert; Lieutenant Colonel Harry Cannon, diver, communications and electronics specialist with a flair for handling business and financial matters; Lisbon Futch, a skilled boatsman with wide knowledge of the channels and shoals in the Sebastian area; Dr. Kip Kelso, scholar and researcher well informed in Spanish history; and Kip Wagner, experienced in the one field in which they all shared a common interest—treasure hunting.

Considering the kind of operation he had in mind, Wagner wondered how well they would work together. Could they stand the long hours, the months of hard work, the probable obstacles and the possible dangers that lay ahead? Or when the going got tough, would they quit in disgust?

Wagner felt that he had to know. He had invested too much in the project to risk losing it because his group of eager treasure hunters could not stand the pressures. Instead of putting them on his choice site south of Sebastian Inlet, he decided to test them first on the picked-over Fort Pierce wreck, where he knew the work would be hard, the obstacles many and the chances of finding treasure virtually nil. If they could weather that, then they would be ready for the real thing.

On a cold, blustery day in January 1960, the group made its first of many exploratory runs out to the wreck north of Fort Pierce in Cannon's cabin cruiser to size up the situation. Enthusiasm compensated for what the fledgling treasure salvagers lacked in equipment. As they peered down through three fathoms of water at the huge pile of heavy ballast rock littering the site, the men were far more speculative about the rewards that might lie beneath that formidable mountain of rocks than about the prodigious job of moving it. Wagner suspected that whatever finds were there would be few and far between; yet he found his friends' excitement infectious. Scores of divers had visited the site, but he doubted that anyone had ever made a thorough search of it. Who could tell what might still be there?

In the weekends that followed, they made repeated trips to the wreck to scout it from above. Meanwhile they scrounged for diving equipment—tanks, regulators, fins, face masks, weight belts—gradually acquiring what they needed, repairing and pooling what they had.

Their greatest need was for a work boat large enough to hold them, their diving equipment and some of the more sophisticated salvage gear they hoped to build. Libe Futch solved the problem when he went to the salvage yards at Norfolk, Virginia, and bought them a forty-foot Navy liberty launch. The boat was little more than a paint-chipped, soot-begrimed hull. But they scraped, patched, painted and overhauled it, added a deck and canopy, and dubbed it the *Sampan*. When they had finished, the vessel looked less like a fugitive from a junkyard and more like a work boat that would do the job for them.

The mechanically minded members of the group improvised a two-inch sand dredge built from junkyard parts. Powered by a tractor engine mounted on the bow of the boat, a pump shot a stream of water through a fire hose connected to the lower end of a piece of stovepipe, creating the suction necessary to vacuum sand from the bottom. It was a Rube Goldberg contraption, but it worked. With this and other pieces of patched or makeshift equipment, the group launched itself into the treasure-salvage business. That March, Wagner received the salvage lease he had applied for almost a year earlier. Every weekend after that was spent on the Fort Pierce wreck, and there was nothing glamorous about what the men did there. It was hard work. The pile of ballast rock that had been carried in the ship's hull to stabilize the vessel was seventy feet long, twenty feet wide and eight feet deep. By midsummer they had cut a ten-foot swath through the middle of it, removing the rock stone by stone, averaging four to five hundred a day. When they reached bottom, the nozzle of the homemade sand dredge was sent down to start eating into the sand. The divers hovered over it anxiously, hoping to see something of value appear. But as the pale yellow grains of sand were sucked up the pipe and discharged a short distance away, there was nothing. The hole grew deeper and the divers grew more intent, but there was no fortune to be found that day. Nor was it to be found in the many days and the many new holes that followed. In the process they unearthed hundreds of pieces of broken Mexican pottery, tiny chips of blue and white china which were later identified as K'ang Hsi porcelain, a truckload of cannonballs, a copper rim and handle, timber fragments and a handful of brass nails. But no treasure.

With their initial enthusiasm slightly dampened, they moved their operations to another part of the ballast pile and started over again, bisecting the big rock heap with another hand-picked trench. As the summer slipped away they continued to burrow through the pile at a snail's speed, until by August they had crisscrossed it so many times with trenches that the ballast heap resembled a cut pie. They had increased their finds by several hundred more pieces of broken pottery and cannonballs, but still no treasure, not even so much as a single coin. By now everyone's spirits were so low that the only thing that kept them going was sheer stubbornness. Then, Harry Cannon found something that suddenly made it all worth while.

Cannon had been excavating a small hole of his own. When the endless chore of rock moving got too monotonous for him, he occasionally slipped away to poke around in his private sand pit. Later, when the others asked him why he persisted in working that one place, Cannon's only comment was that it looked interesting to him.

One day toward the end of the diving season, Cannon left the rock-moving detail and swam off by himself to probe his private place. He had hardly started digging when his crowbar struck something hard. Reaching into the hole, he extracted a fist-sized wedge of blackened metal. Where his bar had scraped it he saw the gleam of silver. Cannon's first impulse was to rush to the surface with his find, but on second thought he returned to the hole, his heart beating in double time as he clawed at the sand. His efforts were rewarded with five more wedges. Then he tucked the pieces under his arms and swam up.

When the *Sampan's* crew saw his find they whooped for joy. Cannon's wedges formed a perfect silver "pie" eight inches in diameter. Someone estimated that a keg of wedges would probably be three layers deep and weigh around a hundred pounds. With that, everyone went over the side hellbent to find the missing layers. By day's end they had found three more wedges, making a total of eight—each one believed to be worth from $500 to $600.

The treasure find did wonders for the men. Their enthusiasm shot back up to normal. They were a close-knit team again, and Wagner decided that their test on the Fort Pierce wreck had amply proved their staying power. Now he felt they deserved to move on to bigger things: the Sebastian Inlet site. But that would have to wait until the following spring. Their diving season was over.

Chapter 11

Whence Came the Golden Dragon?

Those last cold months in 1960 were the longest they ever remembered. The divers itched to get into the water to see for themselves the secret site Wagner had saved for them. But it was out of the question. The wild surf was still on one of its prolonged winter rampages. All the men could do was stand on the beach and stare gloomily at the big waves smashing themselves to smithereens on the hidden limestone ledges flanking the area a few hundred yards offshore.

To keep their minds off the frustrating situation, Wagner kept them busy patching the boat and repairing their equipment. Then, on January 8, 1961, the seas momentarily calmed, and there was no holding the divers. Despite a fifteen-knot wind and frothing whitecaps, everyone piled into the *Sampan* and chugged out through the treacherous crosscurrents of narrow Sebastian Inlet to reconnoiter the site.

Beyond the pass the ocean was calmer, but the bone-chilling wind was whipping foaming combers over the. first and second bars. The wreck site lay between them in the trough.

About 9 A.M. they reached the area two and a half miles south of the inlet and dropped anchor in the relatively calm water separating

97

the two jagged upcroppings of Anastasia limestone lying on either side of them. If the *Sampan* swung fifty to a hundred feet in either direction, it took no vivid imagination to visualize their being disemboweled on the same rocks that had sunk the ship they were seeking.

Cannon and Thompson, the only ones with wetsuits, went over the side to look at the bottom. Visibility below was less than an arm's length, and a strong swell was running. Each time it swept in, the divers grabbed for rock outcroppings to keep from being sucked along with it. If they happened to be caught in the open, the icy water sent them somersaulting toward shore. But in the brief calm between waves, they swam a serpentine pattern over the bottom, searching every shadow for signs of wreckage.

In minutes Cannon spotted something angular, dimly outlined below him. He swooped down to investigate. It was one of the three cannon Wagner had sighted earlier from his homemade surfboard. Cannon surfaced and signaled the *Sampan* to move closer. Then he hailed Thompson and jackknifed down for a closer inspection of the bottom.

Thompson never reached him. Halfway there, as he was finning along just over the rippled white sand, he began seeing scattered objects sticking up out of the bottom. The constant scouring of the big waves had apparently skimmed off several feet of loose overburden from the wreck site. Between trying to keep from being tumbled by the swell and avoiding being sucked out by the undertow, he spotted two curious rocklike objects about a foot and a half thick, and paused to examine them. The blackish green lumps were lightly encrusted with limestone, and he was unsure what they were. But he had no trouble identifying what lay around them in shallow sand pockets—single and clustered pieces of eight. Silver coins were scattered over the bottom, but he decided to salvage the two large objects, if only to learn what they were.

The problem was how to do it. Each of the lumps was almost too heavy to lift. If he swam up to call the boat, he might not find them again. But since that seemed the most logical solution, he surfaced and shouted for the *Sampan*.

Wagner and the others were having trouble hoisting the anchor. Thompson waited about ten minutes to see if they would get started, then dove back down to the bottom, where he almost panicked when he found he had drifted in the strong currents and

98

could not immediately relocate the lumps. Minutes later he found them. He was determined not to leave them again.

Instead, he managed to get both of the bulky weights under his arms and started to walk the bottom toward the boat. After staggering some fifty feet, he was so winded he had to drop one of the lumps. He carried the other back to a rusty mast strap he had seen that might make a good marker. Then he quickly swam to retrieve the one he had dropped, intending to return it to the mast strap. That was when he made his second mistake. He could not find the lump he had dropped.

Thoroughly disgusted with himself, Thompson scooped up a handful of loose coins, swam for the *Sampan*, and flung the coins aboard with a muttered comment about their being so profuse on the bottom that he could collect them with a rake. Then he called for a line and dove again.

He had no trouble finding the mast strap and making the rope fast to the lump, but when he tried to lift the heavy weight while they hauled on the rope from above, the effort was almost too much for him. The lump swung dizzily in the currents, rising and dropping with the pitching boat.

Once on the surface, Thompson started the battle again, kicking furiously with his flippers to push the lump high enough for the others to drag it aboard. Finally, with everyone's help, the feat was accomplished. Thompson followed his find, completely exhausted.

It did not take them long to learn that he had found a cluster of corroded silver coins that weighed seventy-seven pounds and contained an estimated 1,500 to 2,000 pieces of eight.

They congratulated themselves hoarse.

As soon as Thompson caught his breath, he told them about the cluster he had lost. After that it made no difference how cold or rough the water was—divers tumbled off the boat in all directions. Seconds later they surfaced, clutching fistfuls of coins snatched from the bottom. Up and down they went, adding rapidly to the growing pile of silver accumulating on the *Sampan*. They stayed until their teeth chattered; they stayed until they turned blue. After forty-five icy minutes, one of the men found the lump Thompson had lost. Even then it took a blast of foul weather finally to drive them out of the water and force them back to port.

As they counted their day's take that evening, they found they had collected some four thousand silver pieces of eight.

Over the next few weeks, high seas and bad weather prevented the men from returning to the site. Then, when they did return, they were disappointed to find that everything on the bottom had changed. Visibility was about twelve inches, severe wave action had covered the wreck area with a layer of sand, and the coins were more difficult to find. But once the air lift was put to work, the divers were soon picking them up again.

Lou Ullian found a purplish-black lump, which he thought might be another cluster of coins. He examined it, chipping off a corner of the block with his crowbar. Since it looked like rock, he decided it was a piece of coral. He sat on it most of the morning, fanning the sand for coins.

That afternoon when Ullian and Thompson went down to take a last look around the bottom, Thompson spotted the large lump and pointed it out to Ullian, who simply shook his head.

Failing to understand him, Thompson turned the lump over and examined a side Ullian had apparently missed. There, in a small indentation, were the unmistakable shapes of coins.

Ullian's lump was a cluster of corroded coins later found to contain nearly two thousand silver pieces of eight estimated to be worth from $20,000 to $30,000.

Wagner and the others realized that the combined value of their recent finds removed them from the status of amateur treasure hunters. Now they qualified as pros. Since the business of harvesting coins had been so good, they decided to protect their interests by forming a corporation. They named it Real Eight, after the Spanish term for a piece of eight, *ocho reales*. The eight charter members elected officers, making Wagner president, and split a thousand shares of stock among them. After that, for better or worse, they were officially treasure hunters.

The next time they went to work, business could not have been worse. Even their cannon had disappeared. In January the cannon had been lying on the bottom in three fathoms of water. Now, a month later, only the surface buoys that had been tied to them remained, the lines running down to the bottom at two fathoms. That meant the cannon were buried under six feet of sand, thanks to the fickle currents, and so was the rest of the site. The divers would have to move tons of sand before they were in business again.

Once again the mechanical talents of Del Long and Erv Taylor were put to the test with the various sand-moving devices they had built from junk parts. Their first contraption was a two-inch sand pump that worked by centrifugal force. It ran well, but it ate sand too slowly. Their next invention was an air lift that used an old Model T Ford engine for a compressor. This malfunctioned so many times during the trial runs that it was discarded.

In May, Neptune apparently took pity on them, because the sea suddenly cleared the offending tons of sand from the site and left it as clean as before. Jubilantly the divers descended, gazed happily at their exposed cannon and spent the next four days familiarizing themselves with the distribution of the wreck. Before they could dig, however, Neptune changed his mind and once again covered the site with tons of sand.

That was the last straw. The group angrily resolved to find some kind of sand dredge that would do the job. Once again the mechanics cast about for ideas. Taylor had read about an injection dredge used by California divers searching for gold. It involved jetting a column of water up a pipe and creating a strong suction at the intake end for "sniffing" gold out of rock pockets and crevices. The idea looked practical, so Taylor fashioned a similar apparatus, a six-inch diameter, nine-foot-long aluminum tube. Instead of water, a jet of compressed air was shot up the inside of the tube by a two-and-a-half inch fire hose, and the resulting suction was powerful enough to burrow deep holes in the bottom within minutes. Any shells, coins or other treasure sucked up with the sand was caught in a screen basket attached to the outlet. On its trial run, with eighty to ninety pounds of air pressure powering it, the nine-foot-long tube whipped around the bottom like a berserk boa constrictor bent on tossing its operator off its business end. The monster gobbled everything within reach, including cannonballs and incautious hands. But once they learned how to control it, the divers found the dredge worked splendidly. So voracious was its appetite that they affectionately named their mechanical helper "The Hungry Beast."

During this period, Real Eight's relationship with the state was beyond reproach. To oversee the state's quarter share in all finds made, the Internal Improvement Fund selected two eminent archaeologists to work with the salvagers—Dr. William H. Sears,

101

then curator of Social Sciences at the Florida State Museum in Gainesville, and Dr. John M. Goggin, head of the Anthropology Department at the University of Florida and the first professionally trained archaeologist to work in underwater archaeology.

The arrangement worked well. At the end of each diving season the salvagers met informally with the two archaeologists for a division of the treasure and artifacts. Goggin and Sears would select 25 percent of the find for the state's collection, and Wagner would load it into the back of his pickup truck and drive it to Gainesville for them. The articles selected by the two archaeologists consisted mainly of ships' fastenings and gear, armament such as cannon and musket balls, and ceramic fragments—artifacts of historical or scientific value from which archaeologists could reconstruct the past. The salvagers' share was coins and other items of greater material value. Both sides were satisfied with the arrangement. In a letter to the Internal Improvement Fund Director, Van Ferguson, on January 13, 1961, Sears stressed this point:

"The Real Eight Company is doing its work in a scientifically impeccable fashion. Detailed drawings, photographs and other records have been made, and correlated with the specimens recovered. To our best knowledge, this is the first and only wreck in Florida to have been properly investigated, scientifically speaking.

"This company is apparently the only one to attempt to fairly meet their contractual obligations under a salvage lease."

Such praise from a professional archaeologist was not easy to come by. Dr. Sears was later instrumental in gaining cabinet approval for the salvagers' six-year lease extension. Unfortunately, this apparent harmony was not destined to be long lived.

By the end of the summer of 1962, the salvagers had found countless pieces of broken pottery, numerous ship's spikes, silver buckles, twenty cannon scattered over the area and a few thousand pieces of eight. Then, the single most valuable find of all was made before the end of the year. The only trouble was, no one knew where the item had originated, and there was some question where it was found. Wagner's version of the event sounds convincing.

He said that when they wrapped up their diving season in 1962, there was little expectation of finding any more treasure until the weather became fair and the waters cleared again the next spring. Wagner therefore went back to his old habit of prowling the beach with his metal detector, hoping to pick up a few stray coins. One November day, his nineteen-year-old nephew, Rex Stocker, accompanied him on one of his beachcombing trips.

It was just after a strong northeaster had passed, and Wagner reasoned that their chances of finding something were good. He immediately set to work along the water's edge, with his battery bag slung over his shoulder, his earphones on his head and his long-handled, stove-lid-shaped sensor moving just ahead of him like a dog straining at its leash.

Periodically, as the morning wore on, the detector hummed and Wagner stopped to dig. Sometimes he found a bottle cap, sometimes a rusty tin can. But once in a while it was a rectangular piece of eight. Wagner said he began finding them so often that he lost track of time. Lacking a metal detector, Stocker grew restless and began to range well above the tide mark, where Wagner felt sure there were no coins. For the moment, he forgot his nephew as he went on searching.

Suddenly he heard the boy shout. He looked up as the youth came running toward him excitedly with something yellow draped over his arm. Wagner said his first thought was that his nephew had caught a small snake. Then, when he saw what it really was, he could not believe his eyes. It was a long, thin gold chain attached to an unusual gold pendant. Stocker said he had found it up near the bluffs, lying exposed on the sand as if it had been flung there by storm waves.

They hurried home and examined it carefully under a magnifying glass. The finely wrought chain was 11 feet 4¼ inches long, each link faceted with tiny rosettes. The 3-inch gold pendant was shaped like a dragon, with carefully detailed scales running the length of its body. When Wagner blew into its half-opened mouth, it produced a shrill whistle. Part of the dragon's back swiveled out to make a curved toothpick. Its slender tail was shaped into a small spoon, possibly for cleaning wax out of one's ears.

Wagner had the necklace examined by experts. No one had ever seen anything like it before, nor could anyone guess its age or origin. Various museums appraised it at between $40,000 and $60,000. Stocker relinquished his find to the treasure hunters in exchange for forty shares of stock in the company.

There were only two small notes of dissent. Lou Ullian, one of

Real Eight's head divers, said that the dragon pendant had not been found on the beach but had in fact been recovered from the wreck.* And a chart on which the company marked the location of all its finds from the underwater site showed that the dragon pendant had been found in the wreck.

What difference did it make?

About $12,500 worth.

Here is the reason: In the United States, the common law of treasure-trove states that if something of value, defined as treasure, is found on land, it is finders-keepers. However, if that treasure is found offshore on a state's submerged land, then it is a different story. According to Florida's salvage agreement with Real Eight, the state was legally entitled to 25 percent of any such find.

The point, however, was never argued. Officially, Stocker's find was considered treasure-trove. Real Eight later sold the dragon pendant at a New York auction for $50,000.

* Mel Fisher told author Burgess the same thing in 1972.

Chapter 12

Four Fathoms to El Dorado

The salvagers bought a small cabin on the beach near the wreck site and used it as a base of operations. From then on they referred to their valuable offshore property as the "Cabin Wreck." They could have as easily called it the "Silver Wreck," since it had not yet produced any gold, only pieces of eight and artifacts, 25 percent of which was retained by the state as agreed upon in the salvage lease with Florida.

The 1963 season started slowly for the divers, who in the first four months were finding only a nominal number of single silver coins. But the returns rapidly picked up in June with the discovery of more clusters of coins. The first weighed seventy pounds and contained about 1,400 pieces of eight corroded together into a solid mass. Everyone considered the find an omen of good luck. A few days later, in a six-foot-wide area beside a shellrock ledge, they unearthed five more valuable conglomerates weighing between fifty and seventy-five pounds each and increasing their silver hoard by several thousand more coins. Before the day was out, one of the divers had found a silver crucifix encrusted with rainbow-hued shell fragments.

The quantity and frequency of these finds sparked renewed

interest among the members of the group who might not normally work the bottom together. The following weekend everyone turned out, anxious to go down to see what could be found.

Minutes after The Hungry Beast started consuming its usual diet of sand, the pipe suddenly burrowed through a layer of gray clay into a concentration of broken blue and white porcelain. This in itself was not unusual, since fragments of the K'ang Hsi china were common on the site. Higgs reported finding them at the old Spanish camp in 1941, and Wagner knew from his translation of the fleet's manifest lists that the *Flota* vessels had carried shipments of china. But it was what lay immediately under the fragments that surprised the searchers. They began finding larger pieces. First, half a cup; then, a little farther, its other half. Below that lay a complete cup and a bowl. Then as the sand disappeared up the dredge pipe, there gradually appeared horizontal rows of cups and bowls in perfect condition, exactly as they had been stacked in the ship's hold 250 years earlier. Somehow these fragile pieces had withstood for centuries the cataclysmic destruction of the ship and the ravages of time.

The intact china so astounded the divers that they simply stared at their unique find, forgetting the wallowing sand dredge. Abruptly they were snapped out of their reverie by a loud clattering from the dredge.

Horrified, they saw that the unattended Beast was gobbling up whole cups and bowls of invaluable china, rapidly reducing it to fragments that rattled through its long aluminum alimentary canal. Hastily diverting the dredge's voracious maw, the divers rescued the remaining delicate china with careful hands.

They reported that they had found three distinct patterns of china: all white; a blue design on white; and a black enamel with faint gold border decoration. Wagner said in his book that he thought Dr. Kelso first learned of the porcelain in an obscure 1942 Florida historical quarterly. This of course was the Higgs site report. Higgs had identified similar fragments as having come from the K'ang Hsi period (1662–1722). Kelso and Wagner also knew from the old documents that much of it had been recovered by the Spanish salvagers and shipped back to Spain a year after the disaster. Correspondence with a noted authority on the porcelain revealed that at the time of its manufacture it was considered fairly common and inexpensive china destined for sale in Spain. The same china today, however, said the authority, was worth about twenty to twenty-five dollars for a large fragment, more for unbroken cups or bowls. Several museums considered it priceless. For the moment, however, the salvagers were not interested in selling their find. They hoped to keep most of their treasure intact, because the Real Eight members intended to establish a treasure museum.

Not long after finding the porcelain, one of the divers was inspecting a cannon on the bottom when he glimpsed a faint gleam beside its muzzle. Excitedly he fanned away the sand and saw several links of a finely wrought gold chain. Carefully he removed it from beneath the cannon. It was another long necklace containing a pendant that once had miniature oil paintings on its faces. Unfortunately, after its long submersion, only faint tracings of the oil paint remained.

Except for the jewelry, the Cabin Wreck had still not yielded any other gold. Where, wondered Wagner, were the doubloons? Certainly the early Spanish salvagers and the pirates that had worked the wreck had overlooked at least some of them. Were they really working the flagship of the fleet, the one which supposedly carried so much gold and silver? Or was this another ship of the fleet that had carried no gold? It was a strong temptation to let the Cabin Wreck rest while the salvagers investigated some of the other sites Wagner had learned about along the coast. But while the silver kept coming in, he reasoned, why risk valuable time and money elsewhere? After all, he felt, they had hardly scratched the surface of the Cabin Wreck yet. Real Eight stuck with this decision, and before midsummer the group's efforts were rewarded with something more than silver and artifacts.

One day Del Long and Dan Thompson were guiding The Beast over new grazing grounds in nine feet of water when the sand suddenly turned yellow with doubloons. Thompson shouted excitedly into his mouthpiece, and Long streaked for the surface, yelling and waving to the others on shore. Within minutes all were on the bottom, where they formed a circle around the site and swam toward the center of it, picking up doubloons as they went.

Wagner reported that the search turned up twenty-three 4- and 8-escudo gold coins that gleamed as brightly as they had the day they were minted. Before it was over, Long added frosting to the cake by finding a gold ring with an expansion band. As the dredge burrowed a cone-shaped hole in the bottom, Long glimpsed the ring tumbling in slow motion down the sloping sand wall. With perfect timing he thrust out his hand and let it slide onto his little finger.

The gold was a taste of what was to come. Surprisingly, few people outside Real Eight realized what the salvagers—most of whom still retained their regular jobs—had been finding on their weekend treasure-hunting trips. When the *Sampan* and its crew returned to Sebastian Inlet after a day over the wreck, someone around the dock always asked if they had found their pot of gold yet. The usual reply was that they had not, but that they were still looking. Then the divers transferred their sacks of silver coins from the boat to their car without elaborating on the subject.

In 1962 one of the Real Eight members, Lou Ullian, stopped by a dive shop in Los Angeles to look over new equipment. The owner was Mel Fisher, a tall, lean, balding man renowned for his treasure-hunting adventures in various parts of the world. Fisher had never found any gold, but he had an old Spanish silver coin on display that sparked a conversation between the two men. Before it was over, the West Coast treasure hunter had learned about the Florida find and was most interested. A few months later Fisher passed through Florida on his way to the West Indies with an expedition searching for Sir William Phips's fabled Silver Shoals Wreck, believed lost on reefs just north of the Dominican Republic. He stopped to see Wagner, and they talked treasure for hours. He was most impressed by the coins Wagner showed him.

In March 1963, after an unsuccessful treasure hunt on the Shoals, Fisher visited Wagner again, this time with a proposal. He pointed out that Real Eight had more wreck sites than it could work in a lifetime. To spread the work and speed the returns, Fisher offered to bring a group of professional treasure hunters from California to work the other wrecks, splitting any new finds fifty-fifty with Real Eight after division with the state. If the group found nothing, it would get nothing for its efforts.

The idea appealed to Wagner and the other Real Eight members. While details were being worked out, Fisher returned to California, gathered his professionals into a company called Universal Salvage and took them back to Florida, ready to go. He and his attractive wife, Dolores, had sold their West Coast boat, business and home to finance the venture. The group had agreed to work Real Eight's sites for a year without pay. If by the end of that time nothing had turned up, they would call it quits and write the venture off as another unfortunate expedition.

The five men Fisher took with him came from a variety of backgrounds, but their common bond was a hunger for treasure. And they were a talented lot. Rupert Gates, Fisher's second-in-command, was a Stanford graduate with diving credits ranging from the gold-bearing rivers of the western United States to the Mediterranean to Lake Guatavita high in the Andes Mountains of South America. Panamanian-born Demosthenes Molinar, better known as "Moe," was a diesel mechanic turned diver. Jack-of-all-trades Dick Williams had been a railroad diesel engineer, welder, radio operator and electronics repairman. Walt Holzworth was a Pennsylvania Dutch farmer who had moved to California, caught the coin-collecting bug and found himself irresistibly attracted to full-time treasure hunting. Fay Field, an electronics genius, had a hobby to thank for his presence in the group. Field and his wife were avid collectors of the handsome shell of *Spondylus Americanus,* the rare spiny oyster that often inhabits old iron shipwrecks. To find his specimens, Field had to devise a quick way to find shipwrecks. He built a proton magnetometer, a supersensitive instrument that detects deviations in the earth's magnetic field caused by concentrations of iron, as in anchors, cannon, ships' fittings, etc. Fisher immediately saw its application to treasure hunting and persuaded Field to join the group. His electronic detector was destined to revolutionize treasure hunting.

Although the season was almost over, Wagner took Fisher's eager divers to the Wedge Wreck off Fort Pierce to let them test the magnetometer and familiarize themselves with the picked-over wreck where Real Eight had found the silver wedges during their initial work in 1960. No one expected to find anything at the heavily worked site, but Fisher's group got busy with a sand dredge and surprised everyone by uncovering several miniature clay animals and another silver wedge.

Despite increasingly bad weather, the next stop for the salvagers was a site just south of Vero Beach called the Sand Point Wreck. Local divers knew about this wreck at least as early as World War II, when the father of Florida treasure hunters, Art McKee, owner of the McKee Treasure Museum on Plantation Key, salvaged numerous cannon from it and sold them for scrap during the war.

109

Apparently, however, the site had not been worked seriously for treasure, because Fisher and his men found between 1,200 and 1,500 silver coins and three gold doubloons in a few days. Unfortunately, corrosion had so badly deteriorated most of the pieces of eight that few were recognizable as coins. The heavily sulphided wafers of silver were hardly worth cheering about, but in accordance with their agreement Real Eight received half of the find.

For Fisher and his hard-bitten crew it was a long, lean winter. Repeatedly the divers tried to work the wrecks, but the rampaging surf always drove them back. During one attempt, Fisher was slammed against the boat's bulkhead and suffered two cracked ribs. Wagner's men remembered how hard it had been for them during their first year on the Wedge Wreck and tried to bolster the California divers' morale, promising that if they could just last until spring, the reward would be worth it.

No one, in his wildest imaginings, could have guessed just how much that reward would prove to be worth for Fisher's men a few months later. But the fates that were about to guide them to a bonanza had paved the way several years before. The key figures in this historic event were three young men: Bruce Ward, Don Neiman and Frank Allen.

Bruce Ward was a midwesterner from Illinois who had come to Vero Beach in 1955. An active skin diver, he was soon influenced by the local legends of lost treasure and began looking for it at every opportunity. He combed the beach or searched the bottom offshore, using face mask, snorkel and fins and depositing his wreck fragments and artifacts in a peach basket encircled by an innertube on the surface. The more he found, the more treasure hunting intrigued him. He finally quit his job and went to work as a night watchman so that he could devote more daylight hours to his search. One day Ward struck up a friendship with another beachcomber, Don Neiman of Fort Pierce, who hunted fossils and Indian artifacts. Sharing a common interest, they decided to work together. Shortly afterward, just south of Fort Pierce, Neiman found a perfect 8-escudo gold doubloon on the beach. The two jumped for joy. Concentrating their search in that area rewarded them with a few more gold and silver coins. It was enough to make them believe they were onto something hot. Treasure was either close by or not far away, but they needed equipment and financial help to launch any serious attempt to find it.

At this point, Frank Allen of Orlando came to their aid. Allen was a history teacher whose hobby was coin collecting. After seeing Neiman and Ward's coins and hearing their story, he agreed to invest some money in their treasure-hunting venture in exchange for a third of everything they found.

The three formed a company called The Associates. Unaware of the Real Eight lease or of the state laws governing such things, the trio purchased a fourteen-foot boat and diving equipment and went into the treasure-salvage business.

They combed the beach and dived offshore. Their efforts produced a few more coins but nothing as substantial as they had hoped. Obviously they were near a shipwreck, but it soon became apparent that this particular wreck was so badly scattered that about all they could tell about it was that there were objects from a ship on the bottom. The exact location of any concentrated treasure was a mystery they could not solve. They needed more men and better salvage equipment—necessities they could not afford. The three men were forced to make a decision.

They knew about Wagner's work on his sites and that Real Eight had the necessary men and machinery. The question was whether The Associates could reveal to them what they had found, in exchange for a piece of the action.

One August evening in 1963, Ward, Neiman and Allen visited Wagner's home and asked if they could talk with him about some treasure they had found. When he saw their bright gold coins dated 1714 and 1715, Wagner knew that the doubloons had come from the same fleet Real Eight was working.

Understandably the men were vague about the exact location of their find, but they indicated that they were willing to bargain. Wagner learned enough to be convinced that they had indeed stumbled onto something significant.

He called a meeting of the company directors, and several days later Real Eight drew up an agreement with The Associates. After the state had selected its 25 percent, the rest would be divided so that Real Eight could get 60 percent and The Associates 40 percent of everything found.

With the deal made, Ward marked the location of the site on a map of the coast. The Fisher team started searching for the wreck immediately, using their magnetometer. All they found was some metal debris from an old Naval airplane and some unexploded

111

ordnance left over from World War II training held along this part of the coast. The divers combed the area which Ward had indicated as the site of the wreck from September 1963 until January 1964; then they gave up in despair.

Fisher angrily reported to Wagner that they had not found the slightest trace of the ghost wreck and that he did not think it worth trying to go on.

Wagner understood Fisher's position. His divers were working on a percentage. If they found nothing, they got nothing. And for the last few months they had done a great deal of free work. Under the existing agreement with Ward, Neiman and Allen, even if they found something, Universal Salvage's share would be small. As Wagner saw it, the only thing that would keep Fisher's team interested in continuing the search was a change in the agreement.

The Associates were called in for consultation. Wagner explained the problem and offered them three alternatives: share in the search expenses, agree to a change in the present contract, or forget the whole affair.

After some haggling, Ward, Neiman and Allen allegedly agreed to a change in the agreement, under the terms of which Real Eight would get 90 percent and they would get 10 percent. The original letter on Real Eight stationery, with Kip Wagner's signature, was not redrawn. The new arrangement was supposedly a gentlemen's agreement* sealed with a handshake.

Fisher's team returned to the site and began the search again. They trolled their magnetometer head back and forth over the ocean bottom, intently watching the instrument for the slightest indication of a concentration of metal. Months passed and they found nothing. Part of the problem was that at this time they did not use any organized search system. Then, in April, the divers found their first significant evidence of a shipwreck—a scattering of ballast rock on the bottom a half mile north of the area where they had been looking and farther out at sea. Foul weather prevented a closer examination of the site, but when conditions were more favorable a month later, Fisher moved in with a new piece of sand-moving equipment he had built. The new digging system

---

* The matter was later the subject of a suit brought against Real Eight by Ward and Neiman, who in the end received only 10 percent.

used the salvage boat's engine and propeller to shoot a column of surface water down through a metal duct aimed at the bottom. It was affectionately nicknamed "The Mailbox" because of its resemblance to a street postbox. The funneled prop wash reached the ocean floor with such force that it could open an eight-by-ten-foot hole in loose deposits in ten minutes. Although it worked on the reverse principle of the injection dredge, which sucked up sand, the blaster ate holes in the bottom with far greater voracity than Real Eight's Hungry Beast, speeding up Universal Salvage's earth-moving capacity tenfold.

By the end of April, the divers had found about a hundred silver coins around the ballast rocks. Blasting continued until May 8, when one of the men, having moved a short distance away from the work area, was attracted by a dull gleam in the sand. He dug out two solid gold disks, each weighing about seven pounds. Fisher later sold a similar but smaller gold disk with Mexico mint marks for a reported $17,500.

Again the weather prevented an immediate return to the site. When it cleared, the water was so murky that the party could see very little. On a hunch, Fisher suggested moving out farther and punching a hole with The Mailbox. Since luck had favored such intuitions before, they shifted their operations to the east and dug another hole. For two days they found nothing; then, on May 24, they hit it big.

The Mailbox had just opened a deep trench down a ridge between two rocks. Suddenly the divers saw a sight few people have ever seen. The six-foot-wide, fifteen-foot-long cavity glowed yellow with a carpet of gold coins.

Spellbound, they stared at the incredible glory hole they had uncovered; then, like fevered prospectors snatching nuggets from a fresh vein, they began grabbing coins left and right. Rather than chance letting any of the heavy gold slip through their eager fingers and fall back to the bottom to be lost again, each of the divers crammed the coins inside a glove he wore on his left hand. When a diver's glove was filled, he grabbed another fistful in his bare hand and surfaced to unload his find on the boat.

Up and down they went all day long, no one stopping for coffee or lunch. They kept picking coins off the bottom until their arms ached and their wrists were chafed raw from shoving coins into the cuffs of their gloves. But by day's end they had collected 1,033 gold coins. It was the biggest haul that they or, for that matter, any other 20th-century salvager had ever made in Florida.

Their first day's find was so large that Wagner was half afraid to see it continue at that rate for fear it would seriously affect the value of gold doubloons on the world coin market. But he need not have worried. Though their glory hole yielded 900 coins the next day, after that it grew less generous. In a week they had found nearly 2,500 doubloons before the source finally ran dry and they were forced to look elsewhere.

Wagner and Kelso supposed they had found the contents of one chest of gold, practically intact where it had dropped from the ship's disintegrating hull. Surely there were other chests nearby.

The Cabin Wreck was allowed to rest while the salvagers concentrated on the more valuable Fort Pierce gold wreck, which they now called the Colored Beach Wreck. Although the divers continued to turn up a trickle of gold coins, it was nothing compared to their first remarkable strike.

Fearing that news of their finds would attract swarms of pirate divers, Fisher and the others took elaborate precautions to conceal the success of their salvage activities—depositing their treasure in several Fort Pierce Banks and keeping their mouths shut. In fact, their secretiveness about their discovery was one of the things that caused the first trouble between the salvagers and the state.

Chapter 13

Treasure and the State

A seemingly minor but important change occurred in 1963 that was to have considerable effect on the relationship between the treasure hunters and the state. Van Ferguson, with whom the treasure hunters had worked so well, retired as director of the Internal Improvement Fund. He was succeeded by William Kidd, a capable and conscientious man who would soon be nicknamed "Captain Kidd." Since Dr. Goggin had died in 1962, Dr. Sears was handling all the state's negotiations with the treasure hunters. Through the transition in directors of the Internal Improvement Fund, Real Eight continued as before, maintaining its communication with the state exclusively with Dr. Sears.

When, in early 1964, Mel Fisher's group found gold on the wreck south of Fort Pierce, Wagner informed Dr. Sears by telephone that the find would be put into local bank vaults until it could be divided with the state. Sears agreed and acknowledged the arrangement in a return letter. Unfortunately, this information never reached Tallahassee and William Kidd, the new director of the Internal Improvement Fund. Rumors began to fly, and Kidd did not like what he heard. It appeared to him that some company other than Real Eight, which his agency had granted a salvage lease, had found a sizable quantity of treasure and was keeping the find a secret. Moreover, this company was reportedly putting bullion into banks as collateral for loans of operational funds. At this point, Governor Farris Bryant's investigator, Ed Reddick of the Florida Highway Patrol, was called into the case and sent to Fort Pierce to find out what was happening.

Asking discreet questions at various marinas and businesses in that area without revealing the reason for his curiosity, Reddick learned enough to be able to inform Kidd that there was considerably more truth than fiction to the rumor that had reached Tallahassee.

Kidd responded by calling in his office manager, Paul Baldwin, and ordering him to go treasure hunting. He said he had heard that out-of-state salvagers had made a large find in the Fort Pierce–Vero Beach area, and he wanted Reddick and Baldwin to learn whether or not it was covered by state leases.

Reddick was later accused by the salvagers of employing more disguises than Lon Chaney in his effort to get to the bottom of the situation. Sporting a beard, the governor's investigator appeared one day on a sailboat moored close to Fisher's salvage boat, the *Dee-Gee*. With a case of beer clearly in evidence in the stern of the sailboat, Reddick struck up a friendly conversation with one of the divers on the *Dee-Gee*. Presently he was invited aboard, with his case of beer, to see their operations. In the ensuing good cheer that developed in the stern of the salvage boat, no one apparently noticed that the bearded stranger nursed one beer through the whole occasion while he asked seemingly innocent but probing questions about their activities as treasure hunters. As a result, Reddick learned what the group was, what the men were doing in the area and generally how successful they had been.

Not everyone was that cooperative. Baldwin reported later: "We ran into a blank wall everywhere except at three banks—two in Vero Beach and one in Melbourne where some of the treasure had been deposited." Other treasure items were found in the salvagers' homes.

Finally, Reddick and Baldwin went to Wagner with their findings. They said they had evidence that Universal Salvage had been poaching on Real Eight's lease, and they were about to arrest the members of the company.

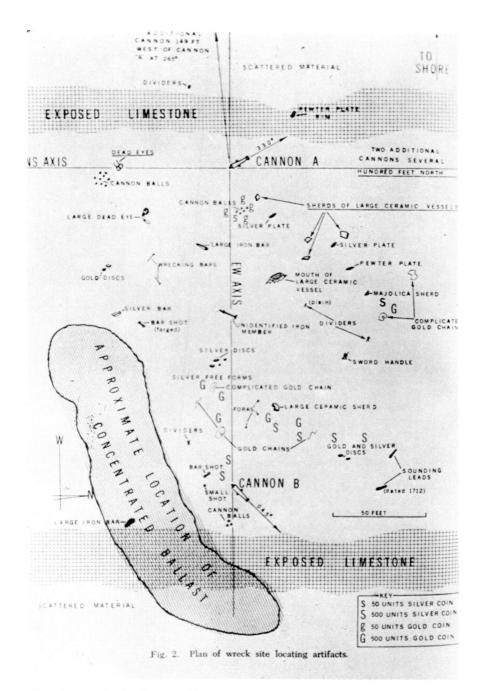

Fig. 2. Plan of wreck site locating artifacts.

Chart showing the distribution and location of artifacts recovered from the Colored Beach Wreck (8–UW–1) in 1964 and 1965. This site is approximately three miles south of Fort Pierce Inlet on the Florida east coast.

Pile of deteriorating iron cannon recovered many years ago from an old shipwreck is an eyesore that Florida's present salvage contract program tries to avoid.

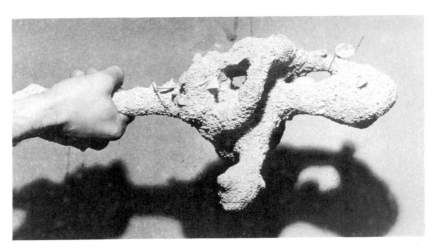

Closeup of a shell- and limestone-encrusted sword hilt recovered from an early-18th-century Spanish shipwreck. At the Florida archaeological laboratory in Tallahassee, the encrustation will be chipped or dissolved off and the metal treated chemically for preservation before the artifact is released for museum display.

Closeup of a religious medal found on one of the 1715 shipwrecks. (Centimeter scale.)

Preservationist and archaeological assistant examine pieces of a huge Ali Baba type jar recovered from one of the early Spanish shipwrecks. Such jars usually carried water or foodstuffs for the long transoceanic voyages.

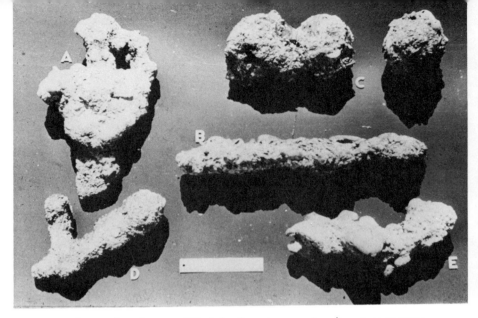

One reason shipwreck artifacts are difficult for divers to recognize—limestone encrustation almost conceals the artifacts' original identities. (A) is a sword hilt, (C) bar-shot or fused cannonballs. The other items are fused spikes and iron ship-fittings.

The sensing element of a magnetometer is lowered overboard as the search begins for a shipwreck. This supersensitive metal detector records magnetic anomalies. It is an indispensable tool for the serious wreck hunter, however, its price tag of $10,000 and up precludes its use by the average amateur.

Treasure hunter Mel Fisher gets ready for a treasure-hunting trip out the mouth of a south Florida inlet to site 8–UW–10, called the Barefoot Mailman Wreck. Note the pair of "dusters" mounted on boat's stern. Lowered over the vessel's propellers, they will be used for excavating the ocean bottom.

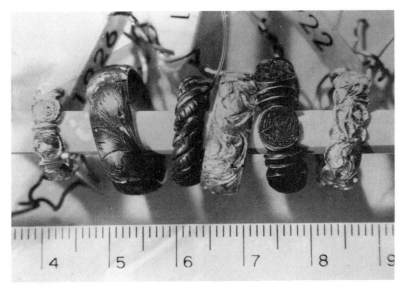

Closeup of a variety of gold rings recovered from the wrecks of the 1715 fleet.

Mexico-mint gold coins of the early 18th century recovered from the Colored Beach Wreck. Top row, 1700–1713; bottom row, 1714 and later. Reading from left to right, the denominations are 8, 4, 2, and 1 escudo.

Reverse faces of two sets of 8-, 4-, 2- and 1-escudo gold coins struck at the Mexico City mint in the early 18th century. Top row minted 1700 to 1713; bottom row, 1714 and 1715.

Two sets of Mexico-mint silver coins of the early 18th century. From left to right, 8-, 4-, 2- and 1-real coins. In Mexico City during the 18th century, the smallest coin at the right could buy more groceries than could be carried home by one person.

Closeup of small gold disk weighing one pound 15 ounces of 22 karat gold, which sold for $17,000. It was recovered from site 8–UW–1, the Colored Beach Wreck.

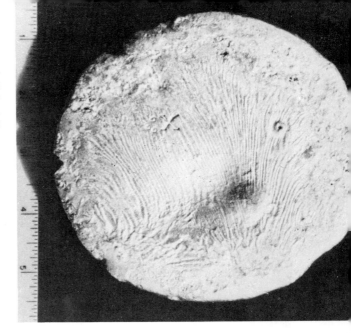

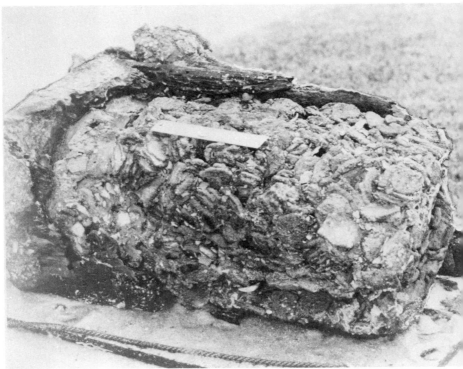

One of the 1,300 cedar chests loaded aboard the *Capitana* of the *Flota* of 1715. Each chest contained three bags of gunnysack-type material, with 1,000 pesos of 4- and 8-real coins in each bag. This 250-pound mass of silver coins is firmly fused together from the action of salt water on the silver. Archaeologists used solvents to separate and clean the coins. The chest was preserved, studied and reproduced for museum display.

Wagner explained that Fisher's team was associated with Real Eight and that as far as he knew no laws had been broken.

He was right, but Real Eight had gone considerably beyond the bounds of its lease in subletting to Universal Salvage. As a result, Mel Fisher's group was salvaging a shipwreck owned by the state of Florida, ignorant of the state laws, rules and regulations governing such an activity. Therefore, in the eyes of the state, Universal Salvage was involved in an illegal activity.

When Reddick and Baldwin confronted Mel Fisher, he told them that he had given forty-six gold coins to his crewmen as a bonus. (All lease agreements with the state specify that "no disposition shall be made of any material recovered" without approval of the state.) One night a short while later, Captain Reddick visited the salvagers' homes and told the treasure hunters to report at once to the sheriff's office at Fort Pierce to be fingerprinted for identification cards. It was after midnight before the fingerprint man showed up. While the incident was embarrassing to those involved, it was entirely within Reddick's power as the governor's investigator to bring it off. The salvagers were told that the state was very much concerned about the lax operation Real Eight had conducted up to that time. No one ever got his identification card, but after the fingerprinting episode, Reddick started getting straight answers from everyone.

The three-week investigation gave rise to sensational news stories. The press generally pictured the salvagers as modern-day pirates reaping out-of-bounds sea treasure with the intention of beating the state out of a fortune. At that time the treasure recovered was erroneously reported to be worth at least a million dollars.

On June 9, Kidd wrote a letter to Colonel H. N. Kirkman, head of the state highway patrol, commending Captain Reddick for his part in the investigation. "This is to advise you," said the Internal Improvement Fund director, "that Capt. Reddick and a representative of this office have during the last week located sizable recoveries of gold and silver, which have been removed from state-owned property. They are now in the process of inventorying and collecting all of this material and storing it in a safe location. . . .

"Let me say," Kidd continued, "that through the efforts of Ed [Reddick] I believe that the state of Florida will recover two or three

117

hundred thousand dollars that otherwise would have been lost.
. . . At the appropriate time I will bring this matter to the attention
of the cabinet."

Apparently the moment never arrived, because the subject was
never mentioned at a public cabinet meeting.

In early June, while Reddick and Baldwin were busy inventorying
the treasure from Fisher's Fort Pierce find, and the newspapers
were playing up the angle that Florida was getting the worst of the
deal in its arrangement with treasure hunters, the Internal Improvement Fund hired someone to look after the state's underwater
archaeological interests. He was Carl Clausen, a marine archaeologist with a master's degree from the University of Florida. On
recommendations that included Dr. Sears's, Kidd had got in touch
with him in Gainesville and asked if he would accept the job of
trying to oversee what was going on. Clausen accepted, and the
governor's cabinet appointed him the archaeologist to supervise the
activities of the salvage contractors.

Not only was this a new position for the recent graduate, but no
one in Tallahassee, certainly not Clausen himself, had much of an
idea what the job would entail. He was green, but he was not an
innocent. He had been well trained professionally by Dr. Goggin,
and he was well acquainted with the realm in which he was to work.
Though born in Texas, Clausen had been raised in Bradenton on
Florida's west coast. As a twelve-year-old in 1949, he was skin
diving and spearfishing when the sport was so new that all of his
equipment was homemade.

When Clausen found he had been hired to do a job nobody
understood, his first request was for over five hundred dollars'
worth of diving equipment so that he could get down and see for
himself what was happening on the wreck sites.

About mid-June he flew to Fort Pierce with William Kidd and
Assistant Attorney General Kenneth Ballenger to meet Paul Baldwin, who was helping Captain Reddick complete his investigation.
The idea was to familiarize Clausen with the people and the
situations involved. Then came the opportunity for the new archaeologist to visit the treasure site and see the salvagers in action.

Everyone motored out in Fisher's salvage boat, the *Dee-Gee*. The
treasure hunters were tense and uneasy with the state people
aboard. While the divers suited up, they kept glancing at the
archaeologist to see, he imagined, if he knew which end to buckle

his weight belt on. Then, instead of revealing what was at that time considered their secret equipment—the blaster—they put over their injection dredges and took the state people down to use them. Clausen was with one of Universal Salvage's best divers, Walt Holzworth, the friendly Pennsylvania Dutchman. Clausen had worked with air lifts before, and the operation of the injection dredge was not much different. As he burrowed down through the sand with the device, out tumbled a small 1-real silver coin about the size of a thumbnail. The archaeologist picked it up and showed it to Holzworth. The treasure hunter stared at Clausen's find, then did a strange thing. He took the coin and scratched it against the side of the dredge!

Clausen learned later that the treasure hunters had purposely put the state people far from the wreck site simply to give them a taste of the procedure. His turning up a coin where none was supposed to have been was the reason for Holzworth's odd reaction.

As soon as the press began printing stories suggesting that the treasure hunters had been taking advantage of the state by seemingly unfair divisions in which Florida got ships' spikes and ceramic sherds—so-called archaeological junk—while the salvagers reaped the real treasure, the state took a closer look at their program. A special advisory committee was set up to examine Florida's relationship with treasure hunters. Out of the chaos several things became clear: 1) For more than three years private salvagers had operated without any direct and continuous supervision from the state. As a result, efforts to audit their books with any accuracy were futile. 2) The policing of salvage operations was so lax that the state learned about the discoveries only by rumor and subsequent investigation by a highway patrol captain. 3) If it had adhered to the letter of the law, Real Eight had no legal right to salvage the Fort Pierce treasure—it had not obtained a pinpoint salvage lease on that wreck site. 4) Until Clausen was hired, the state had no full-time employees to monitor salvage or to oversee the division of treasure and artifacts.

The immediate reaction to all this was to sway judgment too far in the opposite direction. Lacking first-hand experience in the type of commercial salvage operation that Universal Salvage Inc. was mounting for Real Eight on the wrecks, Dr. Charles Fairbanks, chairman of the salvage advisory committee, announced that the

119

state should get 100 percent of the finds and that the locations of all artifacts recovered from the wrecks should be recorded to "the nearest inch" by the salvagers. Dr. Hale Smith, chairman of the Department of Anthropology at Florida State University, the man who had scientifically investigated the Higgs site and was told of the wreck location just offshore, said that the state could have pinpointed and recovered the materials by itself.

Wagner was extremely concerned about the situation because the adverse publicity was driving a wedge between the salvagers and the state. After the initial investigation, Reddick's analysis was that the Real Eight Company could not do the salvage work while Fisher's group, Universal Salvage, could do and was doing it. At that point, William Kidd was on the verge of breaking Wagner's lease over the Colored Beach Wreck incident, with the intention of giving to Mel Fisher the legal rights to salvage the wrecks. If things did not get straightened out in a hurry, Wagner knew he could lose everything he had worked for.

He and Fisher went to Tallahassee to see if they could iron out some of the difficulties with Kidd, but they accomplished nothing. Shortly afterward another attempt was made, this time by several other representatives from Real Eight. Kidd was too busy to see them, so they requested and got an audience with Governor Bryant. After they had explained the whole story to him, then to the attorney general, Jimmy Kynes, the governor asked Kidd to work out a mutually agreeable arrangement with the salvagers.

As a result, an agreement was reached between Real Eight and the state in which the salvagers relinquished their exclusive right to explore the fifty-mile area from Sebastian to Stuart, making it possible for other salvage companies to have leases in the area. In exchange, they received pinpoint salvage leases on the eight wreck sites that the company thought were associated with the 1715 fleet.

After that, except for an occasional flare-up, most of the fireworks died down. The salvagers continued work on the Colored Beach Wreck, but now Clausen accompanied them in an attempt to record some of the archaeological information from the wreck.

Unfortunately, this was not the most ideal situation for either the treasure hunters or the archaeologist. Time was valuable to the salvagers. Any delays to recover artifacts of little monetary value to them were costly. In the circumstances, however, both parties tried to make the best of it. Clausen would try to chart the locations of important artifacts, while the salvagers would periodically pause in their search for treasure to help him haul up anything he could not handle alone. To make matters worse, the wreck was a nightmare. Thanks to the fury of the initial hurricane that destroyed the fleet, coupled with almost two and a half centuries of other natural depredations by everything from ship worms to storm tides, the Colored Beach Wreck was scattered over ten acres of ocean bottom and covered with sand. The site was approximately three nautical miles south of old Fort Pierce Inlet. It lay some 500 to 1,500 feet offshore in eight to twenty feet of water under a white sand bottom punctuated with occasional outcroppings of Anastasia limestone and beds of shell or coquina rock. Wide grooves in the limestone running generally parallel to the beach were filled with sand, varying in depth from several inches to more than five feet. Constant wave action in the area kept the bottom constantly stirred up so that even on a good day maximum visibility was about eighteen inches.

Fisher's fifty-foot Navy launch, the *Dee-Gee*, served as a base of operations. Since the team had had such good luck with their blaster, they relied on it almost entirely for all their excavating. In the beginning there was no set pattern in where they dug. They blasted holes in the bottom wherever intuition directed. It was a haphazard method that sometimes resulted in the salvagers' working areas they had already searched. Now, however, to keep track of new finds, they established a grid system. The east-west base line, or axis, was a length of 3/8-inch chain laid across the bottom between the cascabels of two cannon. A second chain bisected it at right angles in a north-south direction through the cascabel of a shoreward cannon. As work continued out from these base lines, additional lengths of chain would be placed parallel to them at twenty-five-foot intervals.

It was a glamorless, grueling routine. The men would get up at 5:30 each morning and be at the site aboard the *Dee-Gee* at seven o'clock. If the waves were not too bad, the salvage boat would be positioned with three anchors, one off the bow and two off the stern, to keep it from shifting around the site while the excavating went on. The blaster was cranked up, sending its invisible column of water down to the bottom, where it began eating a hole. Divers hovered around the edges of the rapidly growing pit watching intently for whatever might appear. Coins, glassware, pottery sherds, unidentifiable sand-encrusted metal conglomerates and anything even vaguely resembling an artifact were quickly snatched up and deposited in a collecting bag. As the pit deepened, the loose sloping sand walls crept higher, and the divers looked as if they were scratching around in the bottom of a giant ant lion's trap. If something too large to handle appeared in the blue-green world of swirling water and sand, the blaster was shut off until some adequate means was found to raise the item without damaging it. On days of little current, the sand and mud settled back down on the site, creating an eerie gloom around the divers.

With each find, Clausen carefully measured its distance from a chain, shot an azimuth of its position from the boat, and noted the information on a graph chart of the site. This procedure was repeated at each new excavation. The *Dee-Gee* was repositioned by hauling in or letting out on the three anchor lines; then the blaster commenced again. One afternoon while searching among ballast rock, Fisher discovered an object he thought was a waterlogged piece of timber. Instead of being wood, however, the object turned out to be a thirty-five-pound silver bar camouflaged by incrustations.

Clausen had no control over where or how the treasure hunters worked. If they moved too fast for him, he was often left hauling chains and making measurements by himself. Normally he spent six to ten hours a day underwater, surfacing only long enough to grab a bite to eat and to change air tanks. At night there were the artifacts to catalog and care for. The salvagers worked a minimum of sixteen hours a day, twenty to thirty days a month, throughout the diving season, which ended abruptly in late August when two hurricanes—Cleo and Dora—blew in from the Atlantic and put an end to things.

It had been a good year for the salvagers. Clausen had spot-excavated approximately a two-acre square of the ten-acre site. Almost all the wreck material, except the cannon and ballast rock, was removed. Of the five cannon they found, Clausen carefully measured and examined two of them underwater. Almost eight feet long, they were muzzle-loading, smooth-bore weapons typical of the period and capable of firing a variety of projectiles. One still contained a wooden tampion (moisture and dust plug) wedged in its bore. The salvaged artifacts included cannon balls, round shot, bar-shot (two 6- to 9-pound projectiles joined by an iron bar which when fired from a small cannon wreaked havoc among the masts and rigging of another ship), pistol and musket balls, a heavily encrusted sword handle, pottery sherds, four pairs of brass navigational dividers, sounding leads, a pewter plate, lead patches and window cames, wrecking bars, deadeyes and miscellaneous ship fastenings. The treasure items* included several silver knives, forks and spoons, parts of 2 silver candlesticks, 8 pieces of gold chain, 1 silver bar, 6 silver and gold ingots, 16 gold rings, more than 3,700 gold coins and 200 pounds of silver coins.

When the division date for this treasure finally arrived, representatives of the state—a certified public accountant, Captain Ed Reddick, Paul Baldwin and Clausen—met with officials of Real Eight and Universal Salvage at a Vero Beach bank to divide the finds. The problem was that no one there was fully trained and qualified to select artifacts, neither the state representatives nor the salvagers. Clausen was the only one who had any qualifications for identifying, analyzing and determining the scientific value of artifacts, but since he had just come on the scene, he was unsure of his power to affect the situation.

The salvagers took the initiative and tried to make the division as fair as possible by breaking down the treasure into four equal lots. For example, all the coins were stacked in fours according to their dates, denominations and condition; the jewelry and other valuables were stacked in four separate but equal piles along with the artifacts. To a layman this might seem like the easiest and most logical way to make a divison. And it might have been if these items had been anything other than 250-year-old artifacts with individual values. A qualified archaeologist should have been on hand to evaluate all the materials, categorize them, inventory them, and then make the selection for the state on the basis of their scientific and historical value to the people of Florida.

When Clausen realized that, instead, the division was to be the random choice of a layman, and that there was really nothing he could do about it, he left the bank in disgust. He could not conceive of a more illogical way to divide such artifacts.

The state's "share" was then selected by the highway patrolman, Captain Ed Reddick, who chose which of the four stacks of coins he felt he wanted. He did the same with the four piles of valuables.

---

* See Appendix C for detailed description.

In the circumstances, everyone present thought this the best and fairest way of dividing the treasure. Others, however, felt differently. Dr. Charles Fairbanks, chairman of the state advisory committee, reacted quickly with stinging but justified criticism. In a letter to Kidd, he said:

"Dr. Dickinson and I noted that [after Clausen left] no archaeologist or historian was present to make an evaluation of these unique items that could not be divided on a numerical basis. In one case the state apparently received an 8-escudo gold coin as its share of a lot, which included a large bell and a holy medallion. Both the bell and the medallion have a research value far beyond the nominal value of the coin.

"In such cases," said Fairbanks, "an archaeologist or historian from the committee should be present whenever divisions are made to protect the historic values involved."

Such a situation was not to occur again.

Although he later put together what was to be the first bona fide site report* on a shipwreck ever published by a professional archaeologist in the United States, Clausen was disappointed with the meager attempt at archaeological work made on the Colored Beach Wreck. He was more than ever convinced that commercial treasure hunting and underwater archaeology simply did not mix. If a treasure hunter and an archaeologist found a plank on a shipwreck, for example, the archaeologist would try to determine what relationship that plank bore to the ship, observing details, drawing or photographing it in place. The salvager would only be interested in lifting the plank to see if there might be a gold coin under it.

The experiences of that first summer were enough to make Clausen realize that there was much Florida history locked in those wrecks and that commercial salvage was not the way to preserve it.

* Carl J. Clausen, "A 1715 Spanish Treasure Ship," *Contributions of the Florida State Museum, Social Science No. 12* (Gainesville: University of Florida), 1965.

Chapter 14

The Great Florida Gold Rush

William Kidd left the Internal Improvement Fund in 1964 and was replaced by Robert Parker, who inherited all the headaches associated with the job of directing Florida's salvage-lease program. Parker resented the time the salvage-lease program demanded. He tended to ignore problems and adopted a don't-rock-the-boat policy. This laissez-faire attitude toward treasure hunting made him well liked among some of the long-established salvagers. Others, however, criticized him for showing favoritism, allegedly granting salvage leases to the few while refusing the many. But one thing can be said in his favor: Parker realized that the state simply was not equipped to cope with a full-scale gold rush, and that no amount of private or political pressure was going to alter the situation.

That fall Mel Fisher moved part of his operation south to Marathon, where one of his corporations, Armada Research, had leases to search for shipwrecks. When word spread through the Keys that Fisher was invading the area with his sophisticated salvage and detection equipment, many a hard-bitten treasure hunter who had always worked independently without benefit of legal leases was up in arms. Why didn't he stay where he belonged instead of muscling in on their favorite picking grounds?

125

One of the strongest protests was a letter to Governor Bryant from Hugh Brown, then president of the Florida Keys Underwater Guides Association. This loosely organized group of charter-boat captains specialized in taking divers out to the reefs to dive, collect tropical fish or pick up a few artifacts from one of the known wrecks. Brown asked the governor to suspend all leases in the Keys until assurances were made that Fisher's powerful excavating dredges were not destroying shipwrecks that were tourist attractions. Brown pointed out that the underwater guides depended on these wrecks for their livelihood, since they took visitors to see them. One wreck had already been destroyed, he said, and eight others had been damaged by treasure salvagers. Apart from their churning up the wrecks with their air lifts, just what kind of damage the treasure hunters were causing that some of the diving charter captains were not, was not quite clear.

Two months after Brown's letter, Internal Improvement Fund representatives Baldwin (the office manager turned investigator), Ballenger, the assistant attorney general, and Clausen called for a public meeting in Marathon to discuss the problem. Brown, representing the Florida Keys Underwater Guides Association, said that his group was not opposed to operations of the salvage firms but was concerned about whether the wrecks would remain intact, about what would be left after the salvagers got through tearing them apart.

Mel Fisher told the gathering that there were hundreds of shipwrecks in the area and that forty-nine out of fifty his firm had found were left undisturbed because his detection gear did not indicate the presence of gold or silver. "We don't destroy those shipwrecks," said Fisher. "If we detect gold or silver, we bring it up, but we don't pick up cannons or anchors or anything like that."

Incredibly, nine out of ten divers there believed Fisher actually had a device to detect gold and silver. What he really had at this time was a simple but workable homemade version of the proton magnetometer, the device capable of detecting minor but measurable variations or distortions in the earth's local magnetic field caused by large iron objects such as cannon, anchors or small clusters of the iron pins or spikes that held the old ships together.

Ballenger outlined the kinds of salvage leases granted to salvage firms, and Clausen emphasized that the archaeological value of the wrecks was lost when they were picked over and the artifacts removed indiscriminately—whether by treasure hunters or customers of the Underwater Guides Association.

Parker was telephoned a report of the hearing, in which Brown asserted that he was perfectly in accord with the way the salvagers said they were handling the wrecks. Still, there was growing suspicion in Tallahassee that tourists were being allowed to take souvenirs from the wrecks, that in fact this was perhaps one of the lures guides held out to the adventuresome tourist—a chance to go on a "treasure hunt." Moreover, there were even rumors that the guides may have salted the wrecks a little, dropping a few trinkets here and there for customers to find.

The state's special advisory committee recommended that Florida begin a program of underwater investigations and archaeological research on the wrecks in public waters. As usual, the opposition cried that the state was trying to get into treasure hunting for itself, keeping the legitimate treasure hunters out while claiming all finds for the state.

Governor Bryant's reaction was that private salvage companies could do a better job than the state because of the profit motive. "If the state is going out on its own," he said, "it will have to do the exploring as well as the salvaging. We can't wait for someone else to find the treasure and then run out and pirate it."

But how could the state pirate what according to Florida law was already hers?

The monumental misunderstanding of the situation, as reflected in the governor's statement, epitomized the problems in Tallahassee.

Meanwhile, Real Eight was confronted with a problem of its own—a lack of funds. This may sound strange considering the fortune in gold and silver the salvagers had amassed in local bank vaults. But there were bills to be paid, and until some of the treasure could be converted to cash, it was virtually useless to the finders. Converting it to cash, however, presented a problem common to all treasure hunters and diamond dealers: if the value of rare coins or gems is to be maintained, only a few can be allowed on the market at any one time. Real Eight had last disposed of some of its coins in 1961; now it was time to do it again. The salvagers chose a representative collection, including many one-of-a-kind specimens to give the offering depth. They cleaned and polished their choicest items, and that October they went to market.

Henry Christensen, a world-famous coin auctioneer and an authority on Spanish colonial issues, presented the rare collection at an auction in Hoboken, New Jersey. Most of the coins were cataloged at prices of several hundred dollars each. A few were expected to bring well over $1,000 each. The consignment of more than one hundred coins was almost entirely gold, the dates ranging from the 1600s to the early 1700s. All were minted in Mexico or South America, and none was dated later than 1714.

Response to the auction was gratifying. What the salvagers did not know, however, was that the bidders were far more knowledgeable about the offering than anyone had suspected. Without the slightest change of expression, F. Xavier Calico, an eminent collector and coin dealer from Barcelona, Spain, bought the rarest coin of the lot—a round 1695 Carlos II 8-escudo "royal" from the Mexico City mint—for $3,500. None other has ever been found on the wrecks. Another rare item in the collection, unknown to the salvagers before the bidding began, was an almost mint-perfect 4-escudo 1711 gold doubloon estimated in the catalog to be worth $2,000. It sold for $3,600. By the end of the auction, private collectors had bought most of the coins, and the salvagers were richer by $29,000.

Back in Florida, Real Eight and Fisher's company, now called Treasure Salvors, divided the loot according to their various agreements and got ready to harvest more coins. Despite the auction's apparent success, it seemed ironical that after years of hard work recovering a treasure estimated to be worth millions, the most any of the treasure hunters had realized from it was a few thousand dollars already destined to be consumed by the payment of long-overdue bills.

Through 1964, most of the Real Eight crew spent nights and weekends converting a newly purchased boat into a salvage vessel to replace their cherished but frequently unseaworthy *Sampan*. What started out as little more than a fifty-foot copper-sheathed shell with a thirteen-foot beam and a belch-fire engine was by year's end a freshly painted salvage boat with a reconditioned diesel engine, a fiberglassed deck, a pilothouse and steering gear. In honor of her original status she was christened the *Derelict*. Mounted prominently through her side abaft of midship was the pride of Real Eight's ingenious mechanics—a blaster to end all blasters.

Instead of being a square box utilizing the boat's propeller power, as Fisher's device had done, this was a quarter-ton steel cylinder eight feet long and three and a half feet wide, with its four-bladed propeller inside coupled to a 1935 Ford rear-end transmission. Three holes were cut around the cylinder to let in water, and the engine was mounted sideways on the boat. On its first trial the blaster exceeded all expectations. Wagner said it sounded like sixteen jet fighters roaring off the runway at the same time. It blew mud off the bottom of Wabasso harbor for two hundred feet or more. It blasted not only modest holes but elephantine pits. Yet it could be idled down so low that the thirty-six-inch-wide column of swirling water aimed at the bottom became gentle enough to fan sand off a fragile artifact without injuring it. This "Big Bertha" of underwater excavators would soon prove itself in a spectacular debut performance, but not before the state began tightening its salvage program.

In January 1965, Florida's new governor, Haydon Burns, placed a moratorium on all new treasure-salvage leases until he could appraise the situation and determine how the state's position might be improved. Almost all of this evaluation apparently took place in the governor's office. He did, however, come out strongly in opposition to the state's going into the "treasure-salvage business" because he felt it would be too expensive. Finally he called for a program with stronger controls. In response, the state legislature created an Antiquities Commission staffed with state archaeologists, historians, anthropologists, museum curators, geologists and members of the Florida Board of Conservation. These persons were to advise and assist the governor and his cabinet in matters pertaining to the recovery, restoration and protection of all objects covered by Florida's antiquities law, including historic sites, fossil deposits, rare documents and treasure-trove. For administrative purposes the new commission was under Florida's Internal Improvement Fund; however, it would take over from Parker's staff the responsibilities of issuing salvage leases. To strengthen the program, the state hired a ten-man salvage patrol of conservation officers to observe salvage operations and guard against pirating by unlicensed treasure hunters. The Antiquities Commission was under the chairmanship of Dr. J. C. Dickinson, director of the

Florida State Museum, who in his early capacity as head of the state's advisory committee was no stranger to the perplexing problems involving Florida and her treasure hunters.

As soon as possible, Clausen got the ten-man team of conservation officers out of their role of watchmen and into something more beneficial to the program. He suggested that they be put on the salvage boats to record the artifacts recovered. When the state agreed to try this plan, Clausen taught the men how to plot a boat's salvage position on a site, how to fill out field notes and forms and how to care for the artifacts brought up. Eventually the conservation officers were replaced by personnel with some training in archaeological techniques, and they in turn soon trained other technicians in specialized procedures, which program resulted in the basic system still in use.

During the moratorium only three salvage firms had legal instruments to operate: Real Eight Company, which included Fisher's group, Treasure Salvors; the Martin County Historical Society, and the Perdido Corporation. Through the early 1965 diving season, Real Eight's salvage boat, the *Derelict*, alternated between working the Cabin Wreck near Sebastian Inlet and the gold wreck south of Fort Pierce. On May 19, her crew made its first important find. The divers went down 500 feet north of where Fisher's team was working the original hot spot, and struck gold—nineteen doubloons the first day, several more the next week, plus a few hitherto undiscovered cannon, musket balls, pewter plates, ship fittings and two anchors. It was a proper initiation for the new vessel.

The significant distance between the two finds was further evidence of how scattered the wreck was. Apparently the ship struck with such force that she disintegrated, strewing wreckage and treasure over several acres of the bottom. This is why Ward, Neiman and Allen had been unable to pinpoint it and why it was practically anyone's guess where treasure might lie hidden beneath the camouflaging layers of sand.

Wagner said that when it came to predicting where treasure might be, Del Long was either one of the luckiest fellows around, or he was a gifted prognosticator. Not that he made a habit of predicting their good fortunes, but whenever he got "that certain prophetic feeling," the others knew from past experience that it paid to hear him out. For instance, one weekend in late May, Long said he had a feeling that they would strike gold—"right over there." He pointed out a spot about a thousand feet from where the *Derelict* was working.

A couple of days later when the blaster opened a hole not fifty feet from the area Long had indicated, the divers found 130 gold coins in twenty-four feet of water. That night word of the strike went out to the other team members, and the next morning everyone crowded aboard the *Derelict* as it motored out to the site. On station the blaster fired its low-pressure, high-volume jet of water at the bottom that opened a thirty-foot-wide pit. The divers went down, and for the second time in their career, they were stunned by the spectacle of gold coins carpeting the broad white sand depression. Some coins were stacked three and four deep.

It was the gold rush all over again. Divers grabbed coins by handfuls; they lowered buckets and filled them to the brim with doubloons. All day they worked feverishly, gathering gold, hoisting bucketfuls of the precious coins to the surface and dumping them in a golden cascade onto the deck of the *Derelict*. For the second time they had found an underwater El Dorado, and they made the most of it. In that one day they recovered 1,128 gold coins. Nearly half were 8-escudo coins the size of fifty-cent pieces, which from their fine condition were worth anywhere from $500 to more than $2,000 apiece.

As had happened so often in the past, the weather prevented them from returning to the site for the next few days. It was June 3 before they were able to try again, and this time they found only a few coins. Considering how many they had taken the first day, what had happened was no mystery. Once again they thought they might have stumbled onto the scattered contents of a single chest, although strangely enough no such container of coins appeared on the manifest of this ship, which was later identified as the *patache* of the *Flota*. The intensity of the salvagers' initial efforts had simply exhausted the supply of gold coins in that spot. It did not, however, exhaust the hunters' desire to find more. But by now the salvagers were not the only ones with a bad case of gold fever.

When the Fort Pierce treasure strike hit the headlines from coast to coast, the Great Florida Gold Rush was on. Gold seekers came by bus, plane, car and foot. They came in droves—amateur and professional treasure hunters, cranks, con men, crooks and the curious—all converging at the scene of the strike along Florida's

131

southern coasts. They swarmed over the beaches between Sebastian and Wabasso, searching for coins. They shook the sleepy little towns out of their lethargy by buying every piece of scuba and skin-diving equipment local merchants had to offer. They swam or boated out to the Colored Beach Wreck in 1964 and out to the Cabin Wreck in 1965 in such numbers that Treasure Salvors and Real Eight had to shoo them away each time they went to work. They bought every copy they could find of the early version of John Potter's then out-of-print *The Treasure Diver's Guide*, sometimes paying up to $65 for it. The book was in such demand that the local library took its copy out of circulation and made it available for reference only. They bought so many copies of Ralph Odum's copyrighted treasure map entitled "Ye True Chart of Pirate Treasure lost or hidden in the land and waters of Florida" that its printers had to work overtime to fill their orders.

At Fort Pierce city fathers made a bid for the anticipated influx of tourist dollars by dubbing their area "The Treasure Coast." The idea was to attract travelers by circulating the fiction that beachcombing would bring Spanish coins two and a half centuries old as souvenirs.

The rush was overwhelming. The crowds came, looked and spent. Everyone in town talked of Spanish treasure. Newcomers itched to get offshore to see the bottom paved with gold. Rumors spread that new finds not only equaled but exceeded the reported $1.6 million in gold, silver and artifacts recovered by the Real Eight–Treasure Salvors combine. Stories circulated of professional treasure hunters flipping ancient coins for drinks in Fort Pierce bars. Strangers greeted citizens with such jocular queries as "How's the gold today?"

How indeed. It might not have been made in Spain, but it was rolling in. The solitary Fort Pierce coin dealer, who before the rush was doing a penny-ante business, found his trade enlarged 400 percent. Gift shops repeatedly sold out of treasure maps and charts claiming to show the "reefs" that had caused the wrecks. Marinas were doing a land-office business renting everything that would float to sightseers, and there was not an underwater guide from Fort Pierce to Key West who did not have a waiting list of customers as long as his snorkel.

Strangers stalked the beaches, their heads down, eyes scrutinizing the water's edge for gold doubloons winking in the sand like

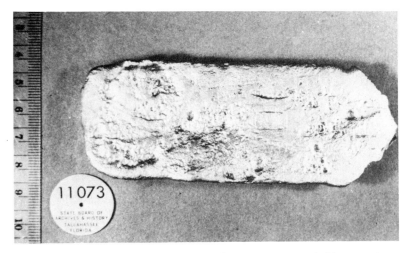

This 21-karat gold bar, weighing 5 pounds 4.07 ounces, probably came from Lima, Peru. It was recovered from the Rio Mar Wreck, site 8–UW–4, probably the wreck of General Echeverz's *Capitana,* just south of Vero Beach, Florida.

This ornate gold crucifix and cross were recovered from the Rio Mar Wreck near Vero Beach in 1969. The crucifix once contained several pearls. The presence of studs on the cross indicates that its entire surface was covered with similar small pearls. These artifacts came from what archaeologists believe are the remains of General Echeverz's *Capitana.*

Artifacts recovered from the Colored Beach Wreck include pewter and silver plates, silver forks and sounding weights.

Pewter and silver plates, cup and silverware recovered from the 1715 wrecks are now on museum display.

Silver plate and silver forks from site 8–UW–1, the Colored Beach Wreck. Arrow points to Mexico City stamp on rim of plate.

Closeups of the handles of three silver forks show the Mexico City mint mark, indicating that the silver from which the forks were made had passed through the mint, and the royal fifth had been paid on it. Other stamps are purity and manufacturer's marks.

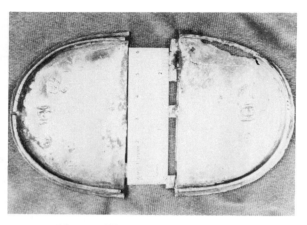

Silver snuff box bears various markings, including the name "Gozalez" or "Gosalez" and the mark of the Mexico City mint from which the silver came.

Closeup of silver moth bottle stopper found on one of the 1715 wrecks.

Marineware bears the various names given it by Clausen to simplify identification of the many ceramic sherds found on the 1715 wrecks and at the site of the Spanish survivors' and salvagers' camp.

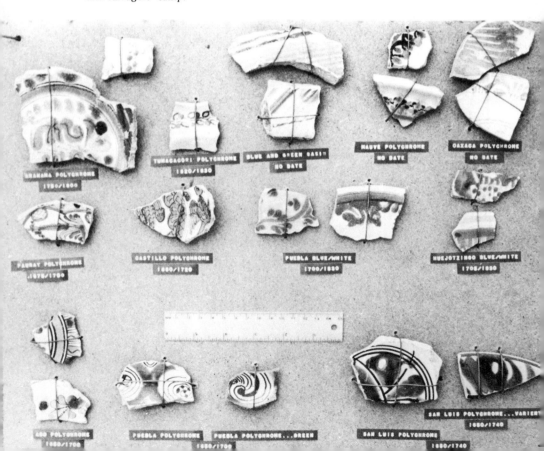

DETAIL OF COUNTERFEIT SPANISH COLONIAL COINS

A. In one series of counterfeit 8-real silver coins the date is 1711, or simply 11, depending on how the counterfeiter trimmed his cast. But the escutcheon or royal shield (the central design under the crown) belongs to a period 75 years earlier. (The components of these shields changed as Spain won or lost possessions or allies and as one king superseded another.)

B. A bead is missing from the decorative semicircle on the left. This could happen in genuine coins, but two such from the same die are seldom found. Yet this defect appears on all the fakes in this series.

C. Areas of unnatural smoothness where defective high spots may have been ground down in the counterfeiting process.

D. When the Spaniards clipped coins to weight, these edges usually turned out convex and dull. When the dies are faked, the edges are straight or concave and sometimes suspiciously sharp in contrast to the otherwise smooth-worn appearance of the coin.

E. OM is the Mexico City mint mark, with F the initial of the assayer. In 1711, however, this mint mark was OXM plus the assayer's initial, which was not F. Assayer F did not make his appearance until several years later.

F. and H. show the crude touch of the counterfeiter on the edge of the shield. The bottom right side of F is not symmetrical with the bottom left side. H betrays a nick which, like the missing bead mentioned above, could happen in one or two coins but not in a series.

G. In this section of the shield, genuine coins show the Lion of Flanders and the Eagle of the Tyrol. Fake coins show only the eagerness of the counterfeiter with a mass of meaningless marks.

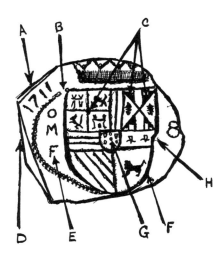

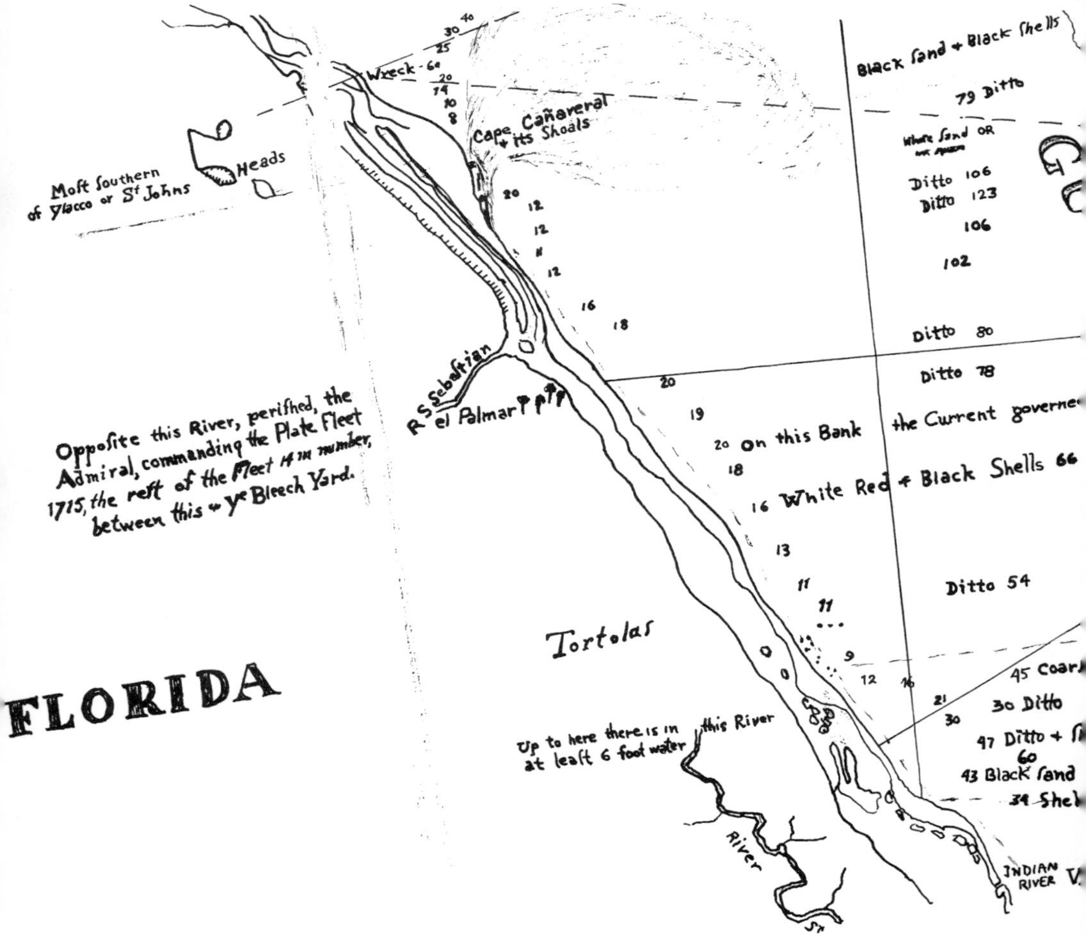
Wreck
Cape Cañaveral + its Shoals
Most southern of Ylacco or St Johns
Heads
R S Sebastian
el Palmar
Opposite this River, perished, the Admiral, commanding the Plate Fleet 1715, the rest of the Fleet 14 in number, between this + ye Bleech Yard.
FLORIDA
Tortolas
Up to here there is in this River at least 6 foot water
River
Black Sand + Black Shells
79 Ditto
White Sand OR
Ditto 106
Ditto 123
106
102
Ditto 80
Ditto 78
On this Bank the Current governe
White Red + Black Shells 66
Ditto 54
45 Coar
30 Ditto
47 Ditto +
43 Black Sand
INDIAN RIVER

Copy of 1774 chart by English cartographer Bernard Romans provided clues to the treasure. On his chart of East Florida Romans noted: "Opposite this River, perished the Admiral, commanding the Plate Fleet 1715 . . . " The river was the Sebastian, and just south of it, along the coast, Wagner found Spanish coins washed ashore from one of the wrecks.

This 155-foot *Almiranta,* or Admiral's flagship, was the type vessel used by the 1715 fleet. Armed with 50 to 60 cannon, such ships carried most of the treasure and served as guard and convoy vessels for the remainder of the merchant fleet. (Illustration by R. Burgess.)

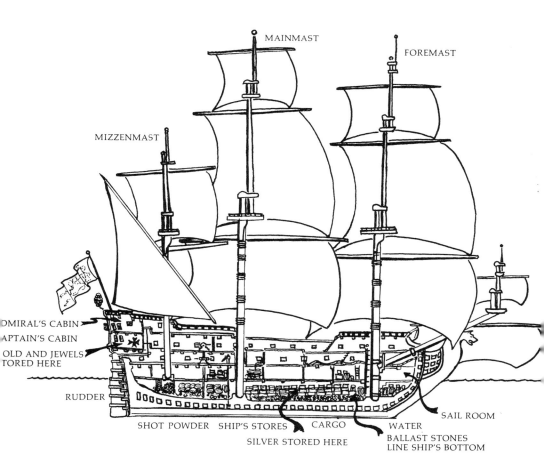

MAINMAST

FOREMAST

MIZZENMAST

DMIRAL'S CABIN

APTAIN'S CABIN

OLD AND JEWELS
TORED HERE

RUDDER

SHOT POWDER   SHIP'S STORES   CARGO   WATER

SILVER STORED HERE

SAIL ROOM

BALLAST STONES
LINE SHIP'S BOTTOM

During height of Florida's treasure-hunting troubles, cartoonists for the *Florida Keys Keynoter* and the *Orlando Sentinel* newspapers kept readers abreast of the situation with these graphic comments.

A Shot Across The Bow

tiny suns. Some, believing that the early birds get the coins, trudged down the breaker-scoured beaches before sunup. Late arrivals had to be satisfied with searching in the dawn patrol's footprinted wake. Bottle caps and seashells were what most found. A very few actually did find coins.

As in most gold rushes, there were those who were eager to sell the searchers gadgets "guaranteed" to find gold. One such "salesman" showed up in town with a forked wand resembling a water dowser's stick, which he said would unerringly point to gold. To prove it he would gather a crowd around him, aim the wand in the general direction of the local bank and gaze triumphantly at the stick leaping and jerking in his hands. Another operator tried to sell a magic pendulum he said would swing until it "sniffed" gold; then it would quickly line up on the precious metal. He also made a note of where the local banks were.

Meanwhile, serious treasure hunters bent on guarding their activities were unnerved by their sudden popularity. When strangers strayed too close to their bailiwicks, they went to elaborate lengths to learn their identities. "You see a man in a white shirt and tie looking for sea shells or sitting back in a thicket, and you tend to get suspicious," said one Fort Pierce man. Some of this paranoia probably stemmed from the state's investigation of the treasure hunters in 1964.

"Every gold rush has produced its crop of con men and counterfeiters, and you can be sure this one will too," prophesied Fort Pierce's *News-Tribune* editor, Tom Cope, long before the Florida gold rush was in full swing. "Fakers are sure to come along with wild claims, looking for sucker financing. There will be lawsuits. Legal salvors or pirates, it's the same story: of all the metals, gold is the one most likely to produce moral blood-poisoning."

Cope's copy was as true as the biblical handwriting on the wall.

The Fisher find was hardly dry before the Neiman-Ward suit hit the headlines. Then, in March 1965, part-time treasure hunter Ray Lorenz went to court to challenge the right of the state of Florida to control offshore salvage and treasure hunting. Lorenz's suit claimed that treasure salvage came under the jurisdiction of the Federal government and that the only right granted to Florida was the right to control the leasing and recovery of natural resources such as sand and gravel lying within its three-mile limit. He insisted the Federal government had granted no right to Florida to issue leases to those who desired to search for abandoned property. Lorenz's case was badly researched and prepared. The suit named as defendants Martin County Judge Mallory Johnson and the trustees of the Internal Improvement Fund, consisting of the governor and state cabinet.

Lorenz, an insurance salesman, said he had been denied a lease to hunt treasure in Martin County, a coastal county located on Florida's lower east coast. The wreck that he reportedly was interested in was supposed to be one of those lost with the 1715 fleet, although there is no support in any of the documents for any 1715 wrecks south of the Fort Pierce wreck. The lease for that area had been granted some years before to the Martin County Historical Society, and Lorenz asked the court to issue a declaratory decree saying that the state had "no right, title, claim or interest" in offshore treasure hunting. A favorable ruling for Lorenz would have thrown out state control over salvage and treasure seekers, resulting in an "open door" policy for all ocean treasure hunters. However, when the suit came up before Circuit Judge Hugh Taylor in Tallahassee, he quickly dismissed it on the grounds that the Federal government was not involved. Lorenz's argument that the shipwrecks were "abandoned property" and not natural resources, thereby making them legal to salvage, was never answered. Though to some this might have seemed a good point, society does not function on the principle of "finders-keepers, losers-weepers," whether a person's car, his money or, as in this case, his American heritage is involved. The decision of the court was a fortunate but hollow victory for the state.

Further confirmation of Cope's predictions that the Florida gold rush would attract more than tourists and publicity began in May 1965, when the *St. Petersburg Times* headlined a news story that seven treasure hunters claimed to have found another rich treasure cache on the wreck of a Spanish galleon they had supposedly discovered ninety miles south of St. Petersburg in the Gulf of Mexico. According to John Sykes, spokesman for the group of St. Petersburg treasure hunters calling themselves the "Lucky Seven," he and his companions (whom he would not name) had located the wreck more than a year before in water so shallow that coins could be picked up by waders. Sykes said his group had applied for a salvage permit from the state about two months before the east

134

coast strike, but it had been held up. Now he felt sure it would be issued.

On learning of the Gulf find, Clausen flew to St. Petersburg with the state's field investigator, Philip Thibedeau, to examine and catalog the treasure. Then, in accordance with state policy, it would be kept in safe-deposit boxes at the First Federal Savings and Loan Association's office there. According to the news story, the artifacts and treasure consisted of three Aztec figurines five to six inches tall, two of gold, one of bronze; an Aztec sacrificial sword with a bronze blade and a silver hilt; and a number of coins, mostly silver pieces of eight dated 1698 and coming from the Mexico City mint.

As soon as Clausen examined the find he suspected that the items were fake. The statement that he and Philip Thibedeau released to the press, however, said only that the state had begun an investigation to check the treasure's authenticity and that there were some points of conflict with the coins found on the east coast.

That was understatement indeed. Twenty-five pieces of eight were found to be spurious; the knight's head on the hilt of the so-called sacrificial sword was thought to have come from a Seaforth's aftershave or cologne bottle, and two of the three small statues represented as being Aztec were believed to be mail-order bookends from Mexico. In addition, hundreds of counterfeit coins similar to the forgeries were being circulated throughout Florida and the southeastern United States.

Doing some backtracking on the suspicious Gulf treasure, the *St. Petersburg Times* reporter learned that Sykes had shown the items to Wallace Minto, a Sarasota metallurgical expert, before the state people saw them. Minto had also suspected that the finds were not genuine. "The sword intrigued me the most," he said. "Although I didn't have an opportunity to touch it, several flaws were evident. The blade was not steel. It was either bronze or copper. They [the treasure hunters] said it was bronze. Bronze swords have not been used since the time of the Romans. It was too soft. The hilt of the sword was shaped in the form of a Teutonic cross which the Spaniards never used and the Germans have only used in modern times. The cross looked very much like a mail-order advertisement of a few years ago for an SS officer's knife."

Minto's observations on the other artifacts were equally interesting: "The figurines were not gold," he said, "but gold plated in a

135

modern style called bright gold. They were also castings. The art of casting was not developed by the Aztecs. [Here, Minto either was incorrect or was misquoted by the newspaper.] The specific gravity was such that I believe these to be brass. The figurines themselves, I am certain, were bookends you could buy through the mail from Mexico a few years ago."

Closer examination of the coins revealed that they had been cast, a process the Spaniards had not used in making their early coins. Instead, they cut them from poured strips of silver, clipped them to legal weight, then stamped them between steel dies. The cast counterfeits had straight, sharp edges all around. The silver was hard rather than soft like pure Spanish silver, which can usually be marked with a fingernail. Some counterfeits also bore file marks, an unmistakable indication that the coins were bogus or at least altered. Less obvious discrepancies were found on the faces of the coins. For instance, one series of fake 8-real pieces was marked with the date 1711, but the crest or royal shield shown on the coin belonged to a period seventy-five years earlier. A bead from a portion of a decorative semicircle was missing. This could happen in genuine coins when there was a defect in the Spaniards' die—but two silver coins from the same die were seldom encountered. Yet the same defect appeared on all the fake coins in the series. Lack of symmetry and a notch in the outline of a coin's embossed shield indicated the counterfeiter's carelessness. Mint marks on the forgeries were OM, with F, the initial of the royal assayer. This was the Mexico City mint. But in 1711, the mark was OXM, and the assayer's initial was not F but J. Assayer F did not appear on the scene until several years later. In some places the counterfeits contained only meaningless marks. Unfortunately, however, the quality of the forgeries, though poor, was still good enough to fool collectors who knew little or nothing about early Spanish coins.

Authorities learned that of the several hundred other counterfeit coins already circulating, most were 8 reals, but there were others of smaller denominations. An indeterminate number of sets containing 1, 2, 4 and 8 reals had been sold to coin collectors along the "Treasure Coast," some for $140 a set. One coin dealer in Fort Pierce even tried to sell sets of the counterfeits after it had been brought to his attention that they were fakes. Considering that each set could have been manufactured for less than five dollars, it was a lucrative business.

Obviously the counterfeiters were capitalizing on the genuine find from the 1715 wrecks off the Florida east coast. Real Eight and Treasure Salvors were in no way involved with the counterfeits. They had too many real coins to bother with fakes. State officials hastened to reassure coin collectors that these companies were "very much above board, very honest and very legal" in selling their original coins. The only fair thing to do was to utilize the newspapers and the various trade journals to point out the difference between the counterfeits and the authentic coins so that these two companies would not be harmed when marketing their merchandise.

The accumulated evidence of the counterfeit coin fraud was turned over to the local Florida state attorney's office, but clamping down on the forgers and making the charges stick proved to be something else again. The counterfeiter could swear in court that he had never represented the coins as genuine, and the dealer could testify that he had been taken in, that he was also a victim. But whether the counterfeits were bought for trading or as an investment, they still represented possible disillusion and financial embarrassment to the dealer.

While these things went on ashore, the salvagers continued searching for more of the real treasure at sea. The *Derelict* routinely worked the Fort Pierce site and the Sebastian Inlet site alternately, depending on which had the clearer water. For a long time the salvagers suspected that since there was no ballast rock around the Cabin Wreck, then there must be another part of it nearby. But where?

They tried to figure out from which direction the hurricane had struck the fleet and where the ship had originally struck bottom. Fisher's crew came up with its magnetometer, a new model, and checked the area but found nothing. They broadened the search, using for the first time, at Clausen's insistence, a pattern. Then, nine hundred feet southwest of their original site, they found some cannon. Real Eight then moved the *Derelict* into the deeper water, and the divers went down. Within minutes they found three silver wedges. Treasure Salvors had discovered an unknown portion of the Cabin Wreck. These finds were soon followed by more. In the next several days, working with Treasure Salvors, Real Eight recovered several hundred loose pieces of eight, three clumps of corroded silver coins and ten 18-inch copper ingots weighing from thirty to seventy pounds each. But this was only the beginning. In the following week the record of their daily finds read like an inventory page from Fort Knox. Besides clumps and wedges, they brought up silver coins by the hundreds. One day's haul alone included 665 *pounds* of silver coins. At approximately fifteen coins to a pound, they had brought up almost 10,000 pieces of eight. A week later their total was almost a ton of silver coins!

Still the silver kept coming up. On July 7, ship's timbers were found; then, four days later, a 125-pound conglomerate of fused pieces of eight, sixty loose silver coins, two silver plates and an apothecary mortar were added to the haul.

So far the Cabin Wreck had produced something of everything—artifacts, china, gold, silver and jewelry. Finding and handling treasure daily destroyed the novelty of it. The salvagers doubted whether the wreck had anything else to offer them that would pique their treasure-jaded senses—but what turned up on July 24 proved them wrong.

Wagner's nephew, Rex Stocker, was examining a freshly blasted hole in the bottom when he saw something too startling to believe—a chest of silver. Without touching it, he rocketed to the surface and yelled out the good news to the divers on the *Derelict*.

Instead of reacting the way he thought they would, the men grinned and told him to go back to work. Everyone knew that treasure chests existed only in fiction. In tropical waters the hungry ship worms would have made quick work of any wooden containers that had fallen into the sea centuries ago.

But Stocker insisted. Finally Del Long consented to go down and look. Seconds later he shot to the surface, shouting that there *was* a treasure chest down there!

No divers ever grabbed their gear and tumbled over the side faster than the crew of the *Derelict* as they followed Long and Stocker back to the bottom.

Half buried in the sand was a blackish-brown wooden packing box just under two feet long, eleven inches wide and nine inches deep. Part of the top, one side and an end were missing, but the original contents were still there—three large clumps of silver coins solidly corroded together. The problem was how to get the 250-pound prize up intact without damaging it.

The divers worked for hours, finishing the work the blaster had begun, digging the chest out of the sand that had protected it from the wood-boring worms for 250 years. A large piece of plywood was brought down from the *Derelict* and slid under the chest; then, with part of the crew hauling on a line from above while the divers guided the plywood platform, the chest was hauled to the surface.

Once the extraordinary find was aboard the boat, the state salvage and exploration agent made sure that it was immersed in water to prevent the wood from drying out and warping before it could be preserved. The salvagers could only guess how many coins the chest contained, but their estimate of 3,000 was close.

The state's documentary research revealed that the chest contained 3,000 Troy ounces of silver in three 1,000-ounce bags. The 250 pounds was in four- and eight- real coins. At fifteen coins to a pound, there were about 3,750 of them in this conglomerate. At the preservation and research station in Tallahassee, the wood was examined and found to be Central American cedar. Precise measurements and a plan of the box were made to show its construction. Before the coins were cleaned and cataloged, a peculiar print of the corrosion products was noticed on one of the clumps. It was an impression of the fabric of the bag that had once held the coins. Clausen made a rubber cast of it, which provided the details for a drawing showing the fabric's intricate weave.

Word of the new find was quickly picked up by the news services. In the glare of publicity that followed, one seemingly insignificant fact was overlooked: besides the chest, the salvagers had found 1,500 loose silver coins that day.

With the August 1 recovery of 4,000 more pieces of eight and the early September visit of hurricane Betsy, the treasure hunters called a halt to the 1965 diving season—one that had netted them more than all the previous years combined. The total find for 1965 was 1,958 pounds 10 ounces of silver coins, or more than 37,000 of them; the 250-pound packing chest of silver coins in clumps; 1,782 gold coins; 41 disks of copper weighing thirty to seventy pounds each; 29 silver wedges; 12 silver "cupcakes" (ingots, so named because of their shape); an assortment of rings, earrings, brooches and miscellaneous jewelry; pieces of K'ang Hsi china, and thousands of historical artifacts, including ships' hardware, fastenings, and armament. Almost all the gold came from the Colored Beach Wreck, designated by the state as site 8-UW-1 near Fort Pierce, and all but a fraction of the silver came from the Cabin Wreck south of Sebastian Inlet, classified as site 8-UW-2.

For the treasure salvagers no other year would ever be quite so rewarding as 1965 in terms of valuables found. From then on it was a downhill slide for Real Eight and Treasure Salvors. Other 1715 wrecks were found and worked, but the treasure hunters' fortunes rapidly waned. In 1966, for example, only 181 gold coins and 123 pounds 14.5 ounces* of silver coins were found. However, a variety of artifacts, including several gold rings, silver wedges and cupcakes were also recovered. In 1967 the total of gold coins fell to 165; artifacts included 2 silver court sword hilts, silver sleeve links, silver crosses, segments of gold chain, 17 gold rings, several silver wedges, cupcakes and small clumps of silver coins. In 1968 the total fell to a low of 62 gold coins, 167 pounds of silver coins, some silverware and miscellaneous small silver and gold items. In 1969 the salvagers shifted their efforts to the Rio Mar Wreck near Vero Beach, possibly the remains of General Echeverz's *Capitana*, and had perhaps what was their second-best year. Although they found only 149 gold coins and 40 pounds 4 ounces of silver coins, they discovered numerous gold bars and valuable jewelry, including gold crosses and crucifixes. (See Appendix D for complete 1969 finds.) In 1970 the salvagers hit a new low, a total of 50 gold coins, 140 pounds of silver coins and approximately the same number of artifacts as in former years. With operational expenses running to hundreds of dollars a day, this kind of treasure hunting was fast becoming a losing proposition. The handwriting was on the wall.

*Avoirdupois.

Chapter 15

Something More
Valuable than Gold

Florida was involved in a hotly disputed double-handed game. On one hand she was licensing treasure hunters to lay waste historically valuable shipwrecks while they searched for coin, and on the other hand, she created the Bureau of Historic Sites and Properties and charged it with the responsibility of salvaging whatever archaeological information could be gleaned from the same sites. The two endeavors were incompatible with each other, but to a certain degree they worked. With but few refinements, mostly in the training of the state's field agents, the procedure was the same as that in use today: 90 percent of the digging by the treasure hunters is done with a blaster blowing a hole in the bottom sediments directly under the boat. Divers bring up all the artifacts and treasure found in the hole when the sand is blown away; then they move the boat to another place, blow the sand clear and again pick up what appears.

Each time artifacts come up from a hole dug by the salvagers, the state's technician, called a Salvage and Exploration Field Agent, takes a position reading with a sextant-like instrument from the stern of the boat on three surveyed landmarks. Later, when the site is being analyzed, the angles he has recorded are plotted on a chart.

The location of the hole that produced the artifacts is found by triangulation. The technician attaches to every artifact recovered a plastic tag with a field inventory number, records where it came from, and sees that the day's archaeological finds are properly handled and stored for later transfer to the Bureau's Archaeological Research and Preservation Laboratory in Tallahassee.

Truckloads of artifacts eventually arrive at Tallahassee's History and Archives Building—the former county jail a few blocks from the capitol—where they are unloaded with the tender care usually associated with handling cases of eggs.

The artifacts are kept in the cellar of the old building, which has been converted into a $70,000 laboratory. In one of the many old jail cells behind thick steel and iron-barred doors, gold and silver coins are cleaned and cataloged. More perishable items are stored underwater in tubs, barrels and vats to await proper preservation and cataloging—a lengthy process which has resulted in a backlog of some 40,000 unprocessed artifacts.

In an effort to keep the salvage program manageable, the state issues salvage leases to only a relatively few firms that show they are qualified to carry out their contractual obligations. All applicants are closely screened. In addition they must put up $5,000 and $15,000 performance bonds with the state and pay $600 for a search contract and $1,200 for an actual salvage contract. A state man then goes along to supervise the salvage work.

When the full procedure of plotting the initial recovery of each artifact is continued on a wreck site over a period of several years, it results in hundreds of location points, which are then plotted on a master chart for the site at the Bureau. This gives the archaeologist an overall picture of the scattered finds and the scope of the wreck under investigation. From it he will learn exactly where the vessel struck and how it began breaking up, which is important in interpreting the disaster historically. The proximity of the artifacts and their relationship to one another suggest possible close relationships aboard the vessel before it wrecked. These are the clues that the archaeologist must have in order to reconstruct the event and learn something about the past which may not yet be known.

Admittedly, this system is rudimentary when compared to the accuracy of land digs by trained archaeologists, or the accuracy obtained by underwater archaeologist Dr. George Bass in some of the University of Pennsylvania's expeditions to the Aegean, but it is as close as the state can get to the real thing under its present program of trying to combine science with commercial salvage.

The simple fact is that a very large chunk of our American heritage is being destroyed while licensed treasure hunters search for coins. And the irony of it all is that treasure hunting is a losing proposition, even for a concern that is working a relatively rich site. Long before the end, Real Eight Company readily admitted that it was spending $10,000 to $15,000 a month to bring up treasure worth in a good month maybe $10,000 to $14,000. As a result, in 1973 the company went bankrupt. What it amounts to is that both the salvagers and the public lose.

The Bureau's hope is that eventually three wreck-containing areas will be set aside by the state. In these areas the wrecks would not be worked for commercial purposes, but would be preserved for scientific research. This is not to suggest that the state go into the salvage business, only that these wrecks be sealed off until trained archaeologists can recover the historical information available from them. Florida waters contain from 1,800 to 2,000 shipwrecks, up to and past the World War II period. Possibly two hundred of these are of archaeological value to us, and a much smaller number have treasure potential. Unless these wrecks are protected, they will be destroyed. And there are no more where they came from.

Despite a growing public awareness of the need to preserve our ecological heritage, few people today are aware that they are losing an important piece of their historical heritage—that which can be found only in period shipwrecks. Public response to this statement might well be, "Who cares? What possible importance or significance is there in sifting through the bones of a ship that sank ages ago?"

An archaeologist or historian might explain by saying that period shipwreck sites constitute an extremely valuable source of information on the periods of exploration, colonization, trade and nationalization of hitherto undeveloped areas of the world. A ship, they might point out, was a single cultural entity; in effect, a "time capsule." It contained everything needed for living in one small area, things that were taken away from man in a moment in time. When these remains are found intact and their significance interpreted, scientists can literally reconstruct the past.

Such answers might be acceptable to academicians, but the lay public can generally understand better if it is given specific examples. The presence of K'ang Hsi porcelain on the 1715 shipwrecks is sufficient to start a chain reaction of dramatic mental pictures when one learns that these pieces afford evidence of a unique trade route beginning in the Orient on the opposite side of the world from where they were found. From them one learns of the fabulous Manila galleon carrying the wealth of the Orient from the Philippine Islands across the Pacific in the longest continuous navigation in the world—a six-month voyage to Acapulco, Mexico. There, the merchandise was sold at a trade fair, the wares destined for Spain packed onto a mule train and carried across the mountains to the Gulf port of Vera Cruz for loading aboard the ships of the *Flota*. From there it went to Havana and then up the Florida Straits to the fleet's destruction by hurricane. Two hundred and fifty years later the delicate porcelain pieces—many still intact in their original packing clay—are found, mute evidence traceable to a Spanish trade route so rich that nations sent squadrons of ships halfway around the world to intercept and capture a Manila galleon. And in the 250-year history of that incredible trade route, they succeeded only four times. Such is the kind of story told by a piece of porcelain.

And there are others, less dramatic, perhaps, but equally important. Certain ceramic types, for example, whose age could be determined within a few years, were found on the wrecks, indicating that Spanish travelers had taken heirlooms with them dating from one hundred years before the storm and the wrecks. Or the surprising discovery of four-tined forks on the 1715 wrecks, when it had been believed that the Spanish used nothing but three-tined forks. That fourth tine bridged an important historical gap. Archaeologists now knew that during the late 17th and early 18th centuries the English were eating with three-tined forks while the Spanish and French were eating with four. The different styles of fork used in these countries reflected custom and usage. The fact that the use of four-tined forks spread from France to Spain and then to England probably indicates the transmittal of other ideas. During the late 17th and early 18th centuries, the concepts of individual rights and laws which are now a part of our western civilization arose in France with the period of Enlightenment, spread to Spain through the political influence of France on that country, and subsequently to England, from which they came to our country. Such small clues as the tine of a fork are often highly significant pieces in a much larger historical puzzle.

Understandably, then, archaeologists are somewhat more than annoyed at the idea of treasure or curio hunters vacuum-cleaning a historically valuable shipwreck for coins, when scientists need every available fragment of evidence left as it was found, in relationship to the whole, if they ever hope to learn anything significant from the find. What archaeologists try to recover from a shipwreck is far more valuable than treasure. Their methods take longer and are considerably more meticulous. Much of what is recovered consists of everyday items that relate to a past historical period, and this is where we are very short. One of the questions most often asked of underwater archaeologists is, "Why do you need these things off shipwrecks when the museums are filled with them?" Unfortunately, our museums are not filled with these kinds of things. The objects that survive in museums and private collections are only the best examples of a culture: the best weapons, the best silverware, the best paintings. These fail to represent a whole culture. To get as accurate a picture as possible, archaeologists have to dig it all, the outhouses as well as the temples. Yet, they are still dealing only with a statistical sample, which is what archaeology is concerned with today. With a shipwreck they are dealing only with the hard parts that survive. And this is usually so limited that every piece counts if the archaeologist is to do a creditable job of bringing forth that culture.

Here is how such an operation would be carried out by a team of archaeologists. Suppose they are looking for a particular wreck to fill out a gap in their records. For example, assume that they have worked an English ship which sank in 1750 and another which sank in 1725 or 1730. To fill a gap in their information and refine their data, they might profitably look for a 1740 English wreck.

The first tip on the general location of such a wreck might come from archival records. An exhaustive search of English sources may be made—in the Public Records Office, admiralty records, Lloyds, the British Museum. Once a likely suspect is found that was lost in Florida waters, all that ship's records are acquired. Usually with the English, court-martial records are extremely useful, so these documents are carefully analyzed, checked and rechecked. From this work will usually emerge several areas, possibly reefs, where the ship might have gone down. Sometimes it is as easy as the name of the reef itself. Looe Key, Triumph Reef, Ledbetter Reef, Carysfort Reef are all areas named for lost ships. Other times it is more difficult. There may be several prime areas in which to look for the wreck.

A search of a suspect area is made by a boat towing a magnetometer. When the instrument detects and records a magnetic anomaly on the bottom, the spot is marked with a buoy, and divers go down to see what they have. It may be nothing more than a cast iron sewer pipe; nine times out of ten it will be a modern wreck. But the tenth time the divers may find what they are looking for—an old wreck, overlaid perhaps by ballast rock.

Next, a test excavation is made and a sample of artifacts taken for examination. Ceramic sherds or other evidence often tells the archaeologist something about the period and nationality of the vessel. Along with other artifacts, ballast stones might be recovered for petrological analysis. Since early sailing vessels tended to carry a particular kind of ballast stone—the size, shape and type varied considerably according to origin—identification and analysis may provide more vital clues to the nationality of the ship.

If the wreck appears to be the one the archaeologists are searching for, another magnetic survey is run on a smaller scale to plot more accurately the ferrous components of the wreck. This is usually done by a boat pulling the sensing element of the magnetometer systematically over the site, using a north-south, east-west grid pattern. Or, conditions permitting, the same grid pattern can be swum by a diver carrying the magnetometer head and working along a compass-oriented single line, which can be moved to ten-foot parallel intervals at the end of each run. Anomalies are recorded on the instrument's moving graph tape on the surface. When the entire area has been checked by the magnetometer, all of the anomalies are then plotted on a chart so that the archaeologist has an accurate record of the ferrous components of the wreck and their relationship to one another. They show the wreck's distribution and the main concentrations or epicenters of iron where the large excavation might begin.

If ballast rocks and wreckage are visible on the ocean floor, an underwater photogrammetric survey of the site follows. This is made in stereo with a six-foot-long winglike metal structure on which two cameras are mounted parallel to each other at opposite ends of the device. As this "wing" is swum through the water on a compass-oriented course at a precise elevation over the site, the two cameras take simultaneous overlapping photographs of everything on the bottom. Later, one set of pictures, fitted together in a mosaic, gives the archaeologist a composite photo-map of the site, while the other is consulted to compute the elevations of any objects extending above the level of the sea floor. Additional photogrammetric photos will be made of features or details of the vessel as they are revealed by the excavation. From these a highly accurate picture of the site emerges. At this point, a sub-bottom profiler may be used to penetrate the sediment over or around the wreck. This device, using low-frequency sound waves, can give the archaeologist helpful information by recording the densities of the sediments in the area.

Using all the information gathered, the archaeologist selects a place on the site where he reasons he can make his most productive excavation, getting the maximum number of artifacts. Before beginning, however, it is necessary for him to find nearby a relatively "clean" area free of artifacts, where ballast stones from the wreck can be placed as they are recorded and removed from the pile. Usually, this will be a wide sandy spot to which all the unwanted remains of the wreck will be eventually shifted when the original site has been completely excavated. Sometimes these areas are covered with three to five feet of sand, which the archaeologist excavates with the blower until bedrock is reached. All artifacts found there are photographed, tagged and removed.

At this stage the archaeologist has a record of what can be "seen" magnetically and a record of what can be seen photographically, and he begins to take off the top layer of ballast rock to learn what lies beneath. As divers remove the stones, they may find artifacts. These are tagged and their location recorded, generally through a photographic grid sometimes set up over the area on a scaffold. This may be a one-and-a-half- or two-meter square aluminum or angle-iron frame enclosing a decimeter square grid. The horizontal and vertical lines of the wire grid serve as a control for photographs or drawings made from above to show the relationship of all visible items within the frame before they are picked up.

Next, the blower aboard the research boat slowly fans sand away from the test site. As artifacts appear, the archaeologist continues to photograph, tag and remove them. Once all the ballast stones

147

have been removed, the divers reach the bottom of the ship, where they may find broken cannon and anchors sometimes carried by vessels as additional ballast. These are photographed in place and removed. Next to be recorded are any timbers and frames remaining from the structure of the ship. These are particularly important, for few details are known about marine architecture prior to 1650.

Most of the productive work on the main part of the site has now been done. There may be other wreckage under the sand along the sides of the wreck, and there is usually a large amount of material fanned out by tides, currents and storms to one quadrant of the main wreck. Although the archaeologist may not want to pick up everything in the fanned scattering, he may wish to place test excavations there. It is therefore possible for him to go from a continuous excavation on the main body of the wreck to a discontinuous one in other areas of the site.

As he works along the edge of the wreck, he will probably uncover remnants of the standing rigging. Areas beyond this may provide parts of the vessel's superstructure. Each new excavation proceeds as with the ballast stones—a gradual layer-by-layer analysis which continues until bedrock is reached or until there is no longer any wreckage to be found.

All recovered artifacts are immersed in containers of salt water aboard the boat and later transported to the laboratory, where they are cleaned, analyzed and restored. After this may come more archival research. If the vessel is one that is known about but not yet identified, the archaeologist may learn the significance of the find and be able to contribute new information from the evidence. All the archaeological and historical data are then written into a wreck report documenting the site.

It is easy to see that this operation is totally incompatible with treasure hunting. However, something must be said for the accomplishments of a state-operated program in which treasure and archaeological artifacts are being recovered simultaneously. Despite its problems and shortcomings, such a program has resulted in Florida's now owning some 50,000 artifacts relating to 17th-, 18th-, and 19th-century shipwrecks worked by treasure-salvage firms under contract to the state. In the nine years this program has been in effect, this policy of paying salvagers for their efforts in recovering underwater treasure has resulted in the state's owning what will one day, with proper exchanges and management, be the

1. Aboard his salvage boat, *Pandion*, treasure salvor Bob Weller prepares to dive on the 1715 Gold Wreck site near Fort Pierce while his wife, Margaret, stands by.

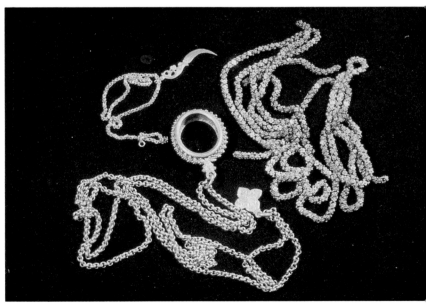

2. This gold locket for religious relics and its gold chain with a gold cross counter-pendant, were recovered from the Rio Mar Wreck just south of Vero Beach. An additional length of gold chain with a dogwood bloom motif, and one with a scimitar toothpick were also among the finds.

All photos by Robert F. Burgess except as noted.

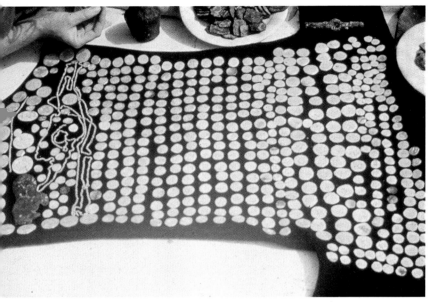

3. The morning's find of gold coins from the Colored Beach (Gold Wreck site) near Fort Pierce lie atop a wetsuit jacket. Treasure Salvors recovered 2500 gold coins a week during their first big strike in 1964.

4. Diver, Mark Yelvington, embraces one of the 1715 canons placed in Key Largo's Pennekamp Coral Reef State Park's public swimming area.

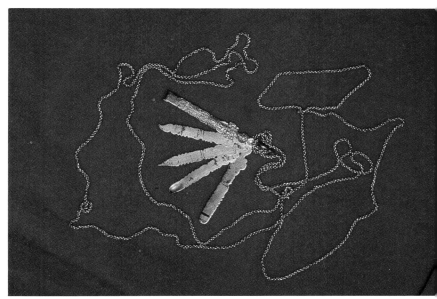

5. Gold manicure set found on the Cabin Wreck south of Sebastian Inlet was part of Florida's share during the 1993 division with Fisher's Salvors Inc. company.

6. Mexico-mint gold coins of the early 18th century recovered from the Fort Pierce Gold Wreck. Top row: 1700-1713; bottom row 1714 and later. Reading from left to right, the denominations are 8-, 4-, 2-, and 1-escudo.

7. Two sets of Mexico City-mint silver coins of the early 18th century. From left to right, 8-, 4-, 2-, and 1-real coins. In Mexico City during the 18th century, the smallest coin at the right could buy more groceries than could be carried home by one person.

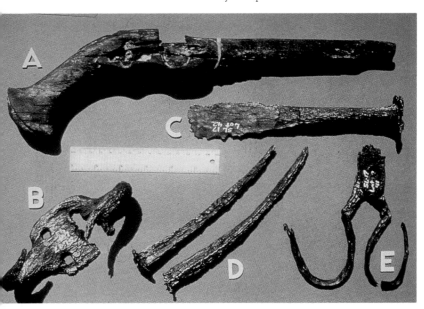

8. (A) Pistol, (B) deck cleat, (C) chisel, (D) deck spikes, (E) shears handle. These artifacts from the 1715 fleet have been cleaned and preserved at Florida's archaeological laboratory and are ready for museum display.

9. Recovered in 1972 by Wagner's Real Eight Company, this religious pendant called a *Venera* was popular in Spain during the 17th to 19th centuries. Surrounding the central religious figure are the words, *Concebida sin pecado orginal* ("conceived without original sin") along with semi-precious stones. The 2¾ x 2-inch 24-karat gold artifact was purchased from the salvors with coins valued then at $12,500 from Florida's 1715 Plate Fleet Collection. The piece is currently on display at Tallahassee's Museum of Florida History.

10. Solid silver artifacts including an ornate court sword hilt and a "puddle" ingot of gold were finds made within recent years by contract salvors on the 1715 sites.

11. Dubbed "Royals" by treasure hunters, gold coins such as this perfectly struck, round 8-escudo piece were extremely rare on the Spanish fleets. Because they are both rare and well-made, such coins today may be valued in excess of $45,000. One non-Royal gold coin in the Florida collection, due to its rarity, is valued at a quarter of a million dollars. This one came from the Gold Wreck site at Fort Pierce.

12. The reverse face of the 1714 8-escudo gold "Royal" minted in Mexico City in 1714, and recovered from the Gold Wreck side near Fort Pierce.

13. This solid gold dragon pendant was the single most valuable item recovered from the wrecks during the 1960s, however, more valuable finds have been made since then. The dragon is a combination whistle, toothpick and ear spoon which hung on a complicated floral pattern gold chain 11½ feet long. The artifact was recovered from the Cabin Wreck just south of Sebastian Inlet and was auctioned into a private Spanish collection for $50,000.

14. Close-up reveals the fine detail of the 11½ foot long chain accompanying the dragon pendant. Note that the alternating pairs of links were given what is believed to be a dogwood flower motif. The artifact's exquisite craftsmanship suggests that it may have been fashioned in the orient and came to the New World aboard a Manila Galleon.

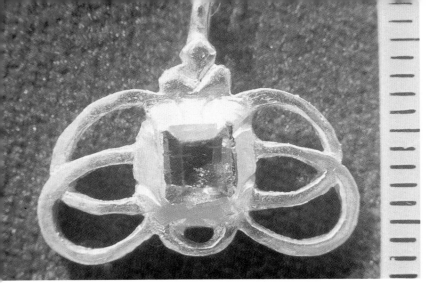

15. This solid gold bee pendant with an emerald body was found on Douglass Beach near Fort Pierce in the 1960s. Treasure salvors soon learned that just offshore lay the widely scattered remains of what they began calling "The Colored Beach" or "Gold Wreck." The emerald is believed to be Columbian because of the characteristic fault discernible in the gem. (Millimeter scale.)

16. When Fisher's blower dusted the sand from one of the Gold Wreck sites, divers were stunned to see the bottom "carpeted in gold." These are some of those coins that Florida received in its division with the treasure salvors.

17. Two sacks of silver coins from the Cabin Wreck which broke out of one of their shipping chests, fell on one another and were "frozen" in this shape by saltwater corrosion.

18. This gold snuff box lid recovered in 1992 from Corrigan's site details mounted huntsmen and dogs. But as we see more clearly in the enlarged sketch, the prey being hunted is human.

19. Though this astrolabe was discovered in 1993 by Fisher's Salvors Inc. on what is called "The Green Cabin Wreck," once believed a 1715 site, this rare navigational instrument is over 400 years old. Dated 1593, it came from the wreck of the *San Martin* which foundered there in 1618. Astrolabes today are valued well over $100,000. This one is now part of the Florida collection.

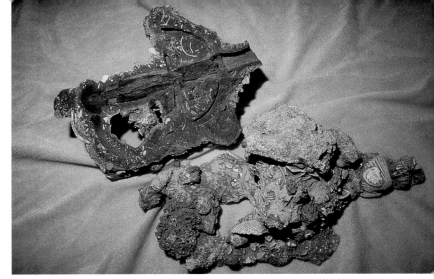

20. When Florida archaeologists sawed this 1715 conglomerate in two they found it concealed the remains of a Spanish rapier's hilt.

21. Using a waterproof metal detector and special digging tool, a treasure hunter searches for Spanish coins and other artifacts along shore opposite the 1715 shipwrecks.

22. These entwined initials carved on the end of a 1715 packing case was probably an owner's identification mark. Salvor's had high hopes the chest contained treasure but instead the contents were hundreds of sail-maker's awls, possibly intended as trade items for St. Augustine.

23. Modern version of the Fisher mailbox blower is a major excavation device. When side handle is pushed forward, elbow pipe end with grill fits around vessel's propeller where the spinning prop's venturi action is directed to the bottom for excavation.

24. A pair of Spanish rapier hilts recovered from the wreck sites were once part of an iron hilt "working" sword, and a gentleman's solid silver hilt court sword.

25. Some idea of a blower's excavation effectiveness is this crater in fairly hard limestone bottom that took a half hour to excavate.

26. Searching for lobsters in the inshore reef, skin divers found this solid gold tray elaborately decorated with a floral motif. Florida officials purchased the unique artifact from the finders with gold coins from the 1715 collection. The tray is now on display at the Museum of Florida in Tallahassee.

27. Rimmed and hinged with silver, this seashell makes an unusual snuff box. One wonders if its owner realized that its unique design identifies it as the deadly poisonous *Conus aulicus* (textile cone) of the Indo-Pacific.

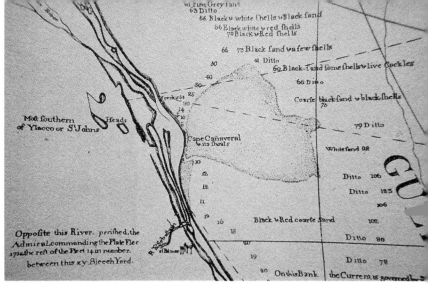

28. These notations by English cartographer Bernard Romans on his chart of 1755 provided clues to the whereabouts of the wrecked 1715 Spanish Treasure Fleet. On beaches just south of Sebastian River, Wagner found coins washed ashore from one of the wrecks.

29. Incredibly, these delicate Kang Hsi porcelain cups not only survived the hurricane's violence but 250 more years on the bottom of the turbulent Atlantic before salvors found them, still in their original packing material. Speaks well of Chinese porcelain packers.

30. Tiny gold scimitar-shaped toothpicks have been found on 1622 Spanish shipwrecks as well as those in 1715, a popular design possibly due to Moorish influence in early Spain.

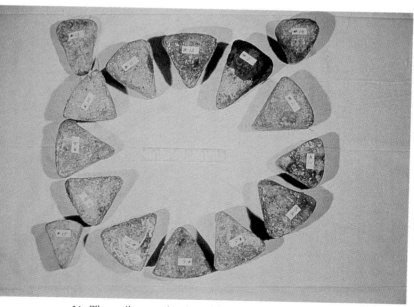

31. These silver wedge-shaped ingots found on the 1715 *Urca de Lima* or Wedge Wreck near Fort Pierce puzzled early finder Kip Wagner until he realized that six of them fitted nicely inside a barrel for shipping. Others were found on the Cabin Wreck south of Sebastian Inlet. Weights vary from one to five pounds each.

32. Mint marks on these silver utensils indicate the Mexico City mint was the source of the silver and that the silver had already had the Royal Fifth paid on it. Other stamps are purity and manufacturer's marks.

33. This gold locket with its glass face is believed to have contained a miniature oil painting surrounded by inset gems. The gold religious medallion could have been part of a rosary, the cup beneath the filigree flower probably containing a pearl.

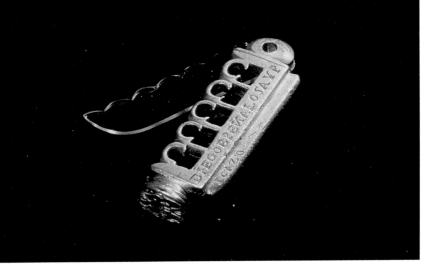

34. With what appears to be an image of a sun and church on one end, perhaps for impressing hot sealing wax, this silver clasp knife found on the Gold Wreck has the name "Diego de Penalosa y Picazo" inscribed on one side and "I give this to you my old friend" in Spanish on the other. One can only guess whether it is the name of the giver or the recipient, but the knife was apparently a gift. Experts believe it had a sheepsfoot blade for utility use, shaped as the plastic replica shown here.

35. Once so encrusted the preservationist thought he had nothing but a lump of limestone, this tiny brass sun-dial was found inside. When the top or "12" of this early 18th century pocket time-piece was pointed north, the indicator shadow told the time by falling on numbers around the instrument's perimeter.

36. Sixty inches of pure beauty, this gold and ebony rosary is one of the most striking treasures ever recovered from the 1715 fleet. The necklace combines intricately designed gold religious medallions with floral motif filigree links to tiny gold floral cups interspersed with ebony beads. Truly a treasure deserving of a museum setting where its uniqueness could to be appreciated by future generations. (Photo credit: Ernie Richards)

37. Jubilant finders of the fabulous gold and ebony rosary, Bob Weller and Whitey Keevan, radiate the kind of joy that climaxes decades of treasure salvaging — when you know you have just found one of the most unique treasures of all time. (Photo credit: John Halas)

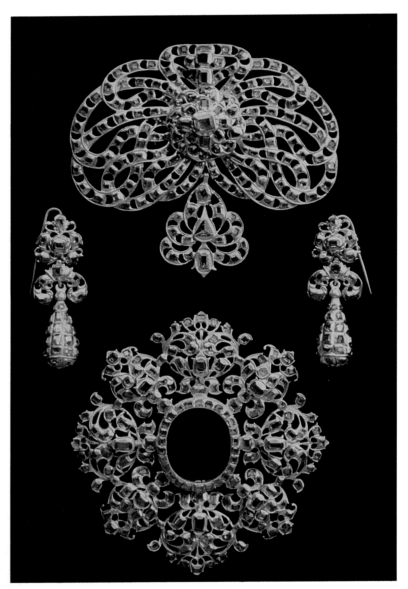

38. When salvors finally investigated shallow inshore reefs, Bob Weller and crew were rewarded with this stunning collection of diamond studded gold brooches and earrings. The ornate wings of the 3.5 by 3.2 inch butterfly brooch at top glitter with 161 diamonds. Diamond total for all the pieces found along with other gold jewelry in that one day's dive: 401 cut stones. Finds worthy of a museum collection. (Photo credit: Bill Moore)

best collection of Spanish colonial coins in the world, primarily because to date the state has kept intact the 25 percent it retains. In other words, Florida citizens can claim as their public property such unique objects as a large medallion bearing a likeness of a woman and a dog, valued at $17,000, and some 1,100 (as of 1969) gold coins, including some extremely rare issues, among which are several Phillip V 8-escudo pieces known to be worth from $10,000 to $15,000. In addition, there is nearly a ton of silver coins which have yet to be analyzed and an assortment of jewelry such as earrings, crosses and rings. The entire collection is valued at an estimated $1,000,000.

No value has yet been set on the historical artifacts, nor is one likely to be. The eventual destinations of all the finds are museums, particularly those of Florida's Division of Recreation and Parks. At present, some of the material is on permanent exhibit at the McLarty State Museum, at Sebastian State Park on the Florida east coast near the site of the old Spanish survivors' and salvagers' camp, and at Pepper Park State Museum, St. Lucie State Park, Fort Pierce. Two other museums now in the planning stage will also have permanent exhibits—one in Key West and another in conjunction with a new History and Archives Building scheduled for completion at Tallahassee in 1976. Three commercial enterprises also house treasure and artifacts recovered by salvagers: The Real Eight Museum of Sunken Treasure at Cape Canaveral, Art McKee's Treasure Fortress at Plantation Key, and Treasure Salvors' exhibit of treasure aboard the *Golden Doubloon*, a 500-ton, 160-foot replica of a Spanish galleon at Key West.

The material presented at the state facilities has been arranged in line with modern museum methods. Instead of being thrown in with a great many similar objects like random gold coins, which are about as impressive to look at as a plaqueful of arrowheads, a few coins may be displayed on a map of the world, for example, showing the products produced by various countries in the year 1715. The museum-goer may be astonished to learn from this display that there was a university at Cuzco, Peru, almost a century before there was one in North America, or that there was a mint in Mexico City striking coins almost 250 years before there was a United States. Instead of just "things" to look at, here will be something to be remembered. Instead of remaining stray items of unrelated interest, the treasure and artifacts will be used to give people an overall picture of history. They will leave this kind of interpretive museum with a better understanding of early-18th-century shipbuilding, trade routes, minting methods and the products of certain sections of the world in early times.

And perhaps, after all the studies are made and all the facts are in, this wealth of historical information from early shipwreck sites will prove to be the most valuable treasure of all.

Chapter 16

Aftermath

After the initial furor of "The Great Florida Gold Rush," things quieted down considerably. Believing that most of the treasure had been found, the major players in this historical scenario went elsewhere seeking their fortunes. Just as they had 251 years earlier when Spain would down its salvage efforts in 1719, leaving the rest to whoever chanced by to pick over the wrecks in the hope of finding overlooked treasure.

After 1719, free-spirited adventurers from as far away as Cape Cod are known to have visited and "fished" the badly scattered wreck sites seeking their fortunes. Most found little if anything for their efforts so they often moved on to the more lucrative business of the day: piracy. Similarly, in 1970, when Mel Fisher moved his operations to Key West to begin the long, costly search for the legendary Spanish treasure galleon *Nuestra Senora de Atocha* lost somewhere in those latitudes in 1622, what was left of the 1715 remnants became the not-so-happy-hunting-grounds of a modern day crop of free-spirited adventures hoping to strike it rich by finding treasure overlooked by the early successful salvors.

Some who searched now were subcontractors who had worked earlier with Fisher or Wagner's Real Eight groups. Others, however, were hot-eyed newcomers looking for more "carpets of gold" but finding instead endless days of crawling around on the rugged limestone bottom in pea-soup visibility bumping an underwater metal detector in front of them. Not quite so devilishly romantic when one considers the blizzard of particles generated by the Fisher-style "mailbox" blower that limits visibility to looking at the bridge of your nose, gloved hands fumbling sharp rocks like a blind man, while ears strain to hear the electronic "beep" of a metallic target in the detector's earphones. A full day of that and one begins to understand some of the realities of treasure hunting. A few months of doing it daily in all kinds of weather, without finding much more than beer cans and fishermen's sinkers, and the romance of treasure diving vanishes faster than last year's income tax return.

But search they did. The short-timers fell by the way, sometimes hardly lasting a season. The more experienced who knew the hardships involved, endured. When Fisher moved to Key West, Kip Wagner's nephew, Rex Stocker, who was said to have found the dragon pendant and chain on the Cabin Wreck beach, now moved his salvage boat and crew onto the formerly lucrative Colored Beach or Gold Wreck site near Fort Pierce. His crew worked it from 1973 to 1976 with little success. No one worked the site during 1977. Then, in 1978 Richard MacAllaster, another experienced treasure salvor who had no illusions about this tough business, contracted to work the Gold Wreck site with his dedicated group of salvors known as the Peninsular Exploration and Salvage Group.

MacAllaster concentrated on developing some system that would enable his people to methodically search the site accurately and completely. No easy undertaking considering that what everyone was looking for—if it was still there—was scattered somewhere over or under 50 acres of ocean bottom whose depth ranged from the beach out to forty feet of water. Paralleling the shore were three wormrock reefs, the shallowest inshore less than a foot from the surface. If the bottom was not crumbly rotten limerock, it was knife-sharp ridged limerock interspersed with clay and sand, sometimes over-layered with black muck, everything pushed around by unpredictable wave surges and currents. For a salvage boat to work the site, it had to be anchored from at least three different points, if not more. Sometimes conditions were so miserable, MacAllaster's 45-foot work boat had to have a spider web of mooring lines. One miscalculation with the boat inshore between those jagged reefs and it could end up the same way as the galleon whose treasure they were searching for.

Before any search began, however, MacAllaster wanted to be sure he knew everything he could about the site. He got as much information from the state as possible, then did a complete magnetometer survey, putting all the "hits" or indications of magnetic anomalies, on an overlay of the detailed chart he drew of the site. On shore he established navigational markers so that by triangulation, his people could carefully pinpoint their search areas on the chart to avoid anyone reworking an area. So accurate was this arrangement that by taking sextant sights on two of their permanent beach marks, a salvor could return to the same spot within a foot of where he had worked the day before.

But all the treasure of value found that first year amounted to little more than nine gold coins, 1,578 silver coins, and two gold rings. After expenses, not much profit.

This suggested that if there was much more to be found, it must be hidden in rock crevices or under some of the overlaying black muck layers which when disturbed totally destroyed any underwater visibility. And naturally, everyone was putting off trying to keep a salvage boat moored near the dangerous inshore rocks or crawling around the buffeting surf zone with metal detectors that often failed to work under these harsh conditions.

MacAllaster knew there had to be something to break them out of their rut. That winter as the usual high winds and seas kept the treasure divers beached, he got together with an electronics genius named Lee Harding who was trying to put together a superior underwater metal detector. Harding's unit soon proved better than anything they had prior to that. It was both sensitive and rugged. It could detect a coin under up to eight inches of rotten rock bottom. It looked like just the thing the salvors needed to work the inshore areas. The rugged instrument needed little adjustment and could be worked even under the cyclonic blasts of a blower excavating the bottom.

One of MacAllaster's team members that year was Bob "Frogfoot" Weller, an ex-underwater demolitions man during the Korean War who had come to Florida with the Honeywell Corporation in 1954. Naturally, Weller soon had a boat and was offshore exploring old shipwrecks. Soon he met up with Craig Hamilton and others with similar interest. On weekends these fellows began looking for and scavenging what they could find off shipwrecks of the Spanish 1733 fleet that had left scattered wrecks close ashore in the Upper Keys. In 1961 Weller was one of five salvager groups actively working the 1733 wrecks. Many artifacts turned up but nothing compared to the treasure Real Eight and Treasure Salvors were soon bringing up off the 1715 wrecks. But Wagner and Fisher had those all sewed up with state salvage contracts. Everyone else had to stay out and continue picking through the 1733 wrecks.

In 1966 Weller formed the Royal Fifth Incorporated and with a 32-foot boat he and others picked away at the already heavily picked over 1733 *El Infante* which was just beyond Florida's three mile limit in federal waters.

Since he now had the crew and the equipment, Weller itched to work more productive sites. Even the inshore 1733 sites were being put off limits by Fisher's exploratory leases with the state. Supposedly Mel now had some twenty-seven shipwrecks waiting to be searched. Surely, reasoned Bob, he would share one of them with Weller's Royal Fifth.

Weller made a dinner date with Fisher. After he and his wife shared a pleasant meal and evening of partying with Mel and Deo Fisher in Vero Beach, a late night walk on a moonlit beach resulted in the two coming to an agreement. Weller's group would work one of the 1733 wrecks that was supposedly in an exploratory lease area contracted to Fisher's Armada Research Company in the Keys. The two groups would share 50/50 on any finds. They made one of Fisher's typical handshake agreements.

The Royal Fifth moved its salvage boat south. Armada Research gave Weller the wreck of *El Sueco*, a 1733 merchantman traveling with the treasure fleet whose remains ended up about 3,000 feet off Conch Key in five to nine feet of water. Found originally in the late 1950s by pioneering treasure diver, Marty Meylach* and his partner, Don Thomas, its location was later revealed to Mel Fisher in another handshake agreement for a share of future finds. No one had yet found much more there than a large pile of ballast rocks welded together by coral.

When Weller's Royal Fifth dived the murky site they took one look at the sixty-foot-long by twenty-foot-wide mass of Spanish river rocks and went to work on it with sledge hammers. First they found only odds and ends but when they whittled down the ballast pile until it was fifteen feet long by five wide, they began finding what had apparently been hidden in the bowels of the ship—pieces of eight all over the place. The treasure was in the lower portion of the rock pile. Everywhere the divers looked they saw silver coins. They brought them up by the bucketsful. Some dated as early as 1727, but most were especially valuable pillar dollars, large round silver coins dated 1732 representing the first milled coins ever

---

Diving to a Flash of Gold by Martin Meylach with Charles Whited, Florida Classics Library, is an excellent narrative history of the early treasure diving efforts on the wrecks of the 1733 Spanish treasure fleet.

minted. It took three days of diving to recover them all. Weller's financial backers were so pleased that they took up Royal Fifth's option for a second year. But that year when Weller set off a demolition charge too close to the stern of his salvage vessel, her seams sprung and she later sank at the dock. At year's end he disbanded the Royal Fifth.

In the next two years, so much publicity followed that find that Weller started a company called Sunken Treasures Reproductions and went into the business of selling reproductions of treasure coins. Later he sold the company and in 1978 MacAllaster phoned him to ask if he cared to get back into the salvaging of the 1715 fleet with him. Weller said he was ready to go and that year he started with the group of the Gold Wreck, at Fort Pierce where most of the gold had been found from the 1715 fleet.

MacAllaster enlisted the aid of other experienced treasure salvors in the same manner he had recruited Weller. Sites were not worked haphazardly but sliced up like a pie with different people and different boats working different areas. No one infringed on another's salvage area unless invited to do so. At season's end, finds were divided with participants according to individual arrangements.

With Harding's superior detectors the salvors were anxious the following spring to look more closely at the more difficult inshore reefs. With its anchors in Deeper water, the group's smaller boat, *Pandion*, a 26-footer, was eased close to the inshore reef. Since the vessel drew less than three inches, it seemed ideal for these conditions. Topside the wave action kept everyone hanging on for dear life, but on the bottom the swells were not that noticeable. *Pandion*'s 24-inch wide blower ate a three-foot-wide hole in the bottom six feet under the boat. Within a week of searching this area which the treasure divers theorized was the original old 1715 shoreline, they found 500 silver coins. Searching southward the next week uncovered five eight-foot-long cannon. That much concentration of iron so disturbed the sensitive metal detectors, that the group moved into deeper water to continue their search. Blowing their way across 25-foot depths of clean bottom, they encountered a large flat rock. A strong signal came from the detector. The divers labored to move the rock aside. When the blower was once again directed into the hole where the rock had been, divers were astonished to see the bottom turn silver. The glory hole contained over 400 silver coins!

From then on things kept trickling in..a crushed pewter mug, an encrusted boarding sword, an ingot of silver shaped like a cupcake. On a good day the divers might find up to 40 silver coins. Other days their

155

strenuous efforts netted them no more than a few rusty beer cans. They all knew what he meant when a salvor shrugged and said, "Well, it's Miller time again."

Uncertainty was the name of the game. Where to hunt in their allocated search area was often guided by someone's hunch. If the hunch was strong enough, everyone went with it. In the business of treasure hunting everyone knew that hunches sometimes paid off in big ways. Nobody knew why they sometimes worked, just that they did. Successful treasure hunters had their antennae out hunting for hunches practically all the time. Mel Fisher's successful hunches were legend.

But it was no hunch that put team members John and Judy Halas offshore in 22 feet of water in their boat *Pandion* one day in late July. It was simply too murky for them to work inshore. So they made their first blow and John dropped down to see what might be there. Fifteen minutes later he was back on the dive ladder grinning and holding up a finely wrought gold ring shaped like angel wings that clasped a 10.5 carat emerald. Moments later, another gold ring appeared. Then Judy got down to the bottom and found a gold earring followed by a gold brooch, another gold ring with four emeralds, and part of a gold money chain. The next day their luck continued. The divers dubbed the site "The Jewelry Flats" because when John and Judy finished after three days of searching they ended up with 27 pieces of worked gold jewelry including a necklace containing a gold Madonna whose crescent-shaped base had once been decorated with six small emeralds, two of which still remained in place. Since everything had been found concentrated in a 20-foot-wide piece of ocean bottom, everyone felt that it probably represented a passenger's personal collection of jewelry.

With that stroke of luck the treasure hunters did what all good treasure hunters do when fate suddenly smiles on them. At the dock each evening after a successful day of recoveries, it was big smiles and drinks all around. Party time!

It was also a strike that heralded more good luck. With hurricane season in full swing and the weather subject to sudden outbursts or abrupt calms, the salvors worked around the temperamental climatic mood swings as best they could. When unseasonable calms flattened the sea, they hurried inshore to scavenge the usual truculent shallows where the pile of cannon rested. With the state's help during one of these calms, they managed to raise all the cannon, and Florida's Division of Archives and History had them moved to the seven-foot depths in the public swimming area at Key

AFTERMATH

Largo's Pennekamp Coral Reef State Park. There, the public could see not rusted cannon or phony concrete ones that later appeared in the state's underwater parks*. There underwater for the first time they could see the real McCoy, unpreserved and unvarnished cannon of the Spanish treasure fleet. The only modern touch that had been added were large sacrificial zinc ingots bolted to each cannon to reduce electrolysis. In no time, the presence of these cannon fired youthful imaginations...negatively in one instance. Since no one had bothered to explain what those large metal ingots were, two youths had to be physically dragged away from one of the cannon because they were trying to wrest off what they believed was a large bar of silver corroded to it's barrel. Argument enough, I suppose, for phony concrete cannon.

Delighted to have the cannons' enormously disturbing magnetic anomaly out of their search area, the treasure hunters grabbed their detectors and eagerly began searching the site where they had rested for 264 years. Hoisting the armament had left zero visibility but that did not deter divers used to working in these conditions most of the time. All they had to do was be able to hear the "beep" of their metal detector through their underwater head phones, and dig down through the mud and sand with their fingers to feel for the metal target. So with storm clouds gathering and the increasingly angry seas of Hurricane David rolling in on them from offshore, the divers crawled around through the underwater murk with their hearts double-timing each time their detectors screamed a "hit." Eager hands clawed up the small disks of metal and slipped them under a wetsuit cuff as they frantically searched for more hits and more coin-like shapes.

No one really knew what they had found until it was all over. Then they climbed back aboard their boat and unzipped their wet suits. Out tumbled the coins onto the deck. All gold! All forty of them! It was happy time again! Hurricane David was chomping on their fantail as the skipper slued Peninsular Salvage's 42-foot work boat *Bamboo Bay* through the pass at Fort Pierce on their last trip of the season. For once it had been a great year producing many fine artifacts, 62 gold coins, 2,500 silver coins and 27 pieces of finely worked gold jewelry. At dock-side with the storm starting to howl in their ears, the grinning divers toasted each other.

---

* Two Florida underwater parks preserving the remains of treasure wrecks with ballast piles and cannon replicas can be seen by the public near Fort Pierce (the 1715 *Urca de Lima*) and off Lower Matecumbe Key (the 1733 *San Pedro*).

Shortly afterward, Hurricane David sank the *Bamboo Bay* at her mooring in the marina. No matter, she would be refloated, patched and ready for the next big season.

In 1980 a moratorium was declared on any salvaging of the 1715 sites. It was a period when Mel Fisher's Treasure Salvors company was engaged in litigation over the right to salvage the sites. Fisher's company had filed an Admiralty Claim on five of the 1715 shipwrecks. When a Federal judge finally ruled in favor of the Admiralty Claim, any other claimants or lease-holders had to work out sub-lease contracts with Fisher's company, or they could not work the sites. It was a legal decision that took much of the responsibility for overseeing the salvage program out of the hands of Florida. No longer would state agents be required to be aboard every salvage boat to make sure everything was done according to how the state wanted it done. In affect, the decision eventually eased Florida out of manipulating the treasure hunting business. Not that any of the current state officials who had been overseeing the program as best they could, were too unhappy over the fact. The mid-1960s hard line bureaucrats had already moved on out of the picture. Newcomers who filled their shoes saw it largely as a gigantic Excedrin headache that no one really wanted anymore anyway.

Chapter 17

Beach Bonanzas

Up to the time of the moratorium groups of salvagers with state salvage contracts had a hard time scratching up enough treasure from the remaining 1715 wreck sites to make expenses. The Cabin Wreck, Kip Wagner's first 1715 wreck site south of Sebastian Inlet which had started it all, had given up over a ton of silver coins to Real Eight salvagers. An amount the site could apparently well afford to give up since Spanish records show that General Ubilla's Capitana, *Nuestra Senora de la Regla*, carried well over 100 tons of silver coins and bars in hundreds of wooden chests similar to the one that had been recovered. So, where was the rest? Did early salvors manage to grapple up the lion's share of it? Or had modern day salvors somehow missed it?

In 1981, long-time salvors John Berrier and D. L. Chaney obtained one of the Fisher sub-contract leases to see if any more silver could be coaxed out of the Cabin Wreck. Their efforts that year yielded a few pieces of worked silver, five gold coins and 140 pieces of eight. Things picked up for the men after the moratorium when everyone went back to salvaging in 1983 and they turned up 1,600 silver coins. The following season they found 2,642 more. Apparently, the *Regla*'s silver was not yet exhausted.

The same year, Roy Volker, also one of the early professional treasure divers who had developed a reputation for doing good professional work, owned a jet-powered salvage vessel that let him and his group work shallow water areas. When he and his men jetted up the shallows of the Corrigan's site 8 miles south of Sebastian Inlet in 1981 the season's efforts netted meager returns: numerous cannon balls, pieces of weaponry, 50 silver coins, a ring and a single gold 8-escudos coin dated 1714. The next season Volker found more armament and 200 pieces of eight. After the moratorium, in 1983, the group returned to Corrigan's and working inshore as usual, turned up thousands of lead grape shot, more small arms items such as trigger guards and flintlock rifle parts along with 1,500 silver coins. Interestingly, Volker not only was finding things hardly 100 feet from shore, but when searching with a metal detector under the wooden walk-over to the beach parking lot beside Highway A1A, one of his group found a gold 1-escudo coin dated 1711.

Over the years, one of the 1715 sites—the *Urca de Lima*—that lay close ashore just north of Fort Pierce, had been picked over by so many divers that almost everyone believed it to be worked out. Everyone except another long-time salvor named Frank Allen. The *Urca* was where Kip Wagner first took Mel Fisher's divers to see if they could turn up anything of value. It was on this wreck that Wagner had recovered fifteen pie-shaped silver wedges believed to have been formed to fit inside a barrel. But outside of these finds and a few scattered silver coins, the wreck seemed barren. Allen's group held an Admiralty Claim on the site in 1979 when they found one more of Wagner's famous silver wedges and little else. But in 1983 the divers looked more closely at what lay between the wreck site and the beach. Less than 100 feet from shore they found a large conglomerate. When it was cracked open, out tumbled 43 uncut Columbian emeralds. The following season several more conglomerates were found and stored in barrels of water for five months before anyone took the time to hammer them open. When finally they did, to everyone's amazement, one of the iron hard clusters of sand, rust, coral and shells nature had welded into an ugly brown mass, yielded to repeated hammer blows and revealed what it had concealed so well for centuries—3,030 glittering uncut emeralds greener than Irish clover! Another iron-hard chunk broke open to reveal 25 gold coins. One wonders how many swimmers over the years wading out from shore to snorkel the wreck had stumbled over those same "ugly rocks". But then, who would have known?

More and more the treasure salvors were learning an interesting fact about all of the sites. Most of the treasure was not in deep water, it was in shallow water...water too shallow even for a salvage boat, coins, worked gold, rings, the contents of a passenger's purse—caught in rock crevices, or covered by layers of sand. For a long time it failed to dawn on searchers that the entire fleet had been blown shoreward, the wreckage and debris pushed by winds and high seas constantly directed toward the beaches, along with the survivors. Only after years of state agents recording exactly where the finds had been made, was it possible for Florida archaeologists to develop computer generated scatter patterns of recoveries.

To everyone's amazement, some of these elongated patterns of recovered treasure touched certain beaches opposite some of the 1715 wreck sites for over a mile!

When treasure salvor Art Hartman became aware of where this occurred, he made good use of the information in 1982 by backing his 86-foot salvage boat stern first up to the beach at Corrigan's site, opposite Winter Beach just south of Wabasso. Once there, he revved up his engines and let their thrust do the rest. Corrigan's, the second 1715 wreck site south of Sebastian is believed to be General Ubilla's Almiranta the *Santo Cristo de San Roman*, that carried the second largest shipment of treasure in the fleet. Only Ubilla's Capitana carried more.

When Hartman's bunch hit the beach rear-end-to, beach strollers probably thought they were witnessing another shipwreck. Either that or the seamen had gone out of their minds. Certainly, with all the roaring of engines, and roiling of waters around the back end of Hartman's big boat *Dare*, the only logical conclusion was that it had run aground and was "spinning its wheels" trying to get off.

Naturally, crowds gathered. With straining anchor lines spiderwebbing seaward, the *Dare*, must have created one heck of a fascinating spectacle as her three engines roared and the big vessel bucked up and down. Meanwhile, her crew stood on the beach eyeballing the muddy mess boiling out from under the boat's stern.

Surely, during the process, some helpful twit on shore standing as close as he dared to this spectacle, must have yelled out, "Hey, you guys stuck or somethin'? Want us to jump in and give ya a push off!"

And one can imagine Hartman and crew grinning nervously but frantically waving off any such offers for assistance, while the perplexed beach-watchers wandered then just what the hell was going on. Should someone call the Environmental Protection Agency, or make a citizen's arrest or something? After all, these guys were just standing there in plain view while their big boat chewed up the beach with its propellers. Sure looked like some kind of environmental foul-up if they had anything to say about it!

Indeed. Eyewitnesses reported that it was a sight to see. Moreover, it paid off big! As the *Dare*'s props slowly dug a 28-foot deep crater under her stern, coins began washing up on the beach. They came so fast and numerously that Hartman's divers were picking them up with their toes. Bystanders were enthralled. Some even got into the act by picking up stray pieces of eight and handing them to Hartman's men. One day his divers were doing something in the water when the prop wash pushed a large conglomerate out of the hole and onto the beach. A newly arrived bystander took one look at it, snatched it up and took off running down the beach with the chunk tucked snugly under his arm like a wide-open receiver tearing for a touchdown. Shouts for him to stop only spurred him to greater speed. The last Hartman saw was sprinter and conglomerate disappearing over the dunes.

Later Hartman learned that the snatch-and-run character had found 52 silver coins in the clump. None was ever recovered.

As for Hartman's beach salvage effort, it paid off handsomely with two palm-sized puddle ingots of gold, twelve 8-escudos gold coins, a long list of unusual artifacts, and 2,000 silver coins. Not bad for a couple days of chewing up the beach. If he could figure how to keep the environmentalists at bay, the shrewd treasure hunter expressed interest in maybe trying it again.

Art Hartman was not the only one who keyed in on the secret of the beaches. There were others in the non-professional treasure hunting public sector who had picked up enough of the gold and silver clues there to know that certain beach sites were bonanzas. All you had to know was where to go, when to go, and how to do it.

Before the determined treasure hunters on land with their metal detectors arrived, however, it was sometimes the weekend lobster divers snooping around those convoluted, work-eaten low-profile limestone reefs that stumbled onto things that most professional salvors find only in their wildest dreams. One such stroke of luck struck three young lobster hunters in 1984. Here's how it began:

It was one of those absolutely perfect days for diving. A rarity for Florida's east coast. But this day the sun glazed a calm Atlantic Ocean gleaming like a giant sapphire as far as the squinted eye could see. The three breathless youths stood on the seven-foot-high sand dunes near Vero Beach and couldn't believe their eyes. Instead of the usual roiled brown water crashing with waves, it now looked perfectly calm and relatively clear with long rows of gentle combers rumbling hollowly down the beach.

Whooping joyfully the three diving buddies charged toward the water, hauling their heavy scuba gear awkwardly with them. Eagerly they donned their equipment at the water's edge, the two experienced divers, Jim Ryan and Randy Lathrop, a bit faster than recently certified Alex Kuze. It wasn't lobster season yet but the divers intended to case the low rocky reef for Florida crawfish so they would be ready when the season opened. The area they had in mind was the inshore rocky nooks and crannies flanking the beach opposite Corrigan's Wreck.

Together the trio made a smooth beach entry, swam out to the low-profile limerock reef in 15 feet of water and dived. Turning north they swam close to the heavily holed surface of the craggy reef covered with a carpet of seaweed. Carefully they peered into the openings for lobsters.

The divers worked their way along this rocky barrier until it began to dwindle away. Then they crossed over it and swam south, examining the face of the reef. Periodically they spotted the antennae of spiny lobsters watching them from various rocks and crevices. Mentally the divers noted their hiding places with the intention of returning after the season opened.

Eventually, the two more experienced divers worked on ahead, leaving Kuze to bring up the rear. Kuze was taking his time, absorbing the scenery, pausing at every crevice to let his eyes adjust to the shadowy interior that might conceal a lobster. At one such crevice, Kuze saw something that was neither fish nor fowl, rock or reef. It was a dull dark yellow, almost amber. Gingerly reaching into the hole, he tugged it out.

It was a thin rather fancily decorated metallic plate that looked too shiny to be anything but somebody's fast food throw-away. Kuze almost tossed it aside but decided instead to at least show it to the others.

When Lathrop realized Kuze was no longer with them, he turned back looking for him. He said later, "I could see Alex swimming toward me out of the blue, and he had something in his hand. As he came into focus I could see a bright yellow object in his hand and a bewildered look on his face."

Hardly even daring to hope that the too-new-looking piece of shiny pressed metal might be worth something, Kuze held out his find questioningly. Suddenly, he was amazed to see Lathrop's eyes grow wide behind his mask as he started yelling into his regulator.

On the surface the three divers knew at once that Kuze had found something a lot more valuable than a throw-away fast food plate. It was an exquisitely carved gold tray shaped like the flat petals of a sunflower. Underneath was a sort of wide pedestal, also of solid gold. When everyone stopped shouting madly for joy, they suddenly realized the full significance of their find.

Obviously they had found treasure, probably from one of the 1715 ships everyone knew had foundered along that coast. But more significantly than that, what they had found was illegal for them to take. They had accidentally picked up a rare and probably very valuable artifact on ocean bottom wetlands belonging to the state of Florida. For all they knew, they were lobstering some treasure hunter's contracted salvage area which was okay. But to do any free-lance treasure hunting in the contracted area and take a piece of property that state officials said repeatedly "belonged to all the people of Florida," was probably some kind of jailable offense.

So, what should they do?

Drop it like a hot potato? Take it to the nearest police station and say, "Hey, look what I just found!" Or jam it in their swim suit and run like hell?

They did the latter. They smuggled their find ashore. At home the three coveted their prize, mulling over their next move. When eventually all avenues and possible repercussions were considered, they made the correct move. They hired a lawyer who reported their find to state authorities.

Those in charge of such affairs then were undecided whether to confiscate the find or to make a more amiable arrangement with the finders.

Fortunately, this was a transitional period when state authorities were beginning to realize that perhaps it would be more beneficial to their interests to work with sport divers who were not intentionally breaking the law, rather than jumping in and prosecuting someone caught with an historical artifact on the state's wetlands. That did not mean that they would not overlook someone, for example, trying to lift and make off with, say, a cannon, or some other object from a wreck site, but it did mean that in such a case as this they were willing to consider all factors and possibly negotiate.

Which is what occurred with the accidentally found gold tray. Rather than confiscate the artifact and punish the finders for taking it from state land already under contract to a treasure salvor, Florida suggested a compromise. The finders *agreed*—and this is the key word since they later argued the state had ripped them off—they all agreed through their lawyer to exchange the tray for one half the appraised value of the find.

The tray was appraised at $23,000. The trio and their lawyer *agreed* to accept six rare 8-escudos gold coins dated 1713 valued together at $12,500. The coins were part of the state's 25% received after a division with Real Eight treasure hunters.

As a result of this exchange, all the divers, including the lawyer gained a share of the treasure; the Florida treasure collection gained a completely unique artifact for its museum, and the public gained by being able to see this remarkable example of early 18th century colonial craftsmanship at the state's public museum rather than have it disappear, as so often happens to unique works of art, into someone's private collection—often outside the country. Today, as Florida slacks off its once rigid control over commercial treasure salvors, it still would appreciate knowing about accidental finds of a unique nature to see if some agreeable means might be found for the state to negotiate a way to include the item in Florida's fine museum collection of historical artifacts in Tallahassee.

Few things did more to excite land-beached amateur treasure hunters who knew a thing or two about what beaches opposite the 1715 wreck sites might reveal, than the Thanksgiving Day storm of 1984.

When it hit the Florida east coast with gale force winds, I should have been leading the crowd with a metal detector in each sweaty hand heading for the "treasure beaches."

Well, I was heading for them all right, but not on a mission for treasure. I was driving down-state to climb aboard one of Blackbeard's 65-foot sailboats for a two week live-aboard dive trip through the Bahama out-islands. I was on assignment for *Skin Diver* so even though I was tempted to alter course, I didn't.

As I rolled southward, however, I wondered if the trip would even take place. My car radio reported that gale force winds and extremely high tides were wracking havoc along Florida's entire eastern seaboard, severely undercutting the coast. I had no idea how severe the storm was until I reached Port Salerno where I was to meet Florida Classics Library publisher, Val Martin, at a favorite seafood restaurant on Indian River which is separated from the Atlantic Ocean only by a narrow string of barrier islands.

By the time I arrived, it was growing dark. As I turned into the restaurant's parking lot my headlights illuminated only the roof of the restaurant. The rest of it was underwater!

Overnighting at Val's place, I phoned Miami the next day to see if our trip was still on. They said it was. Val and I drove to the beach and marveled at the way the seas and winds were gobbling it up. That night Blackbeard's passengers and crew of the *Sea Explorer* were forced to party it up in harbor all night to avoid the high seas. Wisely, no move was made to set sail until everyone was comfortably zonked out, then, around 3:30 A.M. our boat quietly up-anchored and set sail across the high-rolling Florida Straits.

By the time everyone regained consciousness the next morning, the worst of the storm was behind us and we were riding roller-coaster waves full tilt for the Bahamas.

Meanwhile, long before dawn that morning, treasure hunters from all over the state were throwing gear into vehicles and heading for the beaches opposite the treasure wrecks. Sometime later I interviewed a couple of those happy hunters, and they had a tale to tell.

"The Thanksgiving Day storm of eighty-four was the best beach cut we've had in twenty years," said retired Fort Pierce lineman John Durham. "I know where there are wrecks from Miami to Jacksonville. I didn't know where to go first. I did it for ten days and nights. I didn't even come home to go to bed, just slept a bit in my car. I did better with gold in less than an hour at Corrigan's than I've done in all my life. I got nine 8-escudos gold coins (valued then between $6,000 and $8,000 apiece) and nine other coins. I worked the Gold Wreck site but got only a few half reals and ones and twos (silver cob coins valued up to $100 each). A lot of half reals were found 200 yards back in the bushes, I saw a finger bar of gold that was found but I didn't find any. But Corrigan's was really producing. Even the wives were walking along without detectors picking them up. I thought I had cleaned out all the gold coins and told someone where I had found them. They found five more but they were all two-escudos gold coins..."

Durham said he found his large gold coins under 18 inches of sand. If that sounds easy, consider the conditions. Durham parked his car on coastal Highway A1A and walked to the ocean's edge which under normal circumstances is about 40 feet from the sand dunes where a wooden walkway and steps enable the public to cross over the dunes from a small highway parking lot. This time, however, the ocean had moved up to just below the dunes where Durham found a woman standing with a

166

metal detector. "Why aren't you down there looking for coins?" Durham asked.

"I would be but I'm afraid a tree will knock me down," said the woman, referring to numerous large uprooted trees that were rolling back and forth in the seething surf.

Laughing, Durham jumped down on a slender sand spit. Looking back at the woman, he grinned and said, "See...no problem."

That's when the tree hit him and knocked him down. His non-waterproof metal detector wrapped in a plastic garbage bag for protection went one way and he went another. The detector ended up under ten feet of water and had to be retrieved several days later. Drenched, Durham got a spare metal detector out of his car and went back to the fury of the surf, more determined than ever. With winds gusting to 40 miles an hour and a chill factor that made things fairly nippy, Durham once again left the ocean and retreated to his car. This time he came back to the wildly churning surf wearing a diver's wetsuit and a mask. He took off down the beach, dodging the angry seas.

"I may have looked funny," said Durham, "but I was finding coins."

And he was not alone. He said that by mid-morning more than 50 people with metal detectors were searching that same site. They came down the beach in droves. Almost everyone had found some old Spanish coins. Bob Weller said that in the eroded beach area about 900 feet north of the parking lot, beach treasure hunters on that fated Thanksgiving Day found at least 14 gold coins and over 2,000 silver coins. Surely everyone was extraordinarily thankful for that bonanza. Probably one of the most financially rewarding Thanksgivings most of them ever had!

Before it was over, coins were not the only treasure those electronic beachcombers found, nor was it the first time this happened. Three years earlier when a similar storm cut six feet of sand off the beach, Ron Hampton of Tampa was soon there checking the site for treasure. As he swung his detector's sensing unit over the shingle of sand just above the rampaging surf he suddenly got a strong signal in his head phone. Hampton carefully dug into the soft sand. Six inches down he found an ornate gold locket hardly more than an inch long shaped like a tiny rectangular box. Its inside was packed with sand. As he turned it over in his fingers, Hampton was amazed to find that one side of the locket was glass. Behind the tiny window stood a delicately carved ivory figure believed to be the image of a saint. Inscribed on the back of this exquisite locket were these letters: "SN CO FRA SOLA NO." Hampton's research later revealed that the letters translated into the name: "San Francisco de Solano." Born in Montilla, Spain in 1549 and having died in Lima, Peru in 1610, he was supposedly the first saint to visit the new world. The reliquary probably belonged to one of the passengers who perished on General Ubilla's Capitana. Over the years, storm waves had shoved it shoreward the same as they had most of the more moveable shipwreck debris.

Long before things had calmed down after that storm, Frank Giovenco, also from Tampa, was swinging a metal detector in wide arcs over the beach above the thundering surf, where sand dunes had been swept away, something at the base of the vertical wall of sand caught his eye. Bending down he picked up a 1 5/16 by 7/8 inch solid gold cross studded with tiny emeralds.

And now, with this Thanksgiving Day storm Durham was also finding more than treasure. First he found several small cannonballs that he tried to carry in the pockets of an old raincoat he was wearing. But the iron balls tore out the pockets and fell back on the beach. Then Durham uncovered a small iron cannon. Carefully he was metal detecting just out of range of its effect on his detector searching around it for coins when two husky strangers came up to examine his find. One guy carried a mean-looking machete which seemed to be his only treasure hunting tool. (Probably all he needed.) Suddenly the two snatched up the hefty find and ran off with it. Durham stared after them.

"Anybody who could run off with a 350-pound iron cannon as easily as those guys did, I'm not arguing with."

According to dedicated beachcombing treasure hunter, John Durham, the key to successful treasure hunting is to read everything you can find on the subject, get yourself a good, reliable metal detector, and then persistently look for the goodies. Some idea of Durham's persistence is reflected in the fact that before retirement he worked all day and treasure hunted most of the night. Where a sun-cracked old deserted spur of coastal highway A1A crossed a beach opposite a shipwreck site, Durham detected Spanish coins under the baked tar road and dug them out by flashlight at night. On one occasion, believing probably correctly that giant hurricane waves may have tossed valuable coins high into the thick seagrape trees growing do dense on the dunes that walking through them is impossible, Durham crawled through them on his belly. All he needed was enough space for his out-thrust metal detector and his body. On one such foray, he suddenly heard a loud signal, but it wasn't from his head phones. Turning on his flashlight, the determined coin-hunter was shocked to see a coiled rattlesnake directly beneath the sensing coil of his detector. The snake's forceful "signal" was far more meaningful than any Durham might have gotten from his metal detector. Tactfully, he retreated. That ended his nighttime crawls through seagrapes.

On another occasion when Durham shrewdly observed that storm tides had pushed the beach 100 yards inland, he checked the place with his metal detector and found 400 silver coins there.

Quite obviously there is a lesson here for budding treasure hunters of the dry land variety. That lesson is: "Develop a keen sense of observation."

Determined and dedicated hunters such as Durham are thinking about their hobby of metal detecting most of the time. When the subject isn't directly on their mind, it isn't far off. Then their subconscious takes over. But the antennae I told you about that leads treasure hunters to follow their sometime lucky hunches, are always out and working.

For Durham it came once as he was driving down the main street of Sebastian. As he passed a building site his sharp eyes detected odd bluish green patch of ground that had been scraped clean by the blade of a bulldozer. Durham's metal computer instantly processed that meager clue. Blue/green is the color of metal corrosion.

That night in the cover of darkness, Durham with his detector and a companion, returned to the building site to check out the off-colored patch of ground. To their surprised delight, the men saw at the very surface were the dozer blade had shaved open what turned out to be the rotted remains of a cloth bag containing 200 corroded Spanish silver coins clumped together in a single mass. Those that were dated all came from the 1715 wrecks. Durham figured he had found a bag of coins probably hidden by Indian divers forced to help the Spaniards salvage treasure from the wrecks. Interestingly, he said that the building site being cleared with its telltale patch of earth, was directly across the street from the Bank of Sebastian!

Where and how to look for treasure goes back to what John Durham said about reading everything in sight on the subject. Libraries are good starting places. And by all means read John S. Potter Jr.'s *The Treasure Diver's Guide*. It's the bible on the subject worldwide. Florida Classics Library of Port Salerno, Florida, publishes a revised soft-cover edition. Potter's detailed archaeological information is tops, as is his historical data on ships and fleets. Locations, however, are general. More specific information on the history and location of old Florida shipwrecks, is found in the *Divers' and Snorkelers' Guide to Old Shipwrecks of Florida's Southeast Coast*, three combined nautical charts measuring 20" x 28" crammed with old shipwreck information. They focus on Florida's southeast coast from below Cape Canaveral to the upper Florida keys, the so-called "Treasure Coast," where two major Spanish treasure fleets and hundreds of other sailing ships sank close to shore. Thumbnail histories name and locate over 50 old shipwrecks, describing vessels, cargoes, water depths, diving conditions, treasure carried or salvaged. Of special interest to beach hunters are the computer-generated scatter patterns of recovered treasure from the Spanish Treasure Fleet of 1715, some sites touching beaches for over a mile where old Spanish coins, jewelry and artifacts are still found. For those interested in the specifics of this on-going treasure hunt, the charts and guide combo is $14.95 from Spyglass Publications MAP, 308 West Marion Street, Chattahoochee, Florida 32324.

Chapter 18

More Gold
and Mega-finds

Just before the Fourth of July, 1987, I drove down to Fort Pierce to interview Bob Weller and to see what was happening with his group salvaging the Gold Wreck. Bob and his wife, Margaret, have a modest condo there as a base of operations close to where they go offshore to salvage. Bob's attractive wife is a considerable asset to this husband-wife team effort. Not only is she a working treasure diver along with the rest, but her real fame has to do with her legendary shrimp salad the crew gets to enjoy when and if they ever tear themselves loose from the bottom. Personally, I think Margaret Weller's shrimp salad is the secret glue that holds the whole thing together, especially on days when seas are rough and the finds are few.

Weller worked as a member of MacAllaster's Peninsular Salvage for five years, then purchased John and Judy Halas's boat, *Pandion*, and formed his own sub-contracting company, Crossed Anchors Salvage, in 1985. When I caught up to him a couple of years later, *Pandion* had been back and forth to the Gold Wreck off Frederick Douglass Beach so many times that once we cleared the Fort Pierce breakwater, they just turned her loose and she went there by herself.

A gridded copy of the chart MacAllaster and his group had so carefully prepared when they began working the wreck in 1978 was mounted under plastic and thumb-tacked to a board along the starboard bulkhead at eye level.

To me it looked as though someone had stood off 40 paces and peppered it repeatedly with a load of Number 9 bird shot, then drawn a circle around each hit.

Weller explained that those were all the spots they had worked over the years. Each time the boat blew a hole with the mailbox, a diver checked it out carefully with his detector, then the boat was shifted three feet. The new position was then sighted in with a sextant on paired shore markers and another circle went on the chart. Each circle represented a three to four-foot-wide hole and each hole overlapped the next one. In the last six years, Peninsular Salvage had mailboxed 5,000 such craters in the bottom of the 55 acre site.

Weller looked at this graphic journal of their many years' bottom crawling adventures and shook his head. "Not many places left in the scatter pattern to look any more," he commented.

He was right. One was hard put to find any clear, unmarked spot on the chart in the area where they figured the treasure had scattered. However, Weller pointed out some unmarked places in deeper water that he itched to try. It was apparent that MacAllaster's small fleet of salvage boats planned to do it right and leave not a proverbial rock unturned. Their densely circled salvage site reminded me of Carl Clausen's early concern that Real Eight and Treasure Salvor's companies sometimes dug sites they had already worked. In desperation, he told them, "If you do no more than just drop a blue marble in each of the places you work, you won't be doing them over again."

Carl, who had by now gone on to other endeavors, would have been proud of this arrangement. It did not take serious salvors long to understand the need of knowing where they were and what they had done. MacAllester's system worked perfectly.

Most people who know nothing about what a treasure salvor does other than what they read in the newspapers—that the men dive down on a nice white sand bottom in tropical seas and spend their day picking up a fortune in gold and silver coins—would probably be shocked by the slightly less romantic reality of what they actually do.

I thought about this on the *Pandion* as I watched Weller suit up for his first dive. Here it was almost the Fourth of July in southern Florida waters that most people think of as being HOT year around, and this guy is tugging on *layers* of old, scuffed, ripped, and generally scruffy-looking thickly insulated wet-suits. From head to toe, that is. Then, heavy athletic elastic knee protectors went on over all the wet suits. Not that Weller's knees were lacking for rubber protection, but when you spend most of your day underwater in a blizzard of sand, shells and limestone fragments, blindly crawling around over sharp rocks, a normal wetsuit wouldn't last a day. So you try to protect those main bearing points as much as possible. That means hands, knees and elbow pads if you've got them.

As everyone knows, most swimmers not wearing a diver's wetsuit, float easily in salt water. Since water temperatures lower than body temperature soon chill a person, divers try to retain their body heat with neoprene wetsuits. But wearing a quarter inch thick wetsuit makes a diver float like a cork. To off-set that buoyancy he adds a lead weight belt. Ideally, divers want just enough weight so that if they inhale air from a regulator underwater, they rise slightly; or if they exhale they sink. They want neutral buoyancy.

Not so the treasure diver. He can't afford to be even slightly floating or neutral. He has to be negative. He doesn't want to be floating up when he needs to stay down. So he over-weights himself with what looks like a ton of lead. All the better to crawl around the bottom with. The only time those extra weights become a real drag is when he climbs up out of water on the dive ladder leaving behind whatever support the water gave him. He doesn't go far in his super-weighted condition. Which is why the weight belts are the first things shed when the diver emerges from his long time down.

Weller's crew dive shallow water most of the time. but when divers are spending all day underwater, the necessity of scuba tank air-fills becomes impractical. Instead, they use hookah rigs, surface supplied air pumped down to them through a hose connected to their topside compressor usually powered by sturdy Briggs and Statton engines. These rigs provide divers with maximum air for little expense. Also there are no cumbersome scuba tanks to bump against the blower when the water over the search area gets skinny.

Each diver takes his shift on the bottom while the others assist topside. Every ten minutes two tugs on the hose responded to by two tugs from topside signals a move. This is accomplished by hauling in on one 300 foot anchor line astern, while slacking off on another line mooring the vessel in the opposite direction. A third anchor rope usually tethers the boat by its bow.

It is long, arduous work both above water and below. Finds are few and far between. While Weller was working on the bottom, I donned my tank and went down to see if I could get any pictures. I had to be less than twelve inches away from him to even see him. I got a great shot of his knee pad. Or maybe it was his elbow.

After rocking and rolling topside with Margaret and their alternate diver, with the two of them releasing and hauling on the three-way anchor lines shifting the *Pandion* the incremental three feet every ten minutes, taking bearings, refueling the hookah, the diver down blindly but carefully snooping electronically into every invisible nook, cranny and crevice of that rocky bottom with the short-handled detector, by day's end we finally logged the total treasure we had found. It came to one slightly rusty beer can bottom.

Apparently, not my day for recording great treasure finds. But Margaret's shrimp salad was tops!

"Stick around." Bob enthused, "We're going to do a lot better tomorrow!"

We couldn't have done much worse. Unfortunately, I didn't have time to stick around and find out. At home a couple weeks after the Fourth my curiosity got the better of me and I phoned to see if their luck had changed.

"I told you you had better stay," chided Bob. "The day after you left, our diver, Bob Luyendyk thought he had found another beer can bottom but it turned gold on him. It was a fully dated 1712 8-escudos *Royal*!"

I think I yelled into the phone something like "Wowee!" The perfectly struck, round Royals were still so rare that in 1987 they could bring up to $70,000 or $80,000 apiece!

"Wait! Wait! You haven't heard everything!" Weller shouted excitedly over the phone. "Margaret found another Royal just nine days later!" It was a 1711 4-escudos gold Royal this time valued at $40,000 (Why oh why did I go home?) I had to get Margaret on the phone to congratulate her.

"I clutched it so tightly when I brought it up," she told me, "I was afraid I would bend it!"

If I could have sold my typewriter I would have gone right back to Fort Pierce to see if I could better our beer-can-bottom find with a Royal or two myself. Bob's excitement was catching. If we were to get our two excitements together I didn't doubt in the least that I could persuade him to go back down out there at night with me to see what more we could find. When the gold bug bites, abandon all reason. You just keep going back for more. Another hit. They don't call him "Frogfoot" Weller for nothing.

Enthusiastic?

Certainly. How could he help not be? Enthusiasm is one of the primary prerequisites for being a treasure hunter. You *have* to believe. And if you've had as many lucky strikes as the Wellers and some of the others have over a long period of time, you grow to believe that each time down you are going to make the "find" of the season. If not the century. The Wellers know that feeling well. Their find of all time happened just a couple of years earlier.

Bob had noticed that there was an unworked open spot north of the area they called the "Jewelry Flats" where the Halases found 27 pieces of worked gold jewelry. Weller asked MacAllaster if he minded him working it. MacAllaster told him to go ahead and take their vessel the *Defiance*, a 31-foot Bertram and see what he could find. With him went his wife Margaret, and their relief diver, David Ward. Weller had found a single gold coin in that area several years earlier and thought he might start there. But with a strong easterly wind blowing, he missed pinpointing the site by about 60 feet. However by the time the vessel was snubbed down to her anchor ropes, they were in the general area of the unworked spot he had in mind. It was northwest of the "Jewelry Flats" and about 200 feet from any previously worked area.

Down went the *Defiance*'s twin mailboxes and began plowing off the site in earnest. The day turned out to be practically a dud with the exception of three silver coins. With that kind of luck, anyone would have thought it was Friday the 13th instead of Sunday the 13th of July. But come the next day the *Defiance* was back in the same northwest sector on her three-point anchorage. Only difference, the crew had changed. Margaret was now working aboard MacAllaster's salvage vessel *Wag*, helping them lift a couple of old anchors that were bothering the detector search there, so Whitey Keevan had accompanied Weller.

Keevan had just come up from his dive about 11 A.M. and Weller suited up to go down. It was one of those seldom-seen near-perfect days with a balmy five-knot breeze from the southeast and the seas calm. Water depth was 18 feet and Whitey reported unusually good visibility on the bottom. At least 20 feet.

Weller went over the side and down, clutching his short-handled detector. The blowers did their thing and Weller searched. Every ten or fifteen minutes, Whitey shifted the dive boat to an adjoining spot two to three feet away, overlapping the blown holes on the bottom. Four to six feet of sand was being moved off the limestone bottom at each site, the blowers removing it slowly enough with the engines at 600 RPM that Weller had ample time to check out anything that might appear.

For some reason he felt unusually good about where they were and what they were doing. No way could he account for it, except that he knew they were now very close to the site where he had found the gold coin. Maybe it was just the fact that conditions were so unusually good. Or because by noon the underwater visibility had improved to a good fifty feet now. Or maybe it was just a treasure hunter's hunch. Whatever it was, Weller was getting good vibes all over the place.

Then about 1 P.M. came the first hint of what looked like serious bad luck—the starboard stern anchor pulled loose. As the *Defiance* swung, Weller's air hose stretched tight. Topside, Keevan struggled to reset the anchor, getting it to finally hold. Meanwhile, the blowers were excavating another hole 30 feet from Weller who suddenly got a hit with his detector and was struggling against the stretched hose to stay where he was long enough to see what had set off his detector.

Digging down through the loose sand, he found the metal target: a .22 rifle slug. Dejected, he pocketed the item and turned to work his way slowly over to the new hole being dug. A short way away and his detector sang out again. Figuring it was another slug, Weller fanned away six or eight inches of sand down to the target.

But there was no leaden gray chunk of metal there this time. His eyes bulged at the sight of gold filigree shaped like an 8-petal bloom linked to a black ebony bead held by gold cups on each side. The more he fanned, the more of it appeared and the wider Weller's eyes became. One end was hooked under a piece of coral and as he carefully freed it he found himself looking at the most beautiful thing he had ever seen in 26 years of treasure hunting. "I had to admit," he said later, "that my heart was beating like a full dress band!" And no wonder, in his hands he held a 6½" by 8" linked filigree cross of gold and ebony. The four ends of the cross were elaborately worked gold filigree medallions. Eight of the gold-cupped ebony beads alternated with the 8-petal gold filigree floral links forming the main upright of the cross of Christ. The medallion at the base of the cross was the most elaborate of all—loops and swirls of gold strands forming an intricate golden triangle. It appeared to be part of a most extraordinarily fine rosary.

By the time Weller realized what an incredible find he had made, he was breathing doubletime with excitement. Swiftly he swung the detector around the site to see if there might be more. Finding nothing, he made sure he had a good fix on the location, and surfaced.

When Whitey Keevan saw what he came up clutching, his eyes popped open as wide as Wellers.

Bob spit out his regulator and sputtered, "Good, Lord, Whitey, you won't believe this!"

Keevan was too stunned to speak. All he could do was reach down as Weller handed it to him and said, "There's got to be more of it down there." Then he jammed the regulator back in his jaws and down he went.

Back at the spot where he had found it, he began a slow systematic search around the site, expanding his circle searches ever wider until suddenly he got a hit.

Excitedly he fanned his way down through the sand. His spirits fell when he saw he was uncovering a corroded chunk of metal attached to a piece of ship's rigging called a dead-eye. A few feet away he had another false alarm—a second smaller dead-eye. By then he had worked his way back to the new hole the blower had dug, so he came up.

Whitey was beside himself exclaiming over the ornate detail of the medallions. Looking more closely at it now, Weller too was amazed at its detail.

Keevan suited up and went down while Weller radioed the *Wag* which was already heading homeward, to suggest that it might be worth their while to come back and see them.

When they did, MacAllaster shook their hands and said, "That's really something." Everyone was incredulous.

They left clutching the prize in a plastic bag of water. After they were gone, Weller put the *Defiance* in a box search, excavating a square trench down to bedrock. Before long, Keevan surfaced, and right away from the broad grin Weller saw stretched across his face, he knew.

He HAD it! Whitey had found the rest of the rosary, an incredibly beautiful 60-inch long necklace of paired gold-cupped black ebony beads alternating with the eight-petaled filigree links. Closer examination revealed that even the tiny bead cups were shaped like flower petals. The divers spread it all out on a beach towel over the engine cover, then whooped, pounded each other wildly on their backs, and danced an Irish jig or two. Hearing the racket from where they were working 900 feet away on another salvage boat, John Halas and Carl Ward were sure the two had lost their marbles. Weller tried to radio the *Wag* but it had already turned into the marina 45 minutes away and had shut off its radio.

That night, the entire group's jubilation over them finding the complete rosary was borderline ecstatic. The whooping and the dancing and the back-slapping went on long into the night. "It was," as "Frogfoot" Bob Weller said, "a moment that will live forever."

And understandably so. The ornate rosary rivals the dragon whistle necklace that Kip Wagner's Real Eight Company recovered from the 1715 wrecks. It is such a unique work of exquisite art, one hopes that eventually it will not disappear into someone's private collection, but will somehow be part of a collection that will be viewed widely by the public. After all, the public is supposedly the real owner of all such underwater treasures within state or federal jurisdiction.

But only time will tell what will happen to this unusual artifact. When a one-of-a-kind priceless piece such as this is offered for sale, unfortunately the asking price is so prohibitive public museums are seldom the ones standing in line eager to purchase it. Hopefully, however, this magnificent piece will not be lost to the public forever.

After Mel Fisher found the fabulous treasure of *Nuestra Senora de Atocha* under 54 feet of water in Hawk's Channel near the Marquesas Keys west of Key West, intense archaeological work was done by Duncan Mathewson overseeing its recovery. Following the division of treasure with company share-holders, Fisher dissolved Treasure Salvor's Company and moved his family back to the east coast, first near Fort Pierce, later to Sebastian where he renewed his interest in the 1715 wrecks. The family opened a treasure museum at Sebastian and Fisher's daughter, Taffi, looks after it. There is also a conservation laboratory associated with it for processing artifacts recovered by Fisher's current company, Salvors Inc., which has five salvage boats working the 1715 sites. In 1993 Fisher awarded subleases to 47 different companies wanting to work the Treasure Coast. Most of the subcontractors work on the basis of a 50/50 split after its 20% division (formerly 25%) with the State of Florida. Subcontractors wanting exclusive salvage rights to a site, pay Fisher more for it. "There are more people looking than ever before," said James Miller, Director of Florida's Bureau of Archaeological Research in Tallahassee. Miller said the number of subcontractors Fisher makes arrangements with is not something the state has any control over. The important thing is that they live up to the terms of the state's lease with Fisher, including keeping accurate records of where each artifact is found.

Meanwhile, Mo Molinar, one of Fisher's oldest friends and early original Treasure Salvor's member to come east with him, formed his own treasure hunting company. In 1987, with Fisher's old reliable 50-foot salvage boat *Virgilona* which Mo had received as part of his treasure cut, he and his crew subcontracted to work part of the Gold Wreck site with all the other subcontractors working indirectly for Fisher.

The magic wasn't immediate, but things soon began to click for this new group, especially after it was joined by another old-time veteran of the mid-sixties Gold Rush, John deBry.

Molinar's boat and that of salvor Harold Holden were working between the reefs toward shore on the Gold Wreck site when Mo's diver hit a pocket of gold that produced about fifty gold coins of different denominations. The find caused an instant commotion since it was more gold coins than the site had given up at one time in several years. Then, 300 feet away, Holden's boat struck gold, a large ornate oval-shaped gold locket the size of a hen's egg. The domed glass front had protected either a delicate painting or a religious relic inside. Attached to the locket was a delicate 22-karat gold filigree chain twelve feet long ! It was Holden's finest find ever!

Next it was Mo's turn. It looked as though he had tapped into the mint. By day's end his divers had brought up 219 gold coins, worth at the time about $500,000. Not bad for a day's work.

That winter Molinar and deBry formed their own joint salvage operation, the Historical Research and Development Company. What it researched and developed quite quickly was the finding and extracting of more gold coins. But it was John Brandon's boat, *Endeavor* that started the ball rolling as Mo's, Brandon's and Holden's boats all worked the "Bank of Spain" trench at the Gold Wreck, hoping soon to make big withdrawals. John's first came up as a pile of 332 gold 8-escudos coins valued then at about $4,000 apiece. A $128,000 find!

The crews of the other boats all converged on the *Endeavor* to ogle the sight, basking in its golden glow, then it was back to their boats and to work again, hammering at that stubborn Bank on the bottom with their blowers going full bore.

Then it was the *Virgilona*'s turn. Mo's divers got a flipper in the door and began bringing up fistfuls of gold coins. They went up and down so many times to this underwater treasure vault they began to feel they were riding an elevator. In no time the bottom of their drink cooler was layered in gold coins. By day's end their "withdrawal" amounted to a gold snuff box, a gold Maltese Cross with eleven diamonds, and 455 gold coins.

In the next few weeks another 100 gold coins were taken out of the trench before the Bank finally closed.

Brandon's bunch had picked up 34 gold coins from his area and several days later after he moved his boat 1,500 feet to the north and went to work, up came items probably belonging to a passenger. They included a pair of gold thimbles, several 8-escudos gold coins, and two exquisitely braided gold chains bearing small scimitar-shaped toothpicks on each end. Atop each scimitar was a cherub with a bow and arrow.

Days passed, then the Bank opened once more for the salvors. Mo's boat was working near the Junkyard area when the divers uncovered another small Mother Lode. This time it was 122 gold 8-escudos coins, 78 of them dated 1708 and minted in Lima. Quite a rarity. By season's end, Mo's total take amounted to 821 gold coins. Headlines trumpeted "Florida's New Gold Rush."

After that year the gold and silver kept coming in but in smaller dabs and dribbles. Salvors Bill Elam and Carl Lazzeri blew open a hole 100 feet off shore working from their nineteen foot boat *in eight feet of water*, and in one sand pocket they found 33 gold 2-escudos coins from the Bogota mint. Nearby they recovered a three-inch silver disk and 2,000 silver coins.

In 1991, Kane Fisher, Mel's son, moved his salvage boat *Dauntless* to the east coast sites. While recovering tons of conglomerate cannonballs for his father's museum at Sebastian, Kane found an oddity on one of the sites—a conglomerate with strange square holes in it. Closer examination revealed them to be where iron nails had disintegrated, leaving only their shapes. Kane brought the clump aboard as a curiosity but once out of water he saw the edges of gold coins protruding from the mass. X-rays revealed it contained 22 gold 2-escudos coins, each about the size of a nickel. This find made him look again at some of the other debris conglomerates, from which he recovered another 43 gold coins.

These were all great, extremely valuable finds, but bigger and better surprises were just around the corner. The mega finds came in July 1993. Maybe because of sudden calms, July is often a magic month for treasure salvors. This time, Mike Mayer, a diver working for Mel Fisher's Salvors Inc. Company, while looking for 1715 treasure, found 1618 treasure. Sites sometimes overlap, especially at Corrigan's where the supposedly 1715 Green Cabin Wreck north of Corrigan's turned out to be the *San Martin* that sank there in 1618. What Mayer found was the *San Martin's* astrolabe, a circular-shaped navigational instrument of brass or bronze that preceded the sextant. By sighting a known star with the instrument's moveable arm, it pointed to the degrees of latitude scribed on the astrolabe's circular frame.

All navigation in those days was haphazard. Since nobody had yet discovered how to find a ship's longitude position, they had to be satisfied to figure out only it's latitude position. With the astrolabe you could determine where a ship was north or south of the equator, but where it was to the east or to the west on that latitude was anyone's guess. Which is one reason why there were so many shipwrecks.

Today these instruments are valuable because of their rarity. An astrolabe dated 1614 or 1616 with mint mark from the *Atocha* sold for $132,000, and it was broken into six pieces. The one Salvors Inc. found eventually went to the State of Florida in September 1994 as part of the state's portion of the 1993 division with the treasure hunters. It is especially unique because it bears the date "1593" and is believed to be the sixth oldest astrolabe ever found.

That same July, a lightning stroke of fate moved the Wellers and their good ship *Pandion* to investigate the Cabin Wreck near Sebastian Inlet where it all began. There, in a particularly hazardous area between the first and second reef, in only eight feet of water, the Bank of Spain once again graciously threw open its doors and let these intrepid divers sample some of the goodies in its jewelry vault.

Their day's take was spectacular: 18 gold rings; a silver fork, a candelabra, an ornate silver buckle, several silver coins, two 2-inch gold toothpicks, one dragon-shaped with a scimitar for a tail and an earscoop for a tongue; a small gold brooch with 17 diamonds; a pair of three-piece drop earrings, each decorated with 53 diamonds; a 3.5 inch by 2.5 inch gold butterfly whose ornate wings glittered with 161 diamonds; and last but not least, a 3.5 inch wide 22-carat brooch stubbed with 170 diamonds. Bob Weller said the 401 diamonds alone have an estimated value in excess of $1.5 million; along with the other treasure items the find should be worth at least $3 million.

You can imagine how many Irish jigs the *Pandion*'s crew danced *that* night!

Somewhere out in the blue, I know Art McKee, Kip Wagner, and a few hundred other interested souls were watching and smiling.

Meanwhile, the hunt goes on.....

Appendix A

ORDER FROM THE KING
Initiating The *Flota* Portion
Of The 1715 Fleet

"Proyecto of the Crown to the Council of the Indies: 3 March 1712." Printed 28 June 1712, Madrid. Nine pages, translated.

Since the continued navigation to the Indies is the main and most important essential for the good of the Monarchy, its vassals and its commerce, which produces not only the major source of financial help in times of urgency, but the opulent trade of its vassals, who share in its so widespread fruits; and since there follows from the greater security and improvement of the dominions of the Indies and the avoidance of illegal commerce in them . . . His Majesty wishes and orders that, this present year of 1712, there be made ready and sail for the Kingdom of New Spain a flotilla consisting of eight vessels, among which shall be numbered a *Capitana,* an *Almiranta,* first and second *pataches,* and the four listed merchant ships, in the following form:

I. That, for *Capitana* and *Almiranta* of the said fleet, it remains for His Majesty to stipulate the form of those two vessels and their contract, as well as for the persons who must go under orders in them. His Majesty must decide on these points with the greatest dispatch so that these matters might be publicly known.

II. That, with regard to the first *patache,* His Majesty will also advise about it; as to the second *patache,* the Tribunal of the *Casa de Contratación*, using their privilege, may name it and make their selection known. Its owner, however, must be a Spaniard. The choice of a particular vessel to fill this place must, moreover, be made known within thirty days after the publication of this order. It may be up to 200 or even 250 tons capacity. After having given notice of its selection, the Tribunal must furnish precise information about the vessel to the Council of the Indies, which will then inform His Majesty. If the thirty-day term passes without the Tribunal having made any announcement, His Majesty may make the choice, with all the promptness needed to insure the fleet's departure on time. If it appears to the Council that it is His Majesty's will that the first *patache* should not exceed the second in size, the data shall be present for His Majesty's study, when he shall choose to name the vessel.

III. That, for the four merchant ships, which as might be supposed are included in the total of eight vessels, they are hereinafter named by His Majesty. The first shall be that vessel of the 300 tons lading license—a privilege enjoyed by special grant by the Seminary of the City of Seville. This choice must be made within thirty days, under the same above-mentioned requirements for the second *patache* to be chosen by the Tribunal.

The second, named *Nuestra Señora de Regla, San Francisco Xavier y San Joseph,* has as owner D. Pedro Bernardo Peralta y Córdoba and is now found opposite the *Barranco* of the Cádiz interest, having failed to find a place in the last fleet which sailed for New Spain.

The third, named *Nuestra Señora del Rosario, San Francisco Xavier y las Animas,* has as its owner D. Francisco de Chaves Espinosa de los Monteros, and is found at the same place for the same reason.

For the fourth vessel, it shall be that for which His Majesty lately granted concession in the Council *consulta* of 22 December 1711 to

D. Juan de Castro y Aldao. His vessel shall not exceed 400 tons, notwithstanding the fact that His Majesty had previously conceded him the right in the *consulta* of a ship of up to 600 tons. It is now seen that the ship in the said fleet should be of the more moderate size, in order to facilitate its more rapid departure and quick return. It is thus ordered that this ship must expressly make its appearance in the Bay of Cádiz within thirty days of the publication of this order in Seville. If it does not, then the grant shall be rendered null and void for this occasion, although it may be used at a future date. In that event, the billet for this vessel shall remain, in order that the two-thirds lading privilege pertaining to Seville might be fulfilled; the merchants of Seville shall make their ship selection known within eight days following the thirty days. Failing this, then neither party shall any longer possess the right; then His Majesty will choose.

The reason His Majesty has not listed ships corresponding to the two-thirds lading permission of Seville on this occasion is due to the fact that the University of Navigators had advised that they had no ship opposite their Tribunal. For that reason, the grant which pertains to them does not apply. In order that this right should be credited to them for future fleets, it should be well understood that with regard to the billet-space of the wine growers of that city, it should be verified in accordance with their rule and practice. With regard, then, to the 300 tons of the Seminary, they can load in that ship as well as in that of D. Castro y Aldao and in the first and second *pataches* the fruits of the growers in accordance with the rules which ordinarily apply. This leaves for the growers of Cádiz the two ships of Don Pedro de Córdoba and D. Francisco de Chaves, which pertain to that Tribunal.

IV. That, if His Majesty be advised that a ship named *Santo Cristo de San Román,* owner: D. Juan Antonio de Equilaz, which served as *Almiranta* in the fleet under the command of D. Diego de Santillán, His Majesty wishes this vessel to go as *Capitana* or *Almiranta* of this fleet. If the matter is negotiated, and the said D. Juan agrees with His Majesty under the rules and in the form with which a commander whom he wished to go could be named, for this purpose agreement might be reached, in virtue of the power he has before His Majesty to treat of it. If he fails, or excuses himself from performance, His Majesty will have to avail himself of the ship for that purpose under the rules and in the form always practiced for this purpose in similar cases.

If this should happen, His Majesty will then name the person who will go as commander, under the form and circumstances which His Majesty will then declare. His Majesty orders the Council to bring to the Royal notice that which results from the summons made to the said Don Juan Antonio de Equilaz.

V. That the said fleet must go out to sail from the Bay of Cádiz by the last day of July of this year, without any delay. To this end, His Majesty declares that any of the four merchant ships or the two *pataches* which are not promptly ready to receive cargo from the tenth to the fifteenth of June will be excluded from the voyage. For this purpose, His Majesty orders that legal notice of this be given to the shipowners, so that none might plead ignorance of it, and so that it might be known that the fleet will sail without fail on the appointed day with those ships which are ready.

VI. That the body of merchants ought to, and can, carry for trade in the said ships, and in those to be named as *Capitana* and *Almiranta*, all the goods and products which they wish. Before departure they shall pay the same fees and duties fixed and paid in the ships which sailed for New Spain under the command of D. Andrés de Arriola. This shall be done under the same rules, formalities and provisions contained in the *proyecto* agreed upon and fixed for that outfitting, without any departures whatsoever from the *proyecto,* which must be scrupulously observed.

VII. That the same rules and fixed duties may be observed on the return to Spain, without any difference whatsoever, and with equal force with regard to entry and departure from the Indies and to any penalties applicable, whether to this part or to the preceding sixth section.

VIII. That His Majesty will name ministers in Cádiz and Seville to collect the duties of departure and return. The sending of customs-house permits, the readying of ships, and the registers shall be in their charge—all this in conformity with that which was expressed in the last fleet's *proyecto.* The council shall send to each the same instructions, together with copies of the *proyectos* cited, so that they might understand what took place in the dispatch of the last fleet under D. Andrés de Arriola.

IX. That, with regard to the freight rates which merchants must pay to ship-owners for goods, effects and products loaded for the outward, or homeward, journey—these shall be precisely the same prices which were fixed in the *proyecto* of D. Andrés de Arriola's fleet. Thus, questions and embarrassments among merchants and ship-owners can be avoided.

X. His Majesty declares that, in the two ships serving as *Capitana* and *Almiranta*, there shall be loaded on the account of the Royal Exchequer 2,000 *quintales* of mercury, a publication of bulls,* and two years' supply of stamped paper for New Spain. All of this shall be divided so that half of it shall go in each ship. These things shall be taken to Vera Cruz to be delivered to the persons or Ministers destined to receive them. To this end, all of the customary obligations shall be made.

XI. Also, that the first and second *pataches* shall carry for the account of the Royal Exchequer and without cost to it, one thousand *quintales* of mercury—500 in each, and under the same regulations found in the tenth section above.

XII. That the said merchant ships and *pataches* shall pay the Seminary its usual alms-payment, as in other voyages, without altering it, or providing less than in the past.

XIII. That, if the *Capitana* of the Windward Fleet, which has most lately been under the command of D. Andrés de Arriola, arrives in Spain before the date fixed for the departure of this fleet—it is His Majesty's will that this ship with all its equipment and the major and minor officials which sail in her shall be placed in careenage. She shall then be readied, supplied and armed for the account of the Royal Exchequer in the form and under the rules which His Majesty shall prescribe. Then she shall sail back with the two ships named in this fleet. They shall sail under her command and flag as *Capitana*. If His Majesty has already chosen the ships to serve as *Capitana* and *Almiranta*, then the one selected as *Capitana* shall become *Almiranta*, and that chosen *Almiranta* shall become reserve *Almiranta*. This shall be done in such order that there shall follow no prejudice to those already chosen, nor to the *Capitana* of the Windward Fleet during its stay here. Thus will be avoided the

---

* Official documents issued by the Pope.

great expense and harm which would result to the Royal Exchequer, and also the gap which this vessel would leave if it were long missing from the Windward Fleet. It is also the Royal will of His Majesty that, if the said *Capitana* comes in time to return to the Indies with the fleet as its *Capitana,* His Majesty declares that it must carry for the Royal account 3,000 *quintales* of mercury and the duplicate of the publication of bulls which the other two ships must carry, and also the supplies of rigging, fittings, canvas and iron and other things needed for the ships of the Windward Fleet. It shall also carry other items which His Majesty must resolve should be made in those Kingdoms. And if it should appear that this should exceed the load advisable for the said *Capitana* of *Barlovento,* His Majesty will order that it be loaded with those things with which it should be concerned.

XIV. That if His Majesty should resolve that the said *Capitana* of the Windward Fleet shall not return to Spain with the said fleet, the ship which had been serving as *Almiranta* shall again become *Capitana;* the reserve *Almiranta* shall become *Almiranta,* etc.

XV. With regard to the return of the said fleet, it shall remain for His Majesty to send confidential orders when needed and also to advise the riches which they are to bring for the Royal Exchequer, and how much shall be carried in each vessel. The Council shall issue whatever orders might seem appropriate with regard to their fees and other fiscal measures.

XVI. That it is also left to His Majesty to name those persons who shall go as *disputados* [commercial representatives] of the said fleet, under the same regulations and in the same form in which His Majesty named them for the last fleet of D. Andrés de Arriola.

XVII. That, for the execution of and obedience to all that which has been expressed here, His Majesty orders that the Council send copies of these orders to the *Casa de Contratación,* the *Consulado* of Seville, and the same in Cádiz, Puerto de Santa Maria and San Lucar and to the second who shall make it known in the *Junta General de Comercio.* Thus knowing these exact orders, the members of these bodies shall be enabled to make their plans for employment and shiploading of their goods and fruits.

XVIII. And that also the Tribunal is ordered to notify the owners of the ships named in these orders that they should soon be in

Cádiz. Thus within eight days of the receipt of this order they might put their ships into careenage. The owners of other ships yet to be chosen should be advised to do the same. The Tribunal should advise the Council by each mail of the exact status of preparations and the Council shall inform His Majesty. Now His Majesty orders that for no reason nor for any case whatsoever shall any request for admittance to the fleet be considered; His Majesty declares that he shall not augment it, because this best suits His Royal service and the most prompt success of this most important affair. It would only be possible for other ships to go if they go in company with others or if they take registry for ports other than Vera Cruz and do not enter it surreptitiously. Madrid, 3 March 1712. Don Joseph de Grimaldo.

(This is a copy of the original *proyecto* which His Majesty remitted to the Council of the Indies for their obedience and execution. Madrid, 28 March 1712.)
I.G. 2647

Appendix B

FLEET OF GENERAL JUAN DE UBILLA
OUTBOUND FROM CÁDIZ, SPAIN
SEPTEMBER 16, 1712

THE FLOTA

(Some of these ships apparently did not sail with the *Flota*.)

TITLE/POSITION	SHIP NAME	TONNAGE	GUNS/GEAR	OWNER/CAPT.	CARGO	MASTER
Capitana	Nuestra Señora de la Regla, San Dimas y San Francisco San Xavier	471	50	Gen. Ubilla; Capt. D. Luis de Villalobos	Ironwork; varied cargo; 1,000 quintales mercury; bulls & stamp paper	D. Antonio Porflits
Almiranta	Santo Cristo de San Román y Nuestra Señora del Rosario y San Joseph	450	54	D. Juan de Eguilaz	Same as above except 1,000 quint. mercury in 667 containers	D. Bartholomé de Aldadea
First patache	Nuestra Señora de las Nieves	194³/₄	..	D. Francisco de Soto Sanchez	Wine, oil, brandy, 501 quint. mercury in 332 containers	D. Estevan Pieter y Omazur
Second patache	Santo Cristo del Valle y Nuestra Señora de la Concepción	157	..	Capt. Joseph Vaez y Llarena; Capt. Andrés de Conique	Wine, oil, brandy and cloth; 449.5 quint. of mercury	D. Francisco de Paula Moreno

TITLE/POSITION	SHIP NAME	TONNAGE	GUNS/GEAR	OWNER/CAPT.	CARGO	MASTER
Reinforcement	San Juan Evangelista	384	40 "Four anchors and two anchors"	½—D. Rafael de Elira; ½—Dona Josefa de Yriarte	998 quint. of mercury	D. Juan Garcia de la Quadra
First merchant	Nuestra Señora de Regla, San Francisco Xavier y las Animas	. . . .	. .	D. Juan de Castro y Aldao	Wine, oil	D. Antonio Carcas
Second merchant	Nuestra Señora de Regla, San Francisco Xavier y San Joseph	248	. .	D. Pedro Bernardo Peralta y Córdoba	. . . . .	D. Antonio Carca y Peñarrieta
Third merchant	Nuestra Señora del Rosario, San Francisco Xavier y las Animas	151	. .	D. Francisco de Chaves Espinosa de los Monteros	Books, wine, cloth, small cargo	D. Francisco Mauricio del Pozo
Fourth merchant	Santissima Trinidad y Nuestra Señora de la Concepción	. . . .	. .	D. Miguel de Lima	Books, wine, oil, cloth, brandy	D. Juan Antonio LaBiosa

(NOTE: At this time, some changes were beginning to be made in Spanish names; it could be Cristo or Christo; Joseph or José or even Josef.)

Appendix C

THE FLEETS' MANIFESTS IN THE NEW WORLD

CT 2400
Galeones

Loaded at Cartagena, July and August 1714. Ladings certified before the Governor and Royal Officials.

1. CAPITANA (partial lading)
47 leather bags of cacao, equal to 310 *arrobas,* 16 lb.
300 *quintales* of brazilwood
4,695 pesos 6 *reales,* in three gold bars and in doubloons
3,002 pesos 2 *reales,* in two gold bars
1,530 pesos 1¹/₂ *reales,* in one gold bar
2,139 pesos 5 *reales,* in one gold bar and doubloons
18 marks 5¹/₂ oz. of silver
175 pesos 8 *reales* in *plata doble*
5,283 pesos 1¹/₂ *reales* in four bars and doubloons
2,000 pesos: 1,000 in doubloons and 1,000 in *plata doble*

400 pesos in doubloons
1,150 pesos in doubloons
100 pesos in doubloons
210 pesos in doubloons
A gold chain with 50 pesos and 4 *tomines; ley* 20 carats @ 20 *reales,*
worth 126 pesos, 2 *reales.*
Another gold chain with 85 pesos and 1 *tomin; ley* 21¹/₂ carats
[21¹/₂ *reales,* worth 228 pesos, 6 *reales*].
A small gold chain of 10 *castellanos* weight, 3 *tomines* [@17 *reales,*
equals 26 pesos, 6 *reales*].
2. Nao Nuestra Señora de la Concepción—Master, Don Diego
Pablo Soliac. Her register is set up in Cartagena from 17 July 1714 to
20 August 1714.
740 half-hides, in pelt
105 *quintales* of brazilwood
100 *quintales* of brazilwood
8 leather sacks of cacao
2 leather sacks of cacao
1 chest of vanilla
30 *quintales* of brazilwood
700 tanned hides
80 *quintales* of brazilwood
3 leather sacks of cacao
4,714 pesos 3 *reales;* 1 gold bar and doubloons
3,000 pesos in doubloons
25 bales of paper of 32 reams each
6 chests of nails
3 boxes of locks
1 bale of dry goods
She is to be further loaded in Havana with other goods.
3. Fregata—navio Nuestra Señora del Rosario (Almiranta)—
Master, Don Manuel Albarez. Lading at Cartagena, 20 July 1714.
50 *quintales* of brazilwood
20 leather sacks of cacao
1 *cajon* [chest]
650 half-hides; 325 whole ones
4 chests of chocolate
8 leather sacks of cacao
1 chest of gifts
2 chests of shells of Carey

2 little chests and 1 small jar for the Fiscal of the Council of the Indies
4,695 pesos 6 *reales* in 4 gold bars; the rest in doubloons
3,546 pesos 6 *reales* in 2 gold bars; the rest in doubloons
175 pesos in *plata doble*
5,283 pesos 1¹/₂ *reales*; 4 gold bars and doubloons
2,000 pesos in doubloons
75 half-pieces of *crudos* [probably untanned leathers]
3 chests of dry goods
6 barrels of copperas.

The manifest also mentions the "fregata francesa, *El Cierbo*," which was taken on the Porto Bello coast: "this frigate, the said other sloop and frigate, the *Fregata San Miguel*, taken on the coast." Later, this vessel was loaded with 192 *quintales* of brazil-wood.

Mexico 486B
Flota

Loaded at Vera Cruz, 4 May 1715. The officials of the Royal *Hacienda* of this city of the New Vera Cruz and the port of San Juan de Ulúa for His Majesty: Treasurer Francisco San Juan de Santacruz of the Tribunal of the *Contaduria,* member of the Royal *Consejo de Hacienda Contador;* Don Juan de Echagaray, *Factor Veedor;* Don Lorenzo de la Torre, *Caballero* of the Order of Calatrava—both named as Gentlemen by His Majesty—and the official Royal supernumerary, *Pagador* Don Juan Manuel de Santellises:

We certify that in the *Capitana, Almiranta, resfuerzo* and *patache* which comprise the fleet under the command of General Juan Esteban de Ubilla (which is ready to sail on the return voyage to the Kingdoms of Castile) there are loaded, registered and declared, for the account of His Majesty and of the different interested parties and individuals, the quantities of pesos, cochineal, indigo and other items which we will itemize as follows:

FOR THE ACCOUNT OF HIS MAJESTY

The following are divided equally between the *Almiranta* and the *Capitana:*

For the King in *reales* and bars	209,279 pesos 6 *reales* 1 gr.
For the Chamber of the Queen our Lady, in doubloons and *reales*	80,000 pesos
For Salaries of the Council of the Indies	160,248 pesos 6 *reales* 11 gr.
For the Treasury of the Council, benefices	8,800 pesos
For the Secretary of the Council, fines	63 pesos
President of Guadalajara, *reales*	4,279 pesos 3 *reales*
Product of Bulls of the Crusade; *reales* and bars	124,279 pesos 1 *real* 6 gr.
Alms for the Blessed Souls of the *Monte de Piedad*	671 pesos 6 *reales* 6 gr.
Alms for the hospitals of Cádiz and the Royal Hospital in Galicia	8,000 pesos
For the Duke of Tubenasso	5,000 pesos
Of product of Royal mercury, remitted by D. Juan Joseph de Beitia; *reales* and bars	518,469 pesos 3 *reales* 11 gr.
Product of the sales and composition of lands and waters, sent by D. Francisco de Balensuela	24,000 pesos
For the Convent of the *Merced Calcaza* of Madrid, sent by the same	15,831 pesos 4 *reales*
For Vacancies of Bishoprics	6,319 pesos 4 *reales*
For Quarter-vacancies of same	7,232 pesos 4 *reales* 2 gr.
Donation of the ecclesiastical *Cabildo* of la Puebla	2,000 pesos
Donation of *Haciendas*	350 pesos
Donation of the Sr. Archbishop of Mexico	4,000 pesos
For the Royal Treasury of Havana	44,000 pesos
(total)	1,222,824 pesos 3 tomines 5 grains

APPENDIX C

For the Accounts of Private Individuals

Capitana

In coins and bars in 8,086 small chests and sacks 2,559,917 pesos
730 leather bags of fine cochineal
241 leather bags and chests of indigo
23 chests of worked silver
62 chests of gifts
17 chests of vanillas [vanilla beans]
6 chests of chocolate
70 sheets of copper
730 tanned leathers
4 chests of Chinese porcelain
100 *quintales* of brazilwood
9 chests of earthenware vessels
1 small chest of dust [powder?] of Oaxaca
14 earthen jugs of balsam
1 small chest with small gold bars, doubloons and pearls

Almiranta

In silver and bars, in 684 small chests and sacks 2,076,004 pesos
728 leather bags of cochineal
1,702 leather bags and chests of indigo
139 sheets of copper
682 tanned leathers
26 chests of earthenware vessels
48 chests of vanillas
85 chests of gifts
8 earthen jugs of balsam and liquid amber
2 chests with writing desks
40 chests of chocolate and dust of Oaxaca
2 chests of bath oil
30 leather sacks of wild cochineal
12 chests of annatto [a red dyestuff]
53 chests of worked silver
14 chests of Chinese porcelain
80 bales of *lurga* of Talapa
3 folding-screens [?]—*biobos* [sic]
9 leather sacks of cacao

500 *quintales* of brazilwood
31 bales of sarsaparilla

resfuerzo

Coined money (silver) in 81 small chests and loose leather
bags 252,171 pesos
13 chests of worked silver
280 leather sacks of fine cochineal
595 leather sacks of indigo
3,320 tanned leathers
21 barrels and earthen jugs of liquid amber
257 half-hides with hair [pelts]
6 earthen jugs of balsam
198 bales of cathartic
75 chests of earthenware vessels
30 chests of chocolate
19 bales of cacao
22 chests of vanillas
500 *quintales* of brazilwood
11 bales of powdered hellebore root
136 chests of gifts
77 leather sacks and chests of wild cochineal
300 hides with hair [pelts]
3 *biobos* [sic] probably *biombos* [folding screens]
32 chests of Chinese porcelain
65¹/₂ *quintales* of *sarsa* [sarsaparilla?]
2 bales of quinine
1 chest of sugar
2 sheets of copper
4 chests with writing desks
16 chests of copal [a brittle resin]
13 chests of annatto
7 *quintales* of sassafras

patache

In 12 chests and loose sacks 44,000 pesos
63 leather bags of fine cochineal
169 leather bags and chests of indigo
870 tanned hides
8 *alfardas* [wood beams?]

200 *quintales* of brazilwood
9 barrels of liquid amber
25 leather sacks of wild cochineal
58 boxes [chests] of gifts
81 bales of cathartic
18 chests of chocolate
57 *dichos* of earthenware vessels
3 bales of powdered hellebore root
4 trunks
1 bale of quinine
7 chests of Chinese porcelain
8 bales of roots of Michoacán
7 chests of vanillas
11 bales of cacao
12 earthen jugs of oil of *betto*
1 chest of annatto
16 earthen jugs of copal

Inasmuch as the coined and bar silver, the doubloons and gems
and other types of merchandise whose details are itemized above
are those which have been loaded, registered and declared in the
said *Capitana, Almiranta, resfuerzo* and *patache* (for the account of
His Majesty and of private persons) in accord with the details
expressed in the *registros* and in order to advise His Majesty, we
sign this instrument by virtue of the letter of order of the most
Excellent Señor the Duke of Linares, Viceroy of New Spain,
Governor and Captain-General also, under the date of 4 May 1715;
for duplicate we now give this to you by virtue of the order of the
Most Excellent Señor Marquis de Valer, Viceroy, Governor and
Captain-General of this Kingdom. 4 June 1716.

(There follows a summary of all cargoes in total, by type. The
merchandise is not listed again; there is shown below the totals of
bullion, coin, etc., in the four ships.)

The shipments of:
Real Hacienda*   1,222,824 pesos 3 tomines 5 grains
Private Persons   4,932,092 pesos

Total   6,154,916 pesos 3 tomines 5 grains

* The Royal Estate, *i.e.,* The King's share.

Appendix D

DETAILS AND ANALYSIS OF THE RECOVERED TREASURE

Specifically, the treasure included 6 circular-shaped silver ingots, the largest weighing 27 pounds, and 6 similar disks of gold, weighing from 1 pound 15 ounces to 8 pounds 5 ounces; a silver bar weighing 35 pounds 8½ ounces; 11 free-form flat "puddles" of silver weighing together 5 pounds 4 ounces; 16 whole gold rings and the two halves of another; 8 pieces of gold chain bearing an intricate floral design, the longest length 2.04 meters; 3 buckles, two of silver and another of gold; 5 fragmentary silver forks and parts of several silver spoons and knife handles; 2 silver plates; a pair of ornate silver candlestick tops with threaded stems, as if they had been disassembled from their missing bases; several unidentified bullet-shaped objects; 200 pounds of silver coins and slightly more than 3,700 gold coins.

The prevalent form for the bulk precious metals was a circular-shaped ingot with a rounded bottom, evidently formed either by allowing the molten metal to cool in a crucible with a generally rounded bottom or by pouring the metal into a similarly shaped mold. The rough, porous bottoms of most of the ingots indicated that the mold may have been of stone. Markings were found on the top surfaces of the largest of the silver disks. The largest gold disks were stamped with Roman numerals, sometimes followed by from one to three small circles. For example, the gold disk weighing 8 pounds 5 ounces was stamped "XIII" followed by two circles arranged one above the other. Another, weighing 7 pounds 3 ounces, was marked "X" while a third, also weighing 7 pounds 3 ounces, was marked "XI" followed by three circles as well as a ragged assayer's bite where a sample had evidently been clipped from the ingot at the mint by the king's assayer to test the amount of gold in the piece. The smallest gold disk was stamped five times with three stamps. First was a large octagonal stamp near the center of the disk. Inside and slightly below the center of this stamp was a large "S" surmounted by a crown. To the left of the "S" was a small "m," above and below which were round unidentifiable figures, possibly rosettes. To the right was a small letter "o" with the same round figures above and below. These central symbols were enclosed in a border of two ridges, one inside the other, separated by a series of dots. A second stamp across the disk contained the Roman numerals "XXII," below a small crown. The disk was struck twice with this stamp, above and below the large central stamp just described. The third stamp, used both to the right and to the left, was a shield containing a crown above and an almost indiscernible figure below.

The crowns suggest that all of these are probably royal stamps. The "m" and "o" characters identify the piece as originating in, or having passed through, the Mexico City mint. F. Xavier Calico of Barcelona, president of the International Association of Professional Numismatists and an authority on Spanish colonial coins, believes that the large "S" in the center stamp may indicate that the piece dates from around 1700, when Jose Sarmiento was Viceroy of New Spain. Another authority reports that crown seals were used on ingots which had not yet passed through the royal foundry and upon which royal dues were still owed. The Roman numeral stamp "XXII" is believed to indicate the gold content of the disk in carats.

Spectographic analysis indicated that the disks were an approximately half-gold, half-silver alloy. Since all of them received at least one assayer's bite, or *bocado,* the markings may show the purity of the gold in *quilates* or carats, with the small circles representing grains (four per carat). Considering the relatively low gold content of the disk, Clausen felt that the markings represented a stage in the refining of the metal.

The largest disk was marked "1659" or "1699," "01230," and "MI" in three rows on its pitted upper surface. The disk appeared to be gold, but analysis showed over 90 percent silver. The other, smaller disks were unmarked.

The silver bar weighing 35 pounds 8¹/₂ ounces was stamped on the top surface in the upper left-hand quarter with the letters "UUCCCLVCEVALLUS" beside a larger "XC." Another unclear mark appeared below the stamp and there seemed to be no assayer's bite.

Most of the sixteen gold rings found on the site were very small, with simple geometric designs. Four were notable exceptions, however. The most elaborate of these contained a design around the outside of the ring, showing in sequence a cannon, a stack of cannon balls, a powder keg, a pike, a sword, a helmet and sword, a knight's plumed helmet with visor, a bugle, a drum and another cannon. Another ring was fashioned as a pair of hands holding a heart between the finger tips. Two others bore a crudely engraved floral design on a series of round facets, with six sharply pointed pyramids surrounding each ring like short spikes.

On the expanded handles of three of the five fragmentary forks found were three stamps: closest to the tines was the word "Gosalez" or "Gozalez" in a rectangle with the last three letters arranged below the first four. The middle stamp showed the Pillars of Hercules surmounted by a crown. Just below the crown and between the Pillars was an unidentified figure which seemed to be a knight's plumed helmet in outline. Below and between the base of the pillars was a large letter "M." The stamp nearest the end of the handle was all but indiscernible.

The first stamp probably gave the family name of the manufacturers, or less likely, of an owner. The second stamp with crown and pillars when used on manufactured articles may have indicated that the piece was registered and assayed, but had not yet passed through the royal foundry, and that royal dues were still owed. The "M" was the symbol of the Mexico mint. The stamp containing two pillars, a crown and the letter "M" was found on the rim of one of the silver plates after it had been cleaned by electrolysis.

APPENDIX D

Not only was the large number of silver and gold coins found on the Colored Beach wreck valuable to numismatists, but the collection gave archaeologists an invaluable opportunity to learn about dies and minting practices of the early Spanish colonial period. Although the silver was generally damaged from salt water corrosion, the gold coins were in excellent condition. The salvaged specimens represented a broad sample of Spanish colonial coins struck at all mints operating in the New World during the last of the reign of Charles II (1665–1700) and the first fifteen years of the reign of Philip V (1700–1724). Several factors contributed to making this a highly significant numismatic find. The gold coins were in a generally uncirculated condition and included denominations and types previously unknown or of which only a few examples were known to exist. This was true in the case of all the mints, but particularly for those at Bogotá, Colombia, and Cuzco, Peru. The majority of coins, however, was from the Mexico City mint.

Coins struck in New World mints during this period were usually irregularly shaped *macuquinas* or "cobs." The term "cob" comes from the Spanish *cabo de barra,* or "end of the bar," which described a step in the manufacture of the coins. Individual planchets (flat disks of metal ready for stamping as coins) were clipped in succession from the end of a strip of metal. After being trimmed to the proper weights, these irregular blanks were placed between two iron or steel dies into which designs for the coins had been impressed with a variety of puncheons. When forcibly struck, the dies were driven into the metal, producing the finished coins. Carelessness in the way they were struck, together with the fact that many times the planchets were smaller than the area covered by the engraving on the dies, caused most of the coins produced this way to show only part of the die design and seldom the date. The size and shape of the coins were evidently of little consequence. Supported by royal decree, an effort was made, however, to impress the mint mark and the assayer's initial on the coin. Silver, during this period, was minted in the New World in denominations of ½, 1, 2, 4, and 8 reals. Approximately 68 reals were struck from a mark of silver weighing one-half pound. Gold, valued at 16 reals to one escudo, was minted in denominations of 1, 2, 4, and 8 escudos. The 8 escudo was also the *doblon,* equaling sixteen 8-real pieces or "pieces of eight." (For comparative purposes it may be noted that the real had an approximate value of 12¹/₂ cents.)

Spanish colonial coinage at times has enjoyed great influence in other parts of the world, particularly in the Philippines and the Far East, but most importantly perhaps on the currency of the United States, whose first continental currency was made payable in Spanish 8-real pieces or milled dollars. The 2- and 4-real pieces became known as "two bits" and "four bits" respectively in the United States.

About 88 percent of the gold coins found on the Colored Beach Wreck were struck at the mint in Mexico City. Coining operations began there in 1536, although regular issues of gold coins did not begin until 1679. From its beginning, the mint operated as a more or less private enterprise until it was incorporated by decree into the royal treasury in 1732. Coins struck at this mint during the late 17th and early 18th centuries bore on the obverse face a shield showing the coats of arms of territories then under Spanish rule. To the right of the shield was the denomination of the coin, in Roman numerals for gold and in Arabic for silver. On the left were the mint mark and the assayer's initial. The legend around the coin read "Philippus V [or Carlos II] D.G. [date]."

The reverse of the coins usually showed a centered Jerusalem cross, enclosed in a tressure (bordering) design. Around the outside was a continuation of the legend from the obverse, "Hispaniarum et Indiarum Rex."

After 1700, when Charles II, a Hapsburg, died and Philip V of Anjou, a Bourbon, succeeded him, touching off the long, bitter War of the Spanish Succession, Mexico-mint coins reflected the change of monarchy. They are easily identified by the Bourbon shield of Philip V of Spain superimposed on a further modified Hapsburg shield. This remained unchanged until 1714, when the Bourbon device of three fleurs-de-lis was enlarged and other details of the design were made more harmonious.

Of the Mexico-mint coins in the state's 25 percent, about 45 percent, though undated, probably fell into the 1700–1713 period. Seven percent were dated between 1702 and 1713, but the concentration was in the years 1711–1713. This concentration very likely indicates when most of the undated coins were minted. Coins dated 1714 and 1715 made up slightly more than 45 percent of the Mexico-mint coins in the state's share. These dates probably reflect a lack of large fleet movements to Spain during the three to four years before 1715 while the war was still in progress.

Of particular interest was a number of almost perfectly round gold coins struck in the Mexico mint. They were exceptions to the generally crude "cob" coins, and it was obvious that special care had been given to their production. The treasure hunters had found one 1695 8-escudo piece of Charles II, and seventeen others struck during the reign of Philip V—ten 8-escudo coins dated 1702, one 4-escudo coin dated 1713, one 1-escudo and five 8-escudo coins dated 1714. They were "Imperials," thought to have been the first strikes of particularly fine dies and intended as gifts for Spanish royalty. The 8-escudo piece was about the size of a silver dollar. The outer ring of lettering read, "Philippvs∗V∗Dei∗G∗1714 [Philip V, By the Grace of God, 1714]." To the left of the shield was the "M" surmounted by "o," signifying the Mexico City mint, and below this, the letter "J," evidently the mark of the assayer, Jose Eustaquio de Leon. To the right was the Roman numeral "VIII" telling the value, 8 escudos. The shield combined the coats of arms of Spain's provinces and possessions. Centered was the small shield and three fleurs-de-lis of the Bourbons. In the upper left corner of the larger shield, a castle tower symbolized Castile. To the right of this figure, a rampant lion represented Leon; other figures at the bottom represented the Low Countries, then the Spanish Netherlands. Vertical bars at the top right denoted Aragon; and to the right of them, long vertical bars with cross-beams stood for Naples and Sicily.

The mint at Lima, Peru, struck 1-, 2-, 4- and 8-escudo gold coins from the year 1696, in the reign of Charles II, and in that portion of the reign of Philip V covered by the collection. These coins consistently appeared to have been manufactured to higher standards than the coins of any other colonial mint of the time. The design of the coins, although quite different from that of the Mexico mint, did not change appreciably from the late 1690s through the first years of the reign of Philip V.

On the obverse the Lima coins bore the Jerusalem cross with the upper left and lower right quarters occupied by castles; the upper right and lower left quarters by lions inside circles of dots surrounded by the legend "Charles II [or Philip V], D.G. [By the

Grace of God] Hispa [or Hisaniar]." The reverse carried the Pillars of Hercules rising from the sea in front of two horizontal lines. Above the top line in the left corner was the initial of the mint "L," between the columns the value of the coin in Arabic, and to the right the initial of the assayer. On the second line were the letters "P V A," the abbreviation for the motto "Plus Ultra," and the last three digits of the date just above the waves of the sea. Over the Pillars was a crown from the sides of which extended a series of circular dots enclosing all of the above symbols. The legend around the dots read, "Et Indiarum Rex," a continuation of that from the obverse, also enclosed in a dotted circle. In some issues the legend began on the reverse and ended on the obverse face of the coin. The 1-escudo coins also varied, with a single castle and the mint initial on the left, the assayer's initial on the right, and the last three numbers of the date below.

The Santa Fé Bogotá mint in Colombia may have been the first in the New World to coin gold regularly, but there is little positive information available on its minting practices until well into the 18th century. The Colored Beach Wreck yielded 1- and 2-escudo pieces. Previously, rare-coin experts had recorded only one 2-escudo piece of Charles II, and the earliest 1-escudo piece was given as 1736.

These coins were generally crude and irregular. The Spanish arms were incomplete on many specimens, and the coats of arms of the various countries were often incorrectly portrayed. One of the most frequent errors was the reversal in positions of the castles and lions in the arms of Leon and Castile. Occasionally, the entire field was reversed, with Leon and Castile appearing on the right and the cross of the Kingdoms of Naples and Sicily on the left. Lack of consistency in the coins, compounded by poor workmanship, made it difficult to determine their dates of manufacture. Quite possibly the use of unskilled native labor at the mint was responsible for the crude character of the coins.

The mint at Cuzco, Peru, apparently operated for only a few months in 1698. Essentially, coins were like those from Lima with the exception of the mint mark, which was in this case a "C." Previously, only one 2-escudo coin from 1698 was known to exist.

At least ten examples were recovered from the wreck site: a 1-escudo and nine 2-escudo coins. The 1-escudo piece resembled that of Lima, with a single small castle flanked on the left by the mint mark and on the right by the assayer's initial. Underneath were the last three digits of the date.

The division between the state and the salvagers of the 200-odd pounds of silver coins by weight made it impossible for Clausen to learn much about mints, denominations and dates of these coins. His general observations and examination of them, however, indicated that the majority were of Mexican origin dating from 1700 to 1714. A small percentage were from the Lima mint, some from the late 1600s, with an even smaller proportion from the mint at Potosí in present-day Bolivia. Although all three of these mints were striking full series of denominations in silver—$1/2$, 1, 2, 4, and 8 reals—between 1700 and 1714, most of the coins found were 4 and 8 reals.

Despite the lack of variety in common artifacts, those in the treasure category were unsurpassed. The recovered specimens provided first-hand evidence of what actually comprised treasure moving from the New World to Spain during this period. From the large number of Mexican-minted coins in the find, it appears that the wreck was one of the five vessels of the *Flota* under the command of Esteban de Ubilla which loaded at Vera Cruz. The size and number of cannon found indicated that it was probably one of the smaller vessels, possibly a *patache,* and since the vessel had been badly broken up and its contents widely scattered, the early Spanish salvagers had missed getting this treasure.

Appendix E

STATE OF FLORIDA
DEPARTMENT OF STATE
DIVISION OF ARCHIVES, HISTORY AND RECORDS
MANAGEMENT

CONTRACT FOR SALVAGE

No. _____

This INDENTURE made this ____ day of _____ by and between the DEPARTMENT OF STATE, DIVISION OF ARCHIVES, HISTORY AND RECORDS MANAGEMENT, hereinafter called the DEPARTMENT, party of the first part, and _____

_____

hereinafter called SALVAGER, party of the second part (including singular or collective:

WITNESSETH,

That the Department for and in consideration of the sum of *Twelve Hundred Dollars ($1,200.00)* annual rental, and the covenants hereinafter set forth, and under authority of Chapter 267,

APPENDIX E

Florida Statutes, by these presents does hereby grant unto the aforesaid Salvager, subject to the provisions hereinafter set forth, an exclusive contract for exploration and salvage of certain underwater areas and submerged lands in the State of Florida, more particularly described as:

(LEGAL DESCRIPTION)

said area, intended to encompass a shipwreck site, to be explored for salvageable abandoned vessels or the remains thereof, relics, treasure trove and other articles and materials contained in or on the submerged lands aforesaid; said area being State-owned submerged lands in or on which abandoned personal property is acknowledged by the parties hereto to be property of the State of Florida where found; all subject to the rights of the upland owners adjacent to such submerged lands and above the mean high water mark.

TO HAVE AND TO HOLD said contract on the following terms and conditions:

1. The terms of this contract shall be for one (1) year from the date first above written, but subject to renewal at the option of the parties upon such terms and conditions as are agreed upon.

2. The Salvager covenants and agrees as follows:

    (a) to utilize only one vessel to be approved in writing by the Director of the Division of Archives, History and Records Management from which divers will operate i.e. enter or leave the water, or from which any recovery operations contemplated under the terms of this contract will be carried out. This provision does not necessarily preclude the use of additional minor vessels for support purposes, providing no recoveries are made from these vessels and no divers operate from the vessels and permission for their use has been requested from the Division Director and written approval received;

    (b)

    (i) to make reports to the Department under oath at the end of each three months, or more often if either party desires, of operations and findings of all items salvaged and removed, including a list of such materials taken;

(ii) it is declared to be the public policy of the State that all treasure trove, artifacts and such objects having intrinsic or historical and archaeological value which have been abandoned on State-owned submerged lands shall belong to the State of Florida, with title thereto vested in the Department of State, Division of Archives, History and Records Management, for the purpose of administration and protection;

(iii) the Salvager shall be responsible for the safekeeping of all recovered materials unless explicitly relieved of this responsibility in writing by the Director of the Division of Archives, History and Records Management and shall retain them in a place of safety designated in writing by the Director of the Division and stored in a manner prescribed by the Department's Marine Archaeologist, and shall take no action that will alter the place of safekeeping or the form of the materials without the written consent of the Department acting through the Director of the Division of Archives, History and Records Management, or other designated agent;

(iv) the Department shall give to the Salvager 75 (seventy five) per cent of the value of the recovered material divided at any division of materials under this contract as payment for work performed under this contract. Payment to the Salvager by the Department may be in recovered materials or a combination of recovered materials and fair market value at the option of the Department. The selection of a method of division of all articles recovered under this contract shall be made by the Department through the Director of the Division of Archives, History and Records Management. No sale or disposition shall be made by the Salvager of any materials recovered under this contract until a division has been made. It is the intent of the Department that such division shall be made as expeditiously as possible provided, however, that the Department shall have the necessary time to perform such cleaning and scientific and historical evaluation of the materials as the Department shall deem necessary prior to division. The scheduling and location of a division of materials recovered under this contract will be made by the Department through the Director of the Division of Archives, History and Records Management. In the event the parties hereto are unable to reach agreement with respect to the division of salvaged items as set forth above, then a committee of three professional appraisers shall be jointly appointed by the Department and Salvager for the purpose of determining the proper division of the salvaged or recovered items to be made to the Department and Salvager respectively. Payment for the services of the professional appraisers is to be made jointly and equally by the Salvager and the State or any of its agencies having available funds for this purpose as authorized in Chapter 267, Florida Statutes;

(c) to store all material recovered under this contract, whether of a base or precious nature, in a manner prescribed by the Department's Marine Archaeologist. The Department at its own expense may require that all or part of the recovered material be transported to a State Laboratory or other facility for cleaning or preservation for the purpose of scientific or historical evaluation prior to division with the Salvager. It is understood that on occasion severely deteriorated articles may not survive the cleaning process. The Department takes no responsibility in such cases other than accounting for the loss on the inventory furnished the Salvager prior to a division;

(d) to extend all reasonable cooperation to any archaeologist provided by the Department to prepare maps, make site studies, and salvage artifacts in the best interest of the State;

(e) to accurately represent the exact nature of the contractual relationship existing between the Salvager and the Department, giving due credit to the Department in any publication, oral or printed, including films, made by the Salvager or under agreement with the Salvager of any operations carried out or recoveries made under this contract. The wording of such acknowledgement shall be by written approval from the Department through the Director of the Division of Archives, History and Records Management, prior to publication;

(f) to permit the Department or its designated agents to audit the books, accounts and logs of the Salvager in connection with operations permitted under this contract. The Department, at its option, may provide an agent or agents at the home port or ports of the salvage vessel or support vessels operated under this contract, for the purpose of auditing the salvaged material recovered as a result of any or each day's salvage work and for the purpose of observing the operations being conducted by the

Salvager under this contract, including the right of boarding any vessel engaged in salvage operations authorized herein and working under water in actual salvage operations conducted by the Salvager as authorized herein;

(g) to maintain an accurate daily log (in addition to the log provided under Section 4 of this contract) of the operations of the vessels used in the salvage procedures authorized herein, which vessel log shall include an accurate detailed list of all items recovered as prescribed by a duly authorized representative of the Department;

(h) to furnish the Department a good and sufficient surety bond in the amount of Fifteen Thousand Dollars ($15,000.00) to guarantee faithful performance of the covenants of this contract;

(i) to comply with all laws and regulations of the State of Florida relating to conservation of fish, oysters and marine life, all rules and regulations concerning navigation and riparian rights; and all rules, regulations and methods of procedure set forth by the Department to insure the preservation and protection of historic and archaeological sites as contemplated by the terms of Chapter 267, Florida Statutes;

(j) to obtain advance permission from the Department and from the United States Engineers, Department of the Army, before constructing pilings or locks or installing equipment in navigable waters;

(k) to disturb no beds of economically exploitable metals or minerals lying and being in their natural state;

(l) to use no explosives in any of the operations permitted under this contract;

(m) to conduct the operations authorized hereunder in such a manner as to afford protection to the rights of riparian owners.

3. The Log furnished by the Division and kept by the Salvager pursuant to the rules of the Division, will be maintained in accordance with the instructions contained in the Log Book. This Log is the property of the Division and may be removed, used, or otherwise disposed of at the discretion of the Division. Upon expiration or termination of the contract, the blue second sheets of this Log, which it is the Salvager's responsi-

bility to mail to the Division on a weekly basis, become the property of the Salvager and will be returned to the Salvager for disposition.

4. Should the Salvage and Exploration Field Agent, or any archaeologist assigned by the Department, to the salvage site, determine that artifacts or archaeological features discovered or uncovered during recovery operations under this contract are of sufficient scientific or historical importance to the public to warrant special handling or protection, he may order termination of the excavation or recovery operation over an area defined by him. Termination of operations will remain in effect until such time as the Department's Marine Archaeologist determines whether to institute special operational procedures to properly and scientifically record and recover the artifacts or features or until he releases the artifacts and features to normal recovery procedures. This provision is solely intended to protect scientific and historic information relating to the wreck site and is not intended to preclude excavation or recovery operations by the Salvager elsewhere on the site during the time the stoporder is in effect, so long as operations in other areas of the site in no way endanger the artifacts or features being protected.

5. This contract is not subject to assignment in whole or in any part by Salvager; however, employment agreements may be entered into by Salvager subject to the prior written approval of the Director of the Division of Archives, History and Records Management.

6. The State of Florida, acting through any duly authorized agency, reserves the right to enter upon the leased premises to explore for oil, gas and all other naturally occurring minerals, provided such exploration shall not interfere with salvage operations of the Salvager herein.

7. This contract is made subject to any and all prior grants made by the Trustees of the Internal Improvement Fund of the State of Florida.

8. Should the Salvager fail to comply fully with any of the provisions contained herein or any of the Rules and Regulations of the Department, this contract may be immediately cancelled at the option of the Department and the amount of

the bond provided for herein shall be forfeited to the Department.

IN WITNESS WHEREOF, I, Richard (Dick) Stone, Secretary of the State of Florida, have hereunto subscribed my name and have caused the Great Seal of the State of Florida to be hereunto affixed in the City of Tallahassee, Florida on this the _____ day of

_____A.D.,_____ .

_____
Secretary of State

NAME OF COMPANY

By _____
Salvager

ATTEST:

_____

Appendix F

FLORIDA ARCHIVES AND HISTORY ACT

267.011 Short title.—This act shall be known as the Florida Archives and History Act.

History.—§1, ch. 67–50.

267.021 Definitions.—For the purpose of this act:

* (1) ["Division" shall mean the division of archives, history and records management of the department of state.]

(2) "Public record" or "public records" shall mean all documents, papers, letters, maps, books, tapes, photographs, films, sound recordings, or other material regardless of physical form or characteristics made or received pursuant to law or ordinance or in connection with the transaction of official business by any agency.

(3) "Agency" shall mean any state, county, or municipal officer, department, division, board, bureau, commission, or other separate unit of government created or established by law.

(4) "Florida state archives" shall mean an establishment maintained by the division for the preservation of those public records and other papers that have been determined by the division to have sufficient historical or other value to warrant their continued preservation by the state and have been accepted by the division for deposit in its custody.

(5) "Records center" shall mean an establishment maintained by the division primarily for the storage, processing, servicing, and security of public records that must be retained for varying periods of time but need not be retained in an agency's office equipment or space.

(6) "Historic sites and properties" shall mean real or personal property of historical value.

History.—§2, ch. 67–50; §§10, 35, ch. 69–106.

*Note.—§10, ch. 69–106 abolished the board of archives and history and transferred its functions to the division of archives, history and records management of the department of state. The editors have accordingly substituted a definition of "division" for that of "board." The section will be appropriately amended by a subsequent reviser's bill.

267.031 Division of archives, history and records management. —

*(1) There is hereby created a Florida Board of Archives and History which shall consist of the Governor, the Secretary of State, the Attorney General, the Comptroller, the State Treasurer, the Superintendent of Public Instruction, and the Commissioner of Agriculture.

(2) The division of archives, history and records management shall be organized into as many bureaus as deemed necessary by the division for the proper discharge of its duties and responsibilities under this chapter; provided, however, that in addition to the

office of the director, there shall be at least four bureaus to be
named as follows:

(a) Archives and records management;

(b) Historic sites and properties;

(c) Historical museums;

(d) Publications;

(3) (a) An advisory council shall be established to advise and
assist the said division. Members of said council shall be the
director of the Florida State Museum, the State Geologist, the
department heads of the respective established departments of
anthropology and archaeology and history in each accredited
institution of higher education in Florida maintaining such departments which offer graduate degrees in said subjects, the president
of the Florida Historical Society, the president of the Florida
Anthropological Society, the director of the division of recreation
and parks of the department of natural resources, the director of the
board of trustees of the internal improvement trust fund, the State
Librarian, the president of the Florida Library Association and the
director of the university presses of any state university in Florida.

(b) The chairman of said council shall be elected by a majority of
the members of the council and shall serve for two years. If a
vacancy occurs in the office of chairman before the expiration of his
term, a chairman shall be elected by a majority of the members of
the council to serve the unexpired term of such vacated office.

(c) It shall be the duty of the advisory council to provide
professional and technical assistance to the division as to all matters
pertaining to the duties and responsibilities of the division in the
administration of the provisions of this chapter. Members of the
council shall serve without pay but shall be entitled to reimburse-
ment for their necessary travel expenses incurred in carrying out
their official duties as provided by §112.061. The members of this
council shall be organized into subgroups in a manner that will
enable these subgroups to provide professional and technical assistance to each of the four bureaus coming under the jurisdiction of
the division.

(4) The division may employ a director of the division and shall
establish his qualifications. The director shall act as the agent of the
division in coordinating, directing, and administering the activities
and responsibilities of the division. The director may also serve as
the chief of any of the bureaus herein created. The division may

employ other employees as deemed necessary for the performance of its duties under this chapter.

(5) The division shall adopt such rules and regulations deemed necessary to carry out its duties and responsibilities under this chapter, which rules shall be binding on all agencies and persons affected thereby. The willful violation of any of the rules and regulations adopted by the division shall constitute a misdemeanor.

(6) The division may make and enter into all contracts and agreements with other agencies, organizations, associations, corporations and individuals, or federal agencies as it may determine are necessary, expedient, or incidental to the performance of its duties or the execution of its powers under this chapter.

(7) The division may accept gifts, grants, bequests, loans, and endowments for purposes not inconsistent with its responsibilities under this chapter.

(8) All law enforcement agencies and offices are hereby authorized and directed to assist the division in carrying out its duties under this chapter.

History.—§3, ch. 67–50; §§10, 25, 27, 35, ch. 69–106.

*Note.—§10, ch. 69–106, abolished the Florida board of archives and history and assigned its powers, duties, and functions to the division of archives, history and records management of the department of state. Subsection (1) of this section will be repealed by a subsequent reviser's bill.

267.041 Office of the director.—

(1) It shall be the duty and responsibility of the office of the director to render all services required by the division and the several bureaus herein set forth that can advantageously and effectively be centralized. The office shall perform such other functions and duties as the division may direct.

(2) The director shall supervise, direct, and coordinate the activities of the division and its bureaus.

History.—§4, ch. 67–50; §§10, 35, ch. 69–106.

267.051 Bureau of archives and records management.—

(1) It shall be the duty and responsibility of the bureau of archives and records management to:

(a) Administer on behalf of the division the provisions of this section;

(b) Organize and administer the Florida State Archives;

(c) Preserve and administer such records as shall be transferred to its custody, and to accept, arrange, and preserve them, according to approved archival practices and to permit them at reasonable times and under the supervision of the division to be inspected, examined and copied; provided that any record placed in the keeping of the division under special terms or conditions restricting their use shall be made accessible only in accordance with such terms and conditions;

(d) Cooperate with and assist insofar as practicable state institutions, departments, agencies, the counties, municipalities and individuals engaged in activities in the field of state archives, manuscripts, and history, and to accept from any person any papers, books, records and similar materials which in the judgment of the division warrant preservation in the state archives;

(e) Provide a public research room where, under policies established by the division, the materials in the state archives may be studied;

(f) Conduct, promote, and encourage research in Florida history, government, and culture, and to maintain a program of information, assistance, coordination, and guidance for public officials, educational institutions, libraries, the scholarly community, and the general public engaged in such research;

(g) Cooperate with and, insofar as practicable, assist agencies, libraries, institutions, and individuals in projects designed to preserve original source materials relating to Florida history, government, and culture, and to prepare and publish, in cooperation with the bureau of publications, handbooks, guides, indexes, and other literature directed toward encouraging the preservation and use of the state's documentary resources;

(h) Establish and administer a records management program, including the operation of a record center or centers directed to the application of efficient and economical management methods relating to the creation, utilization, maintenance, retention, preservation and disposal of records;

(i) Analyze, develop, establish, and coordinate standards, procedures and techniques of record making and record keeping;

(j) Insure the maintenance and security of records which are deemed appropriate for preservation;

(k) Establish safeguards against unauthorized or unlawful removal or loss of records;

(l) Initiate appropriate action to recover records removed unlawfully or without authorization;

(m) Institute and maintain a training and information program in all phases of archives and records management to bring to the attention of all agencies approved and current practices, methods, procedures and devices for the efficient and economical management of records;

(n) Provide a centralized program of microfilming for the benefit of all agencies;

(o) Make continuous surveys of record keeping operations;

(p) Recommend improvements in current record management practices, including the use of space, equipment, supplies and personnel in creating, maintaining and servicing records;

(q) Establish and maintain a program in cooperation with each agency for the selection and preservation of records considered essential to the operation of government and to the protection of the rights and privileges of citizens;

(r) Make, or to have made, preservation duplicates, or designate existing copies as preservation duplicates, to be preserved in the place and manner of safekeeping as prescribed by the division.

(2) Any agency is hereby authorized and empowered to turn over to the division any record no longer in current official use and the division, in its discretion, is authorized to accept such records and having done so shall provide for their administration and preservation as herein provided and upon acceptance shall be considered the legal custodian of such records.

(3) (a) All records transferred to the division may be held by it in a records center, to be designated by it, for such time as in its judgment retention therein is deemed necessary. At such time as it be established by the division, said records as are determined by it as having historical or other value warranting continued preservation shall be transferred to the Florida State Archives.

(b) Title to any record detained in any record center shall remain in the agency transferring such record to the division.

(c) Title to any record transferred to the state archives, as authorized in this chapter, shall be vested in the division.

(4) The division may make certified copies under seal of any records transferred to it upon the application of any person, and said certificates, signed by the director, shall have the same force and effect as if made by the agency from which the records were

received. The division may charge a reasonable fee for this service.

(5) Any preservation duplicate of any record made pursuant to this chapter shall have the same force and effect for all purposes as the original record. A transcript, exemplification, or certified copy of such preservation duplicate shall be deemed, for all purposes, to be a transcript, exemplification or certified copy of the original record.

(6) It shall be the duty of each agency to:

(a) Cooperate with the division in complying with the provisions of this chapter;

(b) Establish and maintain an active and continuing program for the economical and efficient management of records.

(7) Each agency shall submit to the division in accordance with the rules and regulations of the division a list or schedule of records in its custody that are not needed in the transaction of current business and that do not have sufficient administrative, legal or fiscal significance to warrant further retention by the agency. Such records shall, in the discretion of the division, be transferred to it for further retention and preservation, as herein provided, or may be destroyed upon its approval.

(8) No record shall be destroyed or disposed of by any agency unless approval of the division is first obtained. The division shall adopt reasonable rules and regulations not inconsistent with this chapter which shall be binding on all agencies relating to the destruction and disposal of records. Such rules and regulations shall provide but not be limited to:

(a) Procedures for complying and submitting to the division lists and schedules of records proposed for disposal;

(b) Procedures for the physical destruction or other disposal of records;

(c) Standards for the reproduction of records for security or with a view to the disposal of the original record.

(9) The division may employ a chief of the bureau of archives and records management. The chief shall possess such qualifications as the division may prescribe but shall be qualified by experience and training to administer the functions of the bureau and he shall serve at the pleasure of the division. It shall be the duty of the chief, under the general administration of the director, to supervise, direct, and coordinate the activities of the bureau of archives and records management.

History.—§5, ch. 67–50; §§10, 35, ch. 69–106.

267.061 Bureau of historic sites and properties; state policy, responsibilities.—

(1) State policy relative to historic sites and properties:

(a) It is hereby declared to be the public policy of the state to protect and preserve historic sites and properties, buildings, artifacts, treasure trove, and objects of antiquity which have scientific or historical value or are of interest to the public, including, but not limited to monuments, memorials, fossil deposits, Indian habitations, ceremonial sites, abandoned settlements, caves, sunken or abandoned ships, historical sites and properties and buildings or objects, or any part thereof relating to the history, government and culture of the state.

(b) It is further declared to be the public policy of the state that all treasure trove, artifacts and such objects having intrinsic or historical and archaeological value which have been abandoned on state-owned lands or state-owned sovereignty submerged lands shall belong to the state with the title thereto vested in the division of archives, history and records management of the department of state for the purpose of administration and protection.

(2) It shall be the responsibility of the bureau of historic sites and properties to:

(a) Locate, acquire, protect, preserve, and promote the location, acquisition, and preservation of historic sites and properties, buildings, artifacts, treasure trove, and objects of antiquity which have scientific or historical value or are of interest to the public, including, but not limited to monuments, memorials, fossil deposits, Indian habitations, ceremonial sites, abandoned settlements, caves, sunken or abandoned ships, or any part thereof:

(b) Develop a comprehensive statewide historic preservation plan;

(c) Encourage and promote the acquisition, preservation, restoration and operation of historic sites and properties by other agencies so that such property may be utilized to foster and promote appreciation of Florida history; provided, however, that no acquisition, preservation, restoration, or operation of such sites shall be made by the state and no contribution shall be paid from state funds for such purposes until:

1. A report and recommendation of the advisory council has been received and considered by the division;

2. The division has determined that there exists historical au-

thenticity and a feasible means of providing for the acquisition, preservation, restoration, or operation of such property;

3. The property shall have been approved for such purpose by the division;

(d) Cooperate and coordinate with the division of recreation and parks of the department of natural resources in the operation and management of historic sites and properties subject to the division of archives, history and records management.

(3) The division shall employ a state archaeologist, and such other archaeologists as deemed necessary, who shall possess such qualifications as the division may prescribe. The state archaeologist shall be assigned to the bureau of historic sites and properties and shall serve at the pleasure of the division. The state archaeologist, with emphasis on salvage archaeology, shall conduct an archaeological survey of the state and shall perform such other duties as the chief of the bureau of historic sites and properties may prescribe.

(4) The division may employ a chief of the bureau of historic sites and properties. The chief shall possess such qualifications as the division may prescribe but shall be qualified by experience and training to administer the functions of the bureau and he shall serve at the pleasure of the division. It shall be the duty of the chief, under the general administration of the director, to supervise, direct, and coordinate the activities of the bureau of historic sites and properties.

History.—§6, ch. 67–50; §§10, 25, 35, ch. 69–106.

267.071 Bureau of historical museums.—

(1) It shall be the duty of the bureau of historical museums to:

(a) Promote and encourage throughout the state knowledge and appreciation of Florida history by encouraging the people of the state to engage in the preservation and care of artifacts, museum items, treasure trove, and other historical properties; the display and interpretation of historical materials; the marking and preservation of historical or archaeological buildings and sites; the teaching of Florida history in the schools; the conduct and presentation of historical celebrations and dramas; the publicizing of the state's history through media of public information; and other activities in historical and allied fields;

(b) Encourage, promote, maintain, and operate historical museums, including but not limited to mobile museums, junior museums and an historical museum in the state capital;

(c) Organize and administer a junior historian program in cooperation with the department of education and other agencies, organizations, historical commissions and associations, corporations, and individuals, that may be concerned therein;

(2) The division of archives, history and records management may employ a chief of the bureau of historical museums. The chief shall possess such qualifications as the division may prescribe but shall be qualified by experience and training to administer the functions of the bureau and he shall serve at the pleasure of the division. It shall be the duty of the chief, under the general administration of the director, to supervise, direct, and coordinate the activities of the bureau of historical museums.

History.—§7, ch. 67–50; §§10, 35, ch. 69–106.

267.081 Bureau of publications.—

(1) It shall be the duty of the bureau of publications to:

(a) Promote and encourage the writing of Florida history.

(b) Collect, edit, publish, and print pamphlets, papers, manuscripts, documents, books, monographs, and other materials relating to Florida history, archives and records management. The bureau of publications may establish a reasonable charge for such publications not to exceed the cost of preparation of and publishing said publications.

(c) Cooperate with and coordinate research and publication activities of other agencies, organizations, historical commissions and societies, corporations, and individuals, which relate to archival and historical matters.

(2) The division may employ a chief of the bureau of publications. The chief shall possess such qualifications as the division may prescribe but shall be qualified by experience and training to administer the functions of the bureau, and he shall serve at the pleasure of the division. It shall be the duty of the chief, under the general administration of the director, to supervise, direct, and coordinate the activities of the bureau of publications.

History.—§8, ch. 67–50; §§10, 35, ch. 69–106.

267.09 Certain powers and duties transferred.—

(1) All powers and duties heretofore set forth in chapter 257, pertaining to the state library, insofar as they may relate to historical archives or public records as set forth in chapter 257, are hereby transferred to the division to be administered pursuant to this law.

(2) All the powers and duties heretofore set forth in chapter 592 relating to the division of recreation and parks of the department of natural resources, insofar as they shall relate to historical memorials, shall be transferred to the division to be administered pursuant to this law.

History.—§9, ch. 67–50; §§10, 25, 35, ch. 69–106.

267.10 Legislative intent.—

In enacting this law, the legislature is cognizant of the fact that there may be instances where an agency may be microfilming and destroying public records or performing other records management programs, pursuant to local or special acts; the legislature is further aware that it may not be possible to implement this chapter in its entirety immediately upon its enactment and it is not the legislative intent by this chapter to disrupt the orderly microfilming and destruction of public records pursuant to such local or special acts above referred to; provided, however, that such agencies make no further disposition of public records without approval of the division of archives, history and records management of the department of state pursuant to such rules and regulations as it may establish.

History.—§11, ch. 67–50; §§10, 35, ch. 69–106.

Bibliography

Anderson, Romola and R. C., *The Sailing-Ship, Six Thousand Years of History*, W. W. Norton and Co., New York, 1963.

Atwater, James, "Spanish Gold Two Fathoms Deep," *Saturday Evening Post*, December 12, 1964.

Ault, Warren O., *Europe in Modern Times*, D. C. Heath and Company, Boston, 1946.

Burgess, Robert F., *Sinkings, Salvages and Shipwrecks*, American Heritage Press, New York, 1970.

Clausen, Carl J., "The Proton Magnetometer: Its Use in Plotting the Ferrous Components of a Shipwreck Site as an Aid to Archaeological Interpretations," *The Florida Anthropologist*, Vol. XIX, Nos. 2–3, June–September, 1966.

Clausen, Carl J., "A 1715 Spanish Treasure Ship," *Contributions of the Florida State Museum, Social Sciences*, No. 12, University of Florida, Gainesville, 1965.

Coffman, F. L., *1001 Lost, Buried or Sunken Treasures*, Thomas Nelson & Company, New York, 1957.

Covington, James W., *Pirates, Indians, and Spaniards, Father Escobedo's "La Florida,"* Greater Outdoors Publishing Company, St. Petersburg, Florida, 1963.

Dana, Richard Henry, *Two Years Before the Mast*, Harper and Brothers, New York, 1846.

Defant, Albert, *Volume II of Physical Oceanography*, The Macmillan Company, New York, 1961.

Dickinson, Jonathan, *God's Protecting Providence, Being the Narrative of a Journey from Port Royal in Jamaica to Philadelphia between August 23, 1696, and April 1, 1697* (E. W. and C. M. Andrews, eds.), Yale University Press, New Haven, 1961.

BIBLIOGRAPHY

Editors of the American Heritage, *The American Heritage History of the Thirteen Colonies*, American Heritage Publishing Company, New York, 1967.

Esquemeling, John, *The Buccaneers of America*, George Allen & Unwin Limited, London, 1951.

Fernández Duro, Cesáreo, *Armada Espanola*, Vol. 6, Madrid, 1900.

Goggin, John M., *Indian and Spanish Selected Writings*, University of Miami Press, Miami, 1964.

Higgs, Charles D., "Spanish Contacts with the Ais (Indian River) Country," *Florida Historical Quarterly*, Vol. 21, 1942.

Lever, Darcy, *The Young Sea Officer's Sheet Anchor*, Edward W. Sweetman Company, New York, 1963.

Luce, S. B., *Text-Book of Seamanship*, Cornell Maritime Press, Cambridge, Maryland, 1950.

MacLiesh, Fleming, and Krieger, Martin L., *The Privateers*, Random House, New York, 1962.

Manucy, Albert, *The Houses of St. Augustine 1565–1821*, The St. Augustine Historical Society, St. Augustine, Florida, 1962.

Marx, Robert F., *Shipwrecks in Florida Waters*, Scott Publishing Company, Eau Gallie, Florida, 1969.

Marx, Robert F., *The Treasure Fleets of the Spanish Main*, The World Publishing Company, Cleveland and New York, 1968.

Nesmith, Robert I., *Dig for Pirate Treasure,* The Devin-Adair Company, New York, 1959.

Parry, J. H., *The Age of Reconnaissance*, The New American Library, New York, 1963.

Plenderleith, H. J., *The Conservation of Antiquities and Works of Art*, Oxford University Press, New York and Oxford, 1962.

Potter, John S., Jr., *The Treasure Diver's Guide*, Doubleday & Co., New York, 1960.

Romans, Bernard, *A Concise Natural History of East and West Florida*, A Facsimile Reproduction of the 1775 Edition, University of Florida Press, Gainesville, 1962.

Rouse, Irving, *A Survey of Indian River Archaeology*, Yale University Press, New Haven, 1951.

Schurz, William Lytle, *The Manila Galleon*, E. P. Dutton and Company, New York, 1939.

Shepard, Francis P., *Submarine Geology*, 2d ed., Harper & Row, New York, 1963.

Ships, Paul Hamlyn Limited, London, 1963.

Smith, Hale G., "Two Archaeological Sites in Brevard County, Florida," *Florida Anthropological Society Publications*, Number 1, University of Florida, Gainesville, 1949.

Steel's Elements of Mastmaking, Sailmaking and Rigging (from the 1794 edition), Edward W. Sweetman Company, New York, 1932.

Tooley, R. V., *Maps and Mapmakers*, Bonanza Books, Great Britain, 1962.

Villiers, Captain Alan, and others, *Men, Ships and the Sea*, National Geographic Society, Washington, D.C., 1962.

Wagner, Kip, "Drowned Galleons Yield Spanish Gold," *National Geographic Magazine*, January, 1965.

Wagner, Kip, and Taylor, L. B., Jr., *Pieces of Eight*, E. P. Dutton and Company, New York, 1966.

Weller, Robert "Frogfoot," *Sunken Treasure on Florida Reefs* Revised Edition, Crossed
   Anchors Salvage, Lake Worth, Florida, 1993

Whipple, A. B. C., *Pirate; Rascals of the Spanish Main*, Doubleday and Company, New
   York, 1957.

Worcester, Donald E., and Schaeffer, Wendell G., *The Growth and Culture of Latin
   America*, Oxford University Press, New York and Oxford, 1956.

Other popular books about Florida
published or distributed by
FLORIDA CLASSICS LIBRARY

JONATHAN DICKINSON'S JOURNAL or God's Protecting Providence, A True Story of Shipwreck and Torture on the Florida Coast in 1696

BATTLE OF PENSACOLA — Spain's Final Triumph Over Great Britain in the Gulf of Mexico, by N. Orwin Rush

THE OTHER FLORIDA, by Gloria Jahoda, The "other" Florida is north and west, another country altogether.

MY FLORIDA, by Ernest Lyons, Humorous and philosophical sketches of life in Florida from 1915 to the present.

THE LAST CRACKER BARREL, by Ernest Lyons, Additional essays by the former editor of the Stuart News.

FLORIDAYS, by Don Blanding, Pictures and poetry from a "House in a Hammock." First time available in paperback.

SUWANNEE RIVER — Strange Green Land, by Cecile Hulse Matschat, Life on the river from Okefenokee to the Gulf of Mexico.

THE BAREFOOT MAILMAN, by Theodore Pratt, South Florida during the 1880's when the mail was carried on foot along the beach to Miami.

THE EVERGLADES — River of Grass, by Marjorie Stoneman Douglas, A river seventy miles wide flows through sawgrass to the sea.

CROSSCREEK, by Marjorie Kinnan Rawlings, A narrative of the people, scenery and wildlife of the backcountry of North Central Florida.

EAST COAST FLORIDA MEMOIRS 1837-1886, by Robert Ranson, The story of the Armed Occupation Colony at Ankona, Florida.

THE CAVE DIVERS, by Robert F. Burgess, A History of diving in Florida's caves and sinkholes and the historic artifacts they have yielded.

THEY FOUND TREASURE, by Robert F. Burgess, Accounts of dives to famous wrecks many of which are located in Florida waters.

FLORIDA PARKS — A Guide to Camping in Nature, by Gerald Grow, The most important piece of camping equipment you'll ever need.

THE HISTORY OF JUPITER LIGHTHOUSE, by Bessie W. DuBois

THE HISTORY OF THE LOXAHATCHEE RIVER, by Bessie W. DuBois

SHIPWRECKS IN THE VICINITY OF JUPITER INLET, by Bessie W. DuBois